T H E
"Uncensored War"
THE MEDIA AND VIETNAM

Daniel C. Hallin

New York   Oxford
OXFORD UNIVERSITY PRESS
1986

Oxford University Press

Oxford   New York   Toronto
Delhi   Bombay   Calcutta   Madras   Karachi
Petaling Jaya   Singapore   Hong Kong   Tokyo
Nairobi   Dar es Salaam   Cape Town
Melbourne   Ackland

and associated companies in
Beirut   Berlin   Ibadan   Nicosia

Published by Oxford University press, Inc.,
200 Madison Avenue, New York, New York 10016

Oxford is the registered trademark of Oxford University Press.

Library of Congress Cataloging-in-Publication Data
Hallin, Daniel C.
The "uncensored war."
Bibliography: p.
Includes index.
1. Vietnamese Conflict, 1961–1975—Journalists.
2. Press—United States—History. I. Title.
DS559.46.H35   1986   959.704'38   85-21409
ISBN 0-19-503814-2

Printing (last digit): 9 8 7 6 5 4 3 2 1

Printed in the United States of America
on acid-free paper

To my mother,
EMILY HALLIN,
who taught me to love the written word

Preface

This book was finished in the tenth year after the end of the Vietnam War. The year 1985 was also the year of *Rambo*, and of a number of other celebrations of the Vietnam War in popular culture. It was the year Congress cut off aid to the "Contras" in Nicaragua, and then abruptly reversed itself and approved "humanitarian" aid to support the guerrilla war in that country. The "Vietnam Syndrome" showed signs of giving way to the "Grenada Syndrome": the fear of repeating the Vietnam experience showed signs of giving way to a desire to relive it in an idealized form. The nation seemed deeply confused about its identity as an actor in world politics, and thus particularly vulnerable to appealing myths. So it is a good time to take a sober look back at the nation's consciousness during the Vietnam War itself—which as we shall see, despite the popular image of an independent media demolishing the nation's illusions, was also governed by a powerful mythology, born in part out of the traumas of earlier wars.

But first, acknowledgments are due. This book began as my dissertation at the University of California, Berkeley. My committee there was headed by Jack Citrin, who was my advisor and teacher at Berkeley for ten years, through both my undergraduate and graduate years. Also advising me were Todd Gitlin—whose continuing friendship and whose own work on the media have been extremely important to me—Michael Rogin, and J. Merrill Shanks.

A number of others have also read and commented on portions of the manuscript in one phase or another, including Charles Nathanson, Hanna Pitkin, Samuel Popkin—who has also shared his exceptional knowledge of the Vietnam conflict—Michael Schudson, and especially Michael MacDonald, who has been a part of this project since its beginning. Lawrence W. Lichty has also been an invaluable advisor, sharing what he has learned through many years of studying television coverage of Vietnam.

Thanks are also due to the many people who agreed to be interviewed, most of whom are listed at the beginning of the bibliography. The importance of these interviews may not be immediately evident in the text, because I do not often quote from them directly. But they were an extremely important source of "deep background." I might add here that I am well aware that a discussion as general as this will not do justice to the work of any given reporter, and for that I apologize in advance.

I have also profited greatly from conversations with a number of others, including James C. Thompson, Daniel Ellsberg, Larry Berman, William Gibson, and many veterans I have met over the years.

Susan Rabiner, my editor at Oxford, provided important advice, and Sandra Dijkstra played a key role in moving the manuscript toward publication.

Christy Drale and Delia Guevara made important contributions as research assistants. And this study could never have been done without a great deal of help from the staffs of the Vanderbilt Television News Archive and the Motion Picture and Sound Recording branch of the National Archives. Thanks also to Laura Kapnick, who provided access to the CBS archive.

The reader will find in Appendix A a guide to the many abbreviations which crop up in any discussion of military affairs or government documents.

DANIEL C. HALLIN

August 29, 1985
San Diego, California

Contents

The "Uncensored War"

1

Introduction

Defeat in Vietnam has left the United States deeply divided, and no issue has been more bitterly divisive than the role of the media. At one level, however, there has been remarkable consensus since the end of the war about precisely this issue. In the words of Richard Nixon,

> The Vietnam War was complicated by factors that had never before occured in America's conduct of a war. . . . [T]he American news media had come to dominate domestic opinion about its purpose and conduct. . . . In each night's TV news and each morning's paper the war was reported battle by battle, but little or no sense of the underlying purpose of the fighting was conveyed. Eventually this contributed to the impression that we were fighting in military and moral quicksand, rather than toward an important and worthwile objective. More than ever before, television showed the terrible human suffering and sacrifice of war. Whatever the intention behind such relentless and literal reporting of the war, the result was a serious demoralization of the home front, raising the question whether America would ever again be able to fight an enemy abroad with unity and strength of purpose at home.[1]

And James Reston, writing on the day Communist forces completed their truimphant final drive on Saigon, concluded, "Maybe the historians will agree that the reporters and the cameras were decisive in the end. They brought the issue of the war to the people, before the Congress or the courts, and forced the withdrawal of American power from Vietnam."[2]

Liberals and conservatives disagree about who was being "more honest with the American people" (as Reston put it in the same column) and about the implications of conflict between the media and government—whether it means more vigorous democracy or a decline of "unity and strength of purpose." But it has come to be widely accepted across the political spectrum that the relation between the media and the government during Vietnam was in fact one of conflict: the media contradicted the more positive view of the war officials sought to project, and for better or for worse it was the journalists' view that prevailed

3

with the public, whose disenchantment forced an end to American involvement. Often this view is coupled with its corollary, that television has decisively changed the political dynamics of war so that no "televised war" can long retain political support. These views are shared not only in the United States but abroad as well; it was the example of Vietnam, for instance, that motivated the British government to impose tight controls on news coverage of the Falklands crisis.[3] Back at home, the Reagan administration, with the example of Vietnam once again in mind, excluded the media from the opening phase of the invasion of Grenada.[4]

And the issue of the role of the media in modern American politics goes beyond Vietnam. Vietnam coincided with a number of other dramatic political events in which the role of the media was clearly central. First was the civil rights movement, played out largely on a media stage,[5] then the urban conflicts of the late 1960s, the Democratic Convention in Chicago, the rise of a host of new political movements, and finally Watergate. And the apparently growing prominence of the media coincided with what seemed to be a crisis in political institutions: public confidence in government declined dramatically during these years, public attachment to both political parties weakened, and the political system began a twenty-year period during which not a single president would serve two full terms of office.[6] These developments, along with Vietnam, have provoked a broader controversy about the relation of the media to the institutions of American government.

One of the opening shots in this controversy came in a 1975 study commissioned by the Trilateral Commission on the subject of the "governability" of democracies. The section on the United States, written by Samuel Huntington, argued that the American political system of the 1960s and 1970s suffered from an imbalance between its governing institutions—chiefly the presidency—and its oppositional institutions. Central among these oppositional institutions, which he saw as gaining enormously in power during the Vietnam era, Huntington named the media, with special emphasis on television. Huntington wrote:

> The most notable new source of national power in 1970, as compared to 1950, was the national media. . . . There is . . . considerable evidence to suggest that the development of television journalism contributed to the undermining of governmental authority. The advent of the half-hour nightly news broadcast in 1963 led to greatly increased popular dependence on television as a source of news. At the same time, the themes which were stressed, the focus on controversy and violence, and, conceivably, the values and outlook of the journalists, tended to arouse unfavorable attitudes toward established institutions and to promote a decline of confidence in government. . . . In the 1960s, the network organizations, as

one analyst put it, became "a highly creditable, never-tiring political opposition, a maverick third party which never need face the sobering experience of governing."[7]

Huntington later argued that "crises" like those of the 1960s and 1970s resulted from a hostility to power and authority deeply entrenched in American political culture and expressed particularly strongly by the media.[8] Since the mid-1970s a large body of conservative commentary has expressed this view of the media's role in modern American politics in one form or another.[9]

The journalists and their mostly liberal defenders naturally reject the notion that the media are to blame for any breakdown in the "governability" of American society. "What television did in the sixties," David Brinkley said in a documentary at the end of that decade, "was to show the American people to the American people. . . . It did show the people places and things they had not seen before. Some they liked and some they didn't. It wasn't that television produced or created any of it."[10] This is the "mirror" or "messenger" analogy, which has come to dominate the self-conception of American journalism in the twentieth century, as journalists have come to see themselves as neutral professionals standing above the political fray.

Yet journalists do not like to think—and probably are also too smart to think—of their own political role as purely passive. And simultaneously with the mirror analogy they hold another, older and more activist conception of the role of the "fourth estate": they see themselves as "adversaries" of government and political power, not in the sense of a "maverick third party" contending for a share of power or pursuing policies of its own, but as champions of truth and openness, checking the tendency of the powerful to conceal and dissemble. To quote Reston once again, "The watchdog role has always been there. All you have to do is go back and read Thomas Paine at the beginning of the Republic. This country had a press before we had a government. . . . In general the feeling of reporters is that people with power defend their power, by lies if necessary, and therefore you've got to question them."[11] This is the stuff of which the great tales of journalistic heroism are made. Here is how David Halberstam portrays his days reporting Vietnam for the *New York Times*:

> [T]he White House . . . was putting its word against a handful of reporters in Saigon. In the beginning it looked like an absurd mismatch. . . . It might have been different in other capitals where ambassadors and generals still had a certain cachet, but in Saigon the journalists very quickly came to the conclusion that the top people in the embassy were either fools or liars or both. . . . The reporters were young. . . . [T]hey came

to the story remarkably clean, carrying no excess psychological or political baggage. What obsessed them was *the story*.[12]

Both the messenger and the watchdog analogies have this in common with the conservative view of an oppositional media: they portray the media as an autonomous institution standing *apart* from the institutions of state power. On the surface Vietnam seems the perfect illustration of the separation between media and state in modern American politics. There was in fact persistent conflict and ill feeling between the media and government over Vietnam. The major episodes are well known: in 1962 and 1963 the Kennedy administration made an effort to discredit that young Saigon press corps, which was often at odds with the generals and ambassadors running the war. In 1965, as American troops were committed to what was in effect the first televised war (there had been TV cameras in Korea, but TV news was in its infancy then), CBS enraged Lyndon Johnson by showing American marines setting fire to the thatched huts of the village of Cam Ne with Zippo lighters. In 1968, when the generals were claiming a major victory in the Tet offensive, Walter Cronkite returned from his own inspection of the war to conclude that it had become a "bloody stalemate." In 1971 a major constitutional confrontation erupted when first the *New York Times* and then a series of other papers defied the government to publish the classified history of the war known as the *Pentagon Papers*.

The media had extraordinary freedom to report the war in Vietnam without direct government control: it was the first war in which reporters were routinely accredited to accompany military forces yet not subject to censorship, and it was a war in which the journalists clearly did not think of themselves simply as "soldiers of the typewriter" whose mission was to serve the war effort. This was manifested in dramatic ways, as in the reporting of events like the burning of Cam Ne that would never have made the news in earlier wars. And it was manifested in more subtle but pervasive ways. For example, students asked to compare typical news reporting from Vietnam and World War II often observe that the reporters in Vietnam seem, as one put it, like they "aren't really sure what they're talking about." The impression arises from the fact that World War II stories were typically written without sourcing, as though the journalist could testify to it all personally—though usually with an oblique reference deep in the story to the military communiqué from which the information had actually come. A Vietnam story, by contrast, was typically peppered with attributions, often to unnamed sources not all of whom agreed with one another. This leaves an impression of much greater distance between the reporter and the "war effort," and seems to have the psychological effect of distancing the reader as well. It reflects the fact that reporters treated this war much more as a political issue, subject to the standards of "objective reporting," than previous American wars. Every administration of the Vietnam era had periodic crises in its ability to "manage" this more independent or adversarial news media, and over the years the volume of "negative" coverage increased so dramatically that there seems little doubt that news coverage did indeed contribute to the public war-weariness that eventually made Vietnam a political albatross and forced first Johnson and then Nixon to abandon the effort to win a military victory.

But this is only part of the story. The relation of the modern American news media to political authority is highly ambivalent. In one sense, American journalism has clearly moved toward what one sociologist calls "the ideal type of a differentiated . . . news media structurally free from inhibiting economic, political, solidary and cultural entanglements."[13] The newspaper of the early nineteenth century was directly a political institution, usually backed financially by a party or politician. That of the late nineteenth and early twentieth centuries was often a personal fiefdom in which the political connections and ambitions of the "press baron" routinely intruded into the news (think of *Citizen Kane* or *The Front Page*). The news organization of the late twentieth century is a corporate bureaucracy in which news operations are theoretically run by professional journalists without interference from non-journalists, and submission to political pressures from the outside (though it happens from time to time) is considered a blot on the organization's honor.

Journalism has become "professionalized"; an ethic of political independence has come to dominate the journalist's self-image, and that ethic does, as conservatives have observed, contain a strong streak of hostility toward the holders of political power. This hostility arises in part from the nature of journalism as an occupation. Officials, in their efforts to control political appearances, necessarily challenge the autonomy of the media, and journalists naturally resist. As part of the professional socialization process, moreover, the journalist must renounce precisely the goal of political power which the politician pursues. And consistent with Huntington, the journalists' hostility to power probably also has deep roots in American political culture. The notion of journalistic professionalism arose during the Progressive era, with close ties to the Progressive movement. And one characteristic of Progressivism was a strong individualistic suspicion of the wielders of power in the great organizations, including "big government," that were coming to dominate American society.

But opposites interpenetrate, as Hegel showed us, and things that at one moment seem antagonistic at the next seem united in symbiotic harmony. Simultaneous with the rupturing of the media's old partisan ties and the development of professional autonomy, another major change in journalism was taking place. The relation between the media and political authority was becoming "rationalized" in the Weberian sense: it was becoming depersonalized and depoliticized, in the partisan sense of "political," and the media were becoming integrated into the process of government. A sort of historical trade-off took place: journalists gave up the right to speak with a political voice of their own, and in turn they were granted a regular right of access to the inner counsels of government, a right they had never enjoyed in the era of partisan journalism. The press was recognized as a sort of "fourth branch of government," a part of the informal constitution of the political system; and it in turn accepted certain standards of "responsible" behavior. These standards involved not merely renouncing the right to make partisan criticisms of political authority, but also granting to political authorities certain positive rights of access to the news and accepting for the most part the language, agenda, and perspectives of the political "establishment." This ethic of "responsibility" became particularly powerful in foreign affairs reporting, as World War II confronted the United States with its first great foreign threat since the early-nineteeth century, and the nation emerged from that conflict as the hegemonic power in a nuclear world.

Structurally the American news media are both highly autonomous from direct political control and, through the routines of the news-gathering process, deeply intertwined in the actual operation of government. Culturally and ideologically, they combine the Progressive suspicion of power with a respect for order, institutions, and authority exercised within those institutions that is equally a part of twentieth-century American liberalism.[14] And the individualist suspicion of power has often been displaced in the case of foreign affairs by the nationalism of the Cold War.

The journalists who went to Southeast Asia in the early 1960s were in fact intensely committed to reporting "the story," despite the generals and ambassadors who were telling them to "get on the team." And this did matter: in 1963, when American policy in Vietnam began to fall apart, the media began to send back an image that conflicted sharply with the picture of progress officials were trying to paint. It would happen again many times before the war was over. But those reporters also went to Southeast Asia schooled in a set of journalistic practices which, among other things, ensured that the news would re-

flect, if not always the views of those at the very top of the American
political hierarchy, at least the perspectives of American officialdom
generally. And as for "psychological and political baggage," the reporters also went to Vietnam deeply committed to the "national security" consensus that had dominated American politics since the onset
of the Cold War, and acted as "responsible" advocates of that consensus.

In the early years of the Vietnam war, particularly before the Tet
offensive and the subsequent shift in American policy from escalation
to deescalation, most news coverage was highly supportive of American
intervention in Vietnam, and despite occasional crises, Kennedy and
Johnson were usually able to "manage" the news very effectively.
Americans have been preoccupied since the end of the war with the
question of "why we lost," and this has focused the nation's historical
memory on the political divisions, including those between the media
and the administration, which reached their peak between 1968 and
1972. But if one asks instead how the United States got *into* Vietnam,
then attention must be paid to the enormous strength of the Cold War
consensus in the early 1960s, shared by journalists and policymakers
alike, and to the great power of the administration to control the agenda
and the framing of foreign affairs reporting.

Eventually Vietnam, along with other events of the period, did push
the media in the direction of greater separation from the state. The
peculiar circumstances of that war, for one thing, removed an important
remnant of direct government control over the media: military censorship in wartime. Because Vietnam was a limited war in which U.S.
forces were formally "guests" of the South Vietnamese government,
censorship was politically impractical; the reasons for this will be explored in greater detail below. So for the first time in the twentieth
century the media were able to cover a war with nearly the freedom
they have covering political news in the United States. Probably more
important, as the war ground on (the main difference between Vietnam
and Grenada or the Falklands is that the latter two were short and
relatively costless), and as political divisions increased in the United
States, journalists shifted along the continuum from a more cooperative
or deferential to a more "adversarial" stance toward officials and their
policies. Today journalists often portray the Vietnam/Watergate era as
a time when the media "came of age," by which they mean both that
the media became more autonomous in relation to government and the
professional journalist more autonomous within the news organization.
The decision to print the *Pentagon Papers* is often taken as the symbol
of this change:

> It was, they all thought later . . . the first moment of the [*Washington*]
> *Post* as a big-time newspaper, a paper able to stand on its own and make
> its own decisions. . . . [N]ever during Watergate did [editor] Ben Bradlee
> have to call [publisher] Katherine Graham about whether or not they
> should print a particular story. If you had it, you went with it. It was the
> key moment for the paper, the coming of age.[15]

The change was real, important, and probably lasting. But it also
needs to be kept in perspective. For all the drama of events like Cronkite's Tet broadcast and the battle over the *Pentagon Papers*, the basic
structure of relations between the media and government were not
radically different in later years of Vietnam. Early in the war, for example, the journalists relied primarily on two kinds of sources: government officials, particularly in the executive branch, and American
soldiers in the field—the latter being particularly important in the case
of television. They continued to rely on these same sources throughout
the war; but later on these sources became much more divided, and
many more of them were critical or unenthusiastic about American
policy. The news "reflected" these divisions, to use the mirror analogy.
But that wasn't all; the divisions also triggered a different mode of
reporting.

The "profession" of journalism has not one but many different sets
of standards and procedures, each applied in different kinds of political
situations. It is in these varying models of journalism that the ambivalent
relation between the media and political authority finds its practical
resolution. In situations where political consensus seems to prevail,
journalists tend to act as "responsible" members of the political establishment, upholding the dominant political perspective and passing on
more or less at face value the views of authorities assumed to represent
the nation as a whole. In situations of political conflict, they become
more detached or even adversarial, though they normally will stay well
within the bounds of the debate going on within the political "establishment," and will continue to grant a privileged hearing particularly
to senior officials of the executive branch. The normal routines of the
"fourth branch of government"[16] produced a dramatic change in Vietnam coverage over the years, toward more critical or "negative" reporting. But they also limited that change. The Nixon administration
retained a good deal of power to "manage" the news; the journalists
continued to be patriots in the sense that they portrayed the Americans
as the "good guys" in Vietnam. News coverage in the later years of
the war was considerably less positive than in the early years, but not
nearly so consistently negative as the conventional wisdom now seems
to hold. If news coverage largely accounted—at least as an "intervening

variable"—for the growing public desire to get out of the war, it probably also accounts for the fact that the Nixon administration was able to maintain majority support for its Vietnam policies through four years of war and for the fact that the public came to see the war as a "mistake" or "tragedy," rather than the crime the more radical opposition believed it to be.

It is of course impossible for any single study to deal comprehensively with the media's coverage of Vietnam. The problem is not simply one of volume, though the output of even a single news organization over the years of American involvement in Vietnam is immense. It is also a problem of diversity. Coverage of Vietnam in a liberal "prestige paper" like the *New York Times* was very different from coverage in a conservative paper like the *Chicago Tribune* or the *San Diego Union*, or a small local paper, which perhaps took advantage of "hometowners" in its reportage of local boys "in action," prepared for the use of such papers by the Defense Department.[17] Or contrast a mass-circulation tabloid like the New York *Daily News*, which combined guts-and-glory war reporting ("Wagon-Train GI's Drive Off Red-men") with villification of the "Peaceniks."[18] No doubt coverage appeared very differently on network television than on the local TV or radio news—though virtually nothing of local broadcast journalism has been preserved. The diversity of the media may go a long way toward explaining the pattern of the divisions that eventually emerged, particularly the fact that vocal opposition tended to come from the more affluent and educated parts of the population (in contrast, for example, to the Civil War, with its working-class draft riots). Someone who followed the war in the *New York Times* and *Newsweek* got a much more critical view than someone who followed it in the *Daily News* and *Reader's Digest*.

The most logical focus for a study of Vietnam coverage is television, since its coverage has most often been singled out as the factor that made Vietnam politically unique. But access to television's past is limited. No complete record of the network evening news exists until mid-1968, when the Vanderbilt Television News Archive was established. The networks did not systematically preserve tapes of evening news broadcasts. In 1963, CBS began saving some transcripts and "rundown" sheets (listing the day's stories), though this collection is incomplete. Aside from these transcripts, almost all of the history of TV news before 1968 would have been lost if there had not been such a great controversy over the reporting of Vietnam. But in August of 1965, shortly after the CBS report on the burning of Cam Ne, the Defense Department began filming evening news coverage. This material is incomplete in ways that will be specified later, but it contains most Vietnam coverage and, combined with the CBS transcripts and the Vanderbilt collection, makes possible an analysis of coverage on all three networks from mid-1965.

So this study is divided into two parts. The first is an analysis of *New York Times* coverage from 1961 through mid-1965, based on the reading of all the *Times* coverage during that period (and a look occasionally at other papers). The second deals with a sample of network evening news from August 1965 through the cease-fire in January 1973, and is based in part on a quantitative content analysis of the broadcasts in this sample. Both parts also draw on a set of interviews with journalists (and with a more limited number of officials) involved in the war. Most of these are listed at the beginning of the bibliography, though some preferred not to be identified. The study could of course have dealt with earlier and later phases of U.S. involvement in Southeast Asia, but the volume of material is so huge for the roughly twelve years it does cover that it seemed best to keep it limited.

The four major chapters are arranged chronologically, but each also deals with a certain set of theoretical issues. Chapters 2 and 3, on *New York Times* coverage during the Kennedy administration and the 1964–65 escalation under Johnson, are concerned with the nature of the constraints that kept the news so tightly within official perspectives during those years. Chapter 3 deals with ideology—specifically the ideology of the Cold War; Chapter 4 with the routines of "objective journalism" and the ways in which those routines make it possible for officials to manage the news. These chapters also explore certain factors that caused news management to fail periodically, setting the scene for what would eventually be called the "credibility gap."

Chapters 4 and 5 deal with television coverage before and after the Tet offensive and the political changes of 1968. Far from showing the war literally, without political mediation, televison was particularly patriotic in its early coverage and then, like other media, changed as the political climate shifted at home and among American soldiers in the field. Chapter 4 is concerned with the special characteristics of television's reporting of the war, the different models of journalism applied in different political situations, and another facet of ideology, less articulate but just as important as the Cold War doctrine of containment— the image of war Americans came to hold during World War II and its Cold War aftermath. Chapter 5 is concerned with the causes and the limits of television's disillusionment and shift toward a more critical stance in the later part of the war.

I
ESCALATION AND NEWS MANAGEMENT, 1961–1965

If the press is awaiting a declaration of war before it imposes the self-discipline of combat conditions, then I can only say that no war ever posed a greater threat to our security. If you are awaiting a finding of "clear and present danger," then I can only say that the danger has never been more clear and its presence more imminent. . . . Every newspaper now asks itself with respect to every story: "Is it news?" All I suggest is that you add the question: "Is it in the interest of national security?"

JOHN F. KENNEDY, April 1961[1]

Aside from a fleeting awareness of the Buddhist crisis of 1963, Vietnam probably entered the consciousness of most Americans for the first time in August 1964. On August 5 the lead story in the *New York Times* began:

> President Johnson has ordered retaliatory action against gunboats and "certain supporting facilities in North Vietnam" after renewed attacks against American destroyers in the Gulf of Tonkin.
>
> In a television address tonight, Mr. Johnson said air attacks on the North Vietnamese ships and facilities were taking place as he spoke, shortly after 11:30 P.M. . . .
>
> This "positive reply," as the President called it, followed a naval battle in which a number of North Vietnamese PT boats attacked two United States destroyers with torpedoes. Two of the boats were believed to have been sunk. The United States forces suffered no damage or loss of lives.
>
> Mr. Johnson termed the North Vietnamese attacks "open aggression on the high seas."
>
> Washington's response is "limited and fitting," the President said, and his administration seeks no general extension of the guerrilla war in Southeast Asia.

In the *Washington Post* that day the headline ran, "AMERICAN PLANES HIT NORTH VIETNAM AFTER 2D ATTACK ON OUR DESTROYERS; MOVE TAKEN TO HALT NEW AGGRESSION." The right-hand lead, which like the *Times*'s lead focused on the president's address, termed the incident "the gravest military confrontation since the Cuban missile crisis of 1962." It was accompanied by an analytic article, by Chalmers Roberts, under the head "Firm Stand Is Warning to Hanoi":

> The United States turned loose its military might on North Vietnam last night to prevent the Communist leaders in Hanoi and Peking from making

15

the mistaken decision that they could attack American ships with impunity.

But the initial United States decision was for limited action, a sort of tit-for-tat retaliation, and not a decision to escalate the war in Southeast Asia.

Those views came last night from official American sources who would not let themselves be otherwise identified. But there was no doubt they reflected the views of President Johnson and what was described as the unanimous decision of all the American policy makers meeting in the Security Council.

No one was prepared to say where the President's decision might lead. Yet no one doubted the historic immensity of the step and its possible vast consequences.

The great mystery here was whether the attacks by North Vietnamese PT boats on the American vessels were part of some larger scheme on the Communist side to escalate the war. It was said by American sources that the attacks, clearly not accidental, could be part of some over-all plan.

On virtually every important point, the reporting of the two Gulf of Tonkin incidents (two days before the second incident, which led to American bombing, the destroyer *Maddox*, backed by carrier aircraft, had fought off an attack by three North Vietnamese PT boats, sinking two) was either misleading or simply false.[2] On August 3, following the first incident, the *Times* reported,

> The incident was announced here in an official statement by the Defense Department. . . . The statement said that the destroyer . . . was on a routine patrol when an unprovoked attack took place in the Gulf of Tonkin. . . . Officials here . . . said there was no ready explanation why the PT boats would in effect attack the powerful Seventh Fleet.[3]

In fact, the *Maddox* was on a highly sensitive intelligence-gathering operation, mapping North Vietnamese coastal and air defenses. The day before, two attacks on North Vietnam, part of a campaign of increasing military pressure on the North that the United States had been pursuing since early 1964, had taken place.[4] South Vietnamese patrol boats had carried out an attack on the North Vietnamese island of Hon Me, and Laotian Air Force T-28s had bombed and strafed two villages in North Vietnamese territory near the "Ho Chi Minh Trail." Intercepts of North Vietnamese communications prior to the attack had indicated that the North Vietnamese were speculating about the connection of the destroyer with the South Vietnamese naval operations.

The second attack, which served as the rationale for U.S. retaliation and the passage of the Gulf of Tonkin resolution, probably did not take place at all. The *Maddox* had been joined by a second destroyer, the *Turner Joy*. On the night of August 4 the two destroyers detected unidentified signals on their radar which they interpreted as hostile naval craft. A furious "battle" followed, including aircraft from a nearby carrier, under conditions of great confusion. The sonarman on the *Maddox* detected torpedo after torpedo; but his experience was limited, and many of the crew thought afterwards he was probably picking up the sound of the ship's own propellers, or of water on its hull as it turned to avoid the previous "torpedo." The *Turner Joy* fired furiously, while the *Maddox* had great difficulty finding any targets on its fire control radar. The crew of the *Turner Joy* believed they had sunk one North Vietnamese craft and damaged another, but a search the next morning turned up no physical evidence—no debris, survivors, or oil slicks. Several hours after the engagement the commander of the task force, Captain John J. Herrick, cabled to Pacific headquarters:

> Review of action makes many reported contacts and torpedoes fired appear doubtful. . . . Freak weather effects and overeager sonarman may have accounted for many reports. No actual visual sightings by *Maddox*. Suggest complete evaluation before any further action.[5]

The Pentagon spent a frantic afternoon trying to get confirmation of the attack, and they were still trying when Secretary McNamara gave the order to carry out the retaliatory air strikes. At 8:00 P.M. Washington time, about three and a half hours before the president's address, Herrick cabled:

> *Maddox* scored no known hits and never positively indentified a boat as such. . . . Weather was overcast with limited visibility. . . . Air support not successful in locating targets. . . . There were no stars or moon resulting in almost total darkness throughout action. . . . No known damage or personnel casualties to either ship. . . . *Turner Joy* claims sinking one boat and damaging another. . . . The first boat to close *Maddox* probably fired torpedo at *Maddox* which was heard but not seen. All subsequent *Maddox* torpedo reports were doubtful in that it is supposed that sonarman was hearing ship's own propeller beat.[6]

The most significant inaccuracy in the news of the first acknowledged American combat operation in Vietnam, however, had to do not with events in the Tonkin Gulf but with American policy. Johnson was not lying outright when he reported to the nation that the United States "sought no wider war" in Vietnam. He and his advisors were reluctant to get involved more deeply in Vietnam, and they had not yet firmly decided on the massive escalation that would take place beginning in February 1965. But it certainly was not the case that the first air strike against North Vietnam was merely a "tit-for-tat" retaliation. The administration had been moving throughout 1964 toward a fundamental change in American policy.[7] The covert operations begun in February were part of a systematic program of "increasingly escalating pressure" on North Vietnam. (The document approving this program includes "communications intelligence missions."[8] The *Maddox* was on one of these missions, known as a DESOTO patrol). In March, following intelligence reports of "dramatic Communist gains" in South Vietnam, the Joint Chiefs of Staff were directed to begin planning for possible "retaliatory actions" and "graduated overt military pressures." In April North Vietnam was warned through a Canadian intermediary that "in the event of escalation the greatest devastation would of course result for the DRV itself." And in late May and early June, as specific plans for escalation were reviewed, policymakers discussed obtaining a joint resolution from Congress authorizing increased military involvement in Southeast Asia. Decisions on these plans were deferred in mid-June. "[A] consensus," as one analyst puts it, "was slowly emerging on the eventual need for greater pressures on the North, [but] there was no consensus over how to exert those pressures."[9] When the Gulf of Tonkin incident occurred, however, the draft of the joint resolution was revised and sent to Congress. It was passed—with two dissenting votes in the Senate and none in the House—in an atmosphere of national unity comparable to that of the Cuban missile crisis.

It does not appear that policymakers deliberately provoked the Tonkin Gulf incidents in order to provide a rationale for escalation. Their motivations were no doubt complex. It was an election year, and Johnson may have felt he had little choice but to take some action, lest he hand Goldwater a useful campaign issue: American ships are attacked on the high seas, and the president does nothing. But planned or not, the incidents clearly did give the administration an invaluable opportunity to deepen American commitment without arousing political controversy. "The net effect of the swift U.S. reprisals and the Congressional Resolution," as the *Pentagon Papers* put it, "was to dramatically demonstrate, publicly state and formally record the commitments to South Vietnam and within Southeast Asia that had been made internal U.S. policy" in the spring, when the National Security Council had reaffirmed the aim of preserving an "independent, non-Communist" South Vietnam and approved increased pressures on the North. The *Pentagon Papers* continue:

> They were also conceived and intended as a clear communication to Hanoi of what it could expect if it continued to pursue its current course of action. They were portents of the future designed to demonstrate the firmness of U.S. resolve and the direction its policy was tending. The psychological impact of the raids on the Administration and the American

public is also significant. They marked the crossing of an important threshold in the war, and it was accomplished with virtually no domestic criticism. . . . The precedent for strikes against the North was thus established and at very little apparent cost.[10]

The Gulf of Tonkin incident was a classic of Cold War news management. Through its public statements, its management of information, and its action (there was no "grave military confrontation" until the decision was made to retaliate), the administration was able to define or "frame" the situation in such a way that its action appeared beyond the scope of political controversy.[11] The opening line of the president's address (the text of the speech was printed on page 1 of both the *Times* and *Post*) illustrates well the implications of the package of images the administration had invoked. "My fellow Americans," Johnson began, "as President and Commander in Chief, it is my *duty* to the American people to report that the renewed hostile actions against U.S. ships on the high seas in the Gulf of Tonkin have *required* me to order the military forces of the United States to take action in reply" [emphasis added]. By presenting both the air strikes and the joint resolution as responses to an attack on U.S. forces by a Communist power, the president could claim that events "required" him, in the nonpolitical role of commander in chief, to take the action he did. Many in Congress were nervous about the broad wording of the resolution, which authorized the president to take "all necessary measures to repel any armed attacks against forces of the United States and to prevent further aggression." But the administration argued that any display of disunity would only encourage further North Vietnamese aggression. And in the midst of "the gravest military confrontation since the Cuban missile crisis," few were willing to take the political risk of opposing the president.

An American president, as Richard Neustadt observed in 1960, exercises most of his power indirectly.[12] He does not command; he bargains. He uses his unique structural position, his ability to do things other politicians need done, to induce them either to support or not to oppose his actions. But in foreign affairs, in the early 1960s, presidential power was often exercised in a much more one-sided way. Lyndon Johnson did not have to bargain with anyone to get the Gulf of Tonkin resolution passed. He was, of course, commander in chief of the armed forces. But if it were not for a certain symbolic context that surrounded that role, it would have been nothing more than another source of bargaining power. The president's power in foreign affairs lay in his ability to manipulate symbols, to define events in such a way that he would be considered to have the authority to act not as one politician among others, but as the representative of the nation. What modern scholars sometimes call the "public presidency" existed in an extraordinarily pure and potent form in the Cold War politics of the early 1960s.[13]

The exercise of this kind of symbolic power naturally depended to a large degree on the president's control of the news. But the media are private institutions, protected by constitutional injunctions against government interference, and hence are especially far removed from the president's direct authority. How is it that a president is able to control them as effectively as Lyndon Johnson seems to have done in August 1964?

In the case of the Gulf of Tonkin incident, control of information was clearly an important factor. Journalists had no direct access to any of the details of the incident. They could not talk with the crew or see the cables. They also had relatively little information about what was happening behind the scenes in the administration itself—no way of knowing, for instance, that the text of the joint resolution had been written in the spring, as part of a scenario for a step-by-step escalation of the war. This would change, at least to a degree, later on. Divisions within the administration would increase, and officials involved in bureaucratic conflicts would "leak" much more information about internal policy debates. But in 1964 policy debates were tightly contained, and this greatly enhanced the ability of the president and his top advisors to place any action they took within a context that would guarantee maximum public support.

Control of information by itself, however, by no means explains the effectiveness of their efforts. There was, in fact, a great deal of information available which contradicted the official account; it simply wasn't used. The day before the first incident, Hanoi had protested the attacks on its territory by Laotian aircraft and South Vietnamese gunboats.[14] It was generally known, moreover, and had been reported in the *Times* and elsewhere in the press, that "covert" operations against North Vietnam, carried out by South Vietnamese forces with U.S. support and direction, had been going on for some time.[15] But neither the *Times* nor the *Washington Post* mentioned them at all, either at the time of the incidents or in the weeks that followed, aside from inconspicuous sidebars on Hanoi's "allegations" and a passing reference in James Reston's column.

On the second incident *Le Monde* provides a striking contrast to the U.S. press. "Now that the first armed clashes and the threats have passed," the paper reported on August 8, "it is time to explore the

. . . circumstances in which the 'incidents' in the Gulf of Tonkin took place. As our correspondent in Washington has reported, the American 'dossier' contains serious gaps. Even if Hanoi and Peking need to be taken with a grain of salt in their presentation of the facts, it is nevertheless useful to consider their claims, at least to reexamine the facts such as they can be known."[16] The article went on to review the public statements of Washington, Peking, and Hanoi (Hanoi had acknowledged the first attack on the *Maddox*, but called the second a "fabrication"), concluded that the evidence was fragmentary, and speculated that the incident might have been the product of tension and confusion. Neither the *Times* nor the *Post* made any such analysis of the record. There was even, despite the administration's fairly tight control of information about policy debates, a good deal on the public record that suggested that a change in U.S. policy toward North Vietnam was in the offing, for the administration had at times been using the press to warn North Vietnam of this fact.[17] As we shall see, it is only in the context of a certain political climate and a certain conception of what journalism is about that an administration's control of information can give it this kind of control over the content of the news.

There are, of course, ways an administration can apply direct pressure against journalists and news organizations. It is well known that presidents and other well-placed officials will often use the carrot of access and the stick of its denial to influence coverage; it is a significant punishment to deny a reporter the favors—interviews, "leaks," access to *Air Force One*—granted to his or her competitors. News organizations can also be vulnerable to legal and economic pressures, particularly when they are involved in the government-regulated field of broadcasting, as most now are. In the 1970s the Nixon administration made an effort to mobilize the local affiliates against what it saw as excessively critical coverage by the networks, offering them longer periods between license renewals while warning that local stations would be held responsible in license hearings for the content of network news. It also, through a company headed by Nixon associate Bebe Rebozo, initiated a license challenge against a Miami television station owned by the parent company of the *Washington Post*.[19]

The argument is often made, too—though somewhat vaguely—that personal connections tying top executives in the media to political elites keep the media subservient. This was part (but by no means the strongest part) of C. Wright Mills's classic critique of the media in *The Power Elite*.[19]

There is no evidence, however, that any of these forms of direct influence were at work at the time of the Gulf of Tonkin incident, and in general they are little help in explaining the docility of the press during the years of escalation in Vietnam. Pressures on individual journalists were certainly exercised by the Johnson and Kennedy administrations. But they are far too frail a mechanism to account for the consistent pattern of support for the official perspective that we will trace in the following pages. As for economic and legal pressures against news organizations, these were an innovation of the Nixon administration and were less a source of power (though they were not entirely without effect) than a sign of its erosion; by the Nixon period presidential management of the news was becoming substantially more difficult.

As for the "power elite" model, it rests on a fundamental misunderstanding of the nature of the news organization. There are certainly occasions when top executives intervene in day-to-day news decisions. The publisher of the *New York Times* was involved in a decision to downplay an advance story on the Bay of Pigs;[20] William Paley, chairman of the board of CBS, intervened in 1972 to cut back the second half of a lengthy two-part report CBS News was preparing on the Watergate affair.[21] These interventions and others like them probably have "halo effects," reinforcing among journalists a sense that their autonomy is bounded. They also, however, have important costs.

It is worth pausing for a moment to consider the story of the *Times* report on the Bay of Pigs, for it says a good deal about the nature of social control in American journalism. Early in April 1961 *Times* correspondent Tad Szulc visited Miami on personal business. The coming invasion was an open secret in the Cuban exile community there; there were even pictures of the training bases in the Spanish-language press. And Szulc, who had excellent Cuban sources, was easily able to piece together a story detailing the preparations. This is how Harrison Salisbury recounts the events that transpired in New York:

> The Times bullpen, that is, the major news editors, Theodore Bernstein and Lewis Jordan, two skilled professionals who approached the daily task of "laying out" page one of The Times with the solemnity of open-heart surgeons, placed the Szulc story in column eight of page one and assigned it a four column head. This . . . signified in the typographical symbolism of The Times that it was a story of exceptional importance. . . . The layout of page one was a ritual performed in Bernstein's monastic cubicle at the southeast corner of the third-floor newsroom. . . . Bernstein and Jordan sat down to their task after a general news conference held by managing editor [Turner] Catledge. They worked swiftly and in virtual silence, their minds and news judgments so finely attuned that rarely was there disagreement, and in these rare cases Jordan . . .

quickly deferred to Bernstein, his senior. . . . Catledge was, in theory, of course, free to attend and participate in the process but almost never did. It went forward in what some witnesses felt was the holy hush of the communion, with a subaltern editor or two sitting silently at the table, never uttering a word, drinking in what the participants felt was the ultimate ecstasy of the news process.[22]

But Orvill Dryfoos, the publisher, had meanwhile been on the phone to James Reston, the Washington bureau chief. He and Reston had agreed, he told Catledge, that the story should at least be toned down, lest the *Times* be "blamed for tipping off Castro." All references to the imminence of the invasion and the involvement of the CIA were excised, the size of the head was reduced from four columns to one, and the story was bumped from the right-hand lead to column four. Bernstein and Jordan, Salisbury recounts, were "stunned" by what they saw as an extraordinary intrusion of politics into the news process. "To them the news evaluation process was sacred and they were its high priests. This process had been contaminated by infidels."[23]

The modern American journalist thinks of himself as an autonomous professional. No fact is more central to understanding the politics of the news. The ideology of the "professional" journalist, as Salisbury's shifting metaphors suggest, is ambiguous and contradictory. At one moment Salisbury compares the journalist to a heart surgeon, at another to a priest. He also likens Bernstein and Jordan's decision on the *Times* layout to a "judgment . . . of the Joint Chiefs of Staff in assessing a degree of military alert."[24] We shall see as well that the ideology of the journalist as professional is in important ways a "false consciousness." Based on the idea that "news judgment" can be politically neutral, it not only conceals the process by which the news is shaped politically, but is itself a part of that process. It is, in short, a "myth"— but in a particular sense of that word. Far from being a mere lie or illusion, it is a deeply held system of consciousness that profoundly affects both the structure of the news organization and the day-to-day practice of journalism.

When executives of a news organization intervene directly in editorial decisions, they threaten the very basis of authority within it. This is particularly true when they seem to be bowing to political pressure— or anticipated political pressure—from outside. Modern journalism is a collective enterprise in which the contribution of any individual to the final product is relatively small. It is also an enterprise dedicated, in theory, to the pursuit of truth, in which authority cannot be legitimated by property or political sovereignty. Journalists accept as legitimate the many accommodations they must make in the bureaucratic production of news because they see them as accommodations not to economic or political power, but to the collective standards of journalism. Journalistic autonomy is also the basis of the media's public claim to legitimacy: when questions are raised about the right of "a small group of men" (as Spiro Agnew would later put it) to manage a good part of the society's flow of political information, the media's defenders answer that news judgments are made on the basis of "purely journalistic" standards. Violations of journalistic autonomy disrupt the internal functioning of a news organization, sully its prestige within the larger journalistic community (incidents like the *Times*'s decision on the Bay of Pigs are often publicized extensively within that community), and potentially threaten its public image.

It is rare, therefore, to find power, in the traditional sense of the word, being exercised in the news-making process—rare to find some identifiable person or group, either inside or outside the news organization, making a political decision and enforcing his or her or its will directly on those who produce the final product. Power is exercised indirectly, through the manipulation of symbols and routines of working life that those subject to it accept as their own.[25] Often it simply does not *have* to be exercised: the mechanisms that maintain "control" or "consensus" are strong enough that the media simply do not come into conflict with other established political institutions. Often, too, it seems to have no author, but to lie in structures of consciousness and organization that are larger than all the individuals involved, impelling them forward in ways they cannot control. Johnson and Kennedy both possessed great power of manipulation, but, as we shall see, their freedom of action was sometimes limited by the very factors that gave them their power. The forces that compelled the journalists often compelled the policymakers as well.

The president's power to control foreign affairs news in the early 1960s rested primarily on two factors. The first was the ideology of the Cold War: the bipartisan consensus, forged during the Truman and Eisenhower administrations, that had identified foreign policy with "national security," and hence removed most foreign policy decisions from the agenda of political debate. There were differences, of course, about what exactly "national security" meant and what it required, both in terms of tactics abroad and politics—or the suppression thereof—at home. Kennedy was furious at the *New York Times* for printing the advance story on the Bay of Pigs at all; it is from his speech following this event that the quotation at the beginning of this section is taken. Many journalists in turn were furious when they were asked to suppress information that was clearly no secret to "the enemy" (Castro's sources in Miami were certainly as good as those of Tad Szulc). But on the broad outlines of the Cold War consensus, the journalists and government policymakers were united. It took no arm-twisting to induce reporters to treat mockingly "scare headlines about . . . alleged invasion plans" in the Cuban press, as a *Times* article put it late in 1960,[26] just as it took none to induce them to ignore Hanoi's charges of provocation and fabrication in August 1964. The "responsible journalist" did not give credence to "Communist propaganda"; neither did he quibble when the leader of the "Free World" announced to the nation that "aggression" had occurred. These were core symbols of the journalists' world view, just as deeply held as they were for anyone else in the political establishment.

The second factor, ironically, was professional journalism itself. The assumptions and routines of what is often known as "objective journalism" made it exceedingly easy for officials to manipulate day-to-day news content. There was little "editorializing" in the columns of major American newspapers at the time of the Tonkin Gulf incident: most of the reporting, in the best tradition of objective journalism, "just gave the facts." But they were not just *any* facts. They were *official* facts, facts about what the president said and what "officials here believe." The effect of "objectivity" was not to free the news of political influence, but to open wide the channel through which official influence flowed.

The two chapters which follow will examine Vietnam reporting in the period when the fateful decisions were made to escalate American involvement, beginning in 1961, when the Kennedy administration set aside the limit of 685 foreign military personnel in South Vietnam imposed by the Geneva agreement of 1954, and ending with July 1965, when Lyndon Johnson announced the commitment of ground combat troops in large numbers. The period is complex, illustrating both the extent and the sources of official power over the news, and the roots of the "credibility gap" that would eventually develop. Chapter 2 deals with the Kennedy period, closing with a discussion of the Cold War consensus. Chapter 3 deals with the escalation of 1964–65, and explores in detail the nature of objective journalism. The discussion will focus on the *New York Times*. The *Times* is of course not representative (during the Kennedy period it was the only American daily with a full-time staff correspondent in Saigon[27]); the intent here is to deal with the best of American journalism. It is worth adding that the *Times* was often at the center of controversy, particularly during the Kennedy period, when tensions over Vietnam reporting first began to flare.

2

"A Legitimate Part of That Global Commitment," 1961–1963

I believe that Vietnam is a legitimate part of that global commitment. A strategic country in a key area, it is perhaps one of only five or six nations in the world that is truly vital to U.S. interests. DAVID HALBERSTAM, 1965[1]

After long and solemn deliberations around Reston's desk on January 15, 1962, I was entrusted with a question for President Kennedy that perhaps ten *Times* reporters had honed to what we thought was a fine point. Kennedy could not entirely evade it, we were sure. So as soon as he recognized me later that day, I arose—feeling the cameras aim flatteringly at me—and demanded in my sternest voice: "Mr. President, are American troops now in combat in Vietnam?"

Kennedy looked at me—six feet away and slightly beneath his elevated lectern—as if he thought I might be crazy.

"No," he said crisply—not another word—and pointed at someone else for the next question. TOM WICKER[2]

When the Kennedy adminstration took office in January 1961, it inherited the modest Vietnam Counter-Insurgency Plan which would have increased U.S. aid to the anti-Communist regime of Ngo Dinh Diem by $42 million over the previous yearly total of $220 million. But reports from Vietnam were becoming increasingly pessimistic. By the middle of April the president received from Walt W. Rostow, then deputy to McGeorge Bundy, his special assistant for national security affairs, a report calling the situation in South Vietnam "critical" and citing claims by the National Liberation Front (NLF—the Vietcong, as Americans called them) that it would be able to take power by the end of 1961.[3] From the point of view of Kennedy's advisors the prospect of "losing" South Vietnam seemed particularly ominous at that moment. The Free World, as they saw it, in the wake of Sputnik, the U-2 incident, and reports of a "Missile Gap," was on the defensive in the Cold War;[4]

26

this had been a major theme in Kennedy's 1960 election campaign. And in April, just as Rostow's report was reaching the president, the administration was facing two serious foreign policy setbacks: the disaster of the Bay of Pigs and a civil war in Laos in which it was becoming increasingly clear that anti-Communist forces backed by the United States could not hold their own against a coalition of neutralists and Communists.

So officials felt that it was important to show "firmness" in Vietnam, and the administration began moving toward a major expansion of American involvement. The key decision came in November, following a fact-finding mission by Rostow and General Maxwell D. Taylor, the president's military advisor. Taylor and Rostow confirmed the earlier assessment that an expanded American involvement was essential to prevent the collapse of the anti-Communist government, and recommended that an "initial" force of 6,000 to 8,000 U.S. troops, including some combat infantry, be sent immediately. Kennedy deferred a decision on combat troops, but accepted other recommendations of the Taylor-Rostow report, including the dispatch of American-piloted aircraft and a substantial increase in the number of advisors and logistical and support personnel. The decision was open-ended: additional troops were routinely approved after November, and by October 1963 the number of American military personnel—still officially described as "advisors"—had risen from 685 at the beginning of 1961 to nearly 17,000.

The announcement of the Taylor-Rostow mission generated a flurry of publicity about the conflict in Vietnam—which, overshadowed by crises in Berlin, the Congo, and Laos, was not a major issue in the fall of 1961. But this publicity was focused primarily on the question of combat troops, and when the president let it be known that he did not intend to send them, Vietnam faded quickly from the news. The decision to expand the U.S. military mission, which was announced on November 16, made page 1 of the *New York Times*, but it was placed below the fold, and the next day Vietnam was gone from the headlines. In December, when the aircraft ferry *Core* sailed up the Saigon River carrying two U.S. Army helicopter companies which would provide the first "direct military support" to the Saigon government, not only advising but carrying South Vietnamese troops into battle, the *Times* carried the story on page 21.[5] (The docking of the *Core* became legendary among journalists as a symbol of the government's lack of candor. As the ship towered "high above the surrounding rice paddies," an American information officer is said to have told reporters, "I don't see any aircraft carrier."[6])

The consensus on America's "global commitment" was so powerful in the early 1960s that as long as the Vietnam War remained small, the administration had little trouble with the press. With the security of the Free World in the balance—as none doubted it was—who could quibble about sending a few hundred advisors to assist a pro-Western government threatened by Communist guerrillas? The decisions of November 1961, as the authors of the *Pentagon Papers* put it, "stirred very little fuss and (considering their retrospective importance), not even much interest. . . . There is simply nothing much to say about them: except that they were apparently taken for granted at the time."[7] Even if journalists had been skeptical about the emerging policy, which they were not, with no significant debate about it either in Congress or in the administration, it simply was not "news."

As the war became more costly and its conduct more controversial, this would begin to change. American combat deaths—there were 31 in 1962 and 77 in 1963[8]—and the dramatic expansion of the American role not only put the war in the news, but began to strain relations between journalists and the administration, which continued to maintain publicly that American forces were not in combat. Consensus in Washington began to break down, making the war a political issue and hence more newsworthy than it had been before, though the degree of opposition was still very limited. And a serious break in consensus began to develop in Vietnam itself, where the American mission became increasingly divided over tactics, progress assessments, and U.S. policy toward the Diem regime, which by the spring of 1963 was embroiled in a bitter and dramatic political conflict with its Buddhist opposition. The conflict among American officials in the field, who were the primary source of Vietnam news, weakened the administration's ability to manage news coverage even before the heavily covered Buddhist crisis, provoking a bitter confrontation between the administration and the Saigon press corps. As intense as it was, however, the conflict between the administration and the press over Vietnam must be kept in perspective. It was a conflict over tactics, not principles. It threatened neither the Cold War consensus itself nor the premise that American intervention in Vietnam was a "legitimate part of that global commitment."

"President Kennedy Is Known to be Reluctant . . ."

Despite the strength of the Cold War consensus (which will be explored in greater detail later in this chapter), the Kennedy administration did not consider the home front entirely secure, and its public information policies were generally designed to keep American involvement in Vietnam out of the news. This is not to say that efforts to restrict news coverage were motivated entirely by considerations of domestic politics. There were, of course, restrictions on information about military operations, technology, intelligence, and so on, as there are in all wars. But these do not concern us here: as we shall see, the administration's most important efforts at news management had nothing to do with military secrets, nothing to do really with *secrets* at all. Their objective was to play down the whole issue of Vietnam, to keep the extent of U.S. involvement out of the headlines. The North Vietnamese and the guerrillas in the South were well aware that beginning in December 1961 they were fighting Americans more and more. Indeed, they were being "sent a signal" of American resolve. Nevertheless, it made a good deal of difference to the administration whether this information was on page 1 or page 21 of the *New York Times*. To some extent news management had diplomatic objectives. The South Vietnamese government was extremely sensitive about appearing dependent on and subservient to the United States; this required discretion both in criticism of the South Vietnamese and in discussing the extent to which the United States was carrying the burden of the war. The United States also wanted to maintain the appearance of complying with the Geneva accords of 1954, which limited the size of foreign military missions in Indochina, though American intervention, relying as it did on extensive military hardware and conspicuous Westerners to run and maintain it, made this more or less hopeless.[9]

But Kennedy was also concerned, as was every president of the Vietnam era, to keep the war out of domestic politics. Ironically, it was to a large extent the very strength of the Cold War consensus that gave him reason to fear the consequences of a public debate on Vietnam. That consensus was at once empowering and constraining, a source of control over public opinion and a force that threatened, or so officials believed, to run out of control as it had done during the McCarthy era, to the misfortune of the Truman administration. The strength of Cold War ideology combined with another important aspect of the American political consciousness of the early 1960s to place the administration between the cliffs and the whirlpool: the unpleasant memory of Korea.[10] Vietnam was by no means America's first unpopular war; it was not even the first unpopular war of the Cold War era. Public opinion is complex and volatile, and it is impossible to characterize in a simple way the extent of public unhappiness with the Korean War, but in many polls a majority, and in all a substantial minority, of the public felt the United States had made a mistake getting involved in Korea.[11] Democratic politicians, moreover, remembered Korea as a major factor in the defeat of the Truman administration in 1952. And Korea brought into political discourse an important principle whose relevance to Vietnam was unmistakable: never fight a limited land war in Asia. It was opposition from the Right, not the Left, that the Kennedy administration feared most. Eventually, Kennedy would face some criticism from liberals within his own party and from the liberal press, including the *Times*, over specifics of Vietnam policy, particularly support for Diem. But on the broad outlines of that policy, the liberals were with him. What the administration feared was that Vietnam would arouse the Right, which would put it under intense pressure, on the one hand, not to appear "soft on Communism" and, on the other hand, not to become involved in a limited war.

One sure way to arouse the Right was to reject military advice. But that was precisely what Kennedy had done following the Taylor-Rostow report. General Taylor, Secretary McNamara, and the Joint Chiefs of Staff (JCS) had all advised that the American effort in Vietnam could not succeed without the introduction of ground combat troops. Taylor cabled from the Philippines, "I have reached the conclusion that the introduction of a U.S. military task force without delay offers definitely more advantages than it creates risks and difficulties. In fact, I do not believe our program to save SVN will succeed without it."[12] And Secretary McNamara told the president, on behalf of himself and the JCS, "The chances are against, probably sharply against, preventing [the fall of South Vietnam] by any measure short of the introduction of U.S. forces on a substantial scale."[13]

So the Taylor-Rostow mission required a bit of fancy footwork with the press. Even before Taylor had returned from Vietnam the White House had begun telling reporters privately that the president *and* General Taylor were "increasingly reluctant" to send American troops. In the middle of October the *Times*, in one of several stories quoting "high administration sources," reported:

> Military leaders at the Pentagon, no less than General Taylor himself, are understood to be reluctant to send organized U.S. combat units into Southeast Asia. Pentagon plans for this area stress the importance of countering Communist guerrillas with troops from the affected countries, perhaps trained and equipped by the U.S., but not supplanted by U.S. troops.[14]

On November 4, after Taylor returned to the United States, the *Times* reported:

The General declined to comment directly on whether he would recommend sending United States combat troops. . . .

However, when General Taylor was reminded at the airport that his remarks before leaving Saigon had been interpreted as meaning that Ngo Dinh Diem's problem was not manpower, the General replied:

"That is correct. It is a populous country."

Officials said it was correct to infer from this that General Taylor did not look favorably on the sending of United States combat troops at this time. . . .

Although some officials in the White House and State and Defense Departments are known to favor the dispatch of American forces, there would be considerable surprise here if General Taylor recommended such a move.[15]

And on November 16, when the decisions were announced, reporters were told the president had followed General Taylor's advice:

President Kennedy has decided on the measures that the United States is prepared to take to strengthen South Vietnam against attack by the Communists.

The measures . . . closely followed the recommendations made by General Maxwell D. Taylor, the President's military advisor.

The United States plans do not include the dispatching of combat units at this time. They call for sending several hundred specialists . . . to train the forces of President Ngo Dinh Diem. The plans also call for fairly large-scale shipments of aircraft and other special equipment.

Officials emphasized that the President and the National Security Council had not foreclosed the possibility of sending ground or air combat units if the situation deteriorated drastically. The President, it was said, does not wish to bind himself into a "never position."

However, the President and General Taylor agreed, according to reliable information available here, that the South Vietnamese government is capable of turning back the Communist threat.[16]

This was the first case of government "management" of Vietnam news, and it was in many ways typical of what was to follow. Its purpose was to keep the issue off the agenda of political discussion. In order to defuse the issue politically, it was essential that major policy decisions appear routine, incremental, and automatic. This in turn required that policy debate within the administration be kept out of the public eye. It also required that an appearance of crisis be avoided, which meant that the pessimistic intelligence reports which preceded this and every major escalation of the war were kept secret. The emphasis in published news reports at the time of the Taylor-Rostow mission was on the strength of the Saigon government, not the imminent possibility of its defeat, which had led to the mission to begin with.

Defusing Vietnam as a political issue also required concealing the actual scope of the decisions made and of those contemplated for the future. The public handling of the Taylor-Rostow mission is an excellent example of the usefulness of establishing a comparison level in advance of a decision, or of utilizing one once it has fortuitously been established. Given the speculation about the possibility that troops would be sent to Vietnam, the news that the president had decided only to send equipment and "a few hundred specialists" seemed reassuring. The first major decision to escalate in Vietnam thus appeared in the news as a decision *not* to escalate. There was no hint at the time that the November decision was open-ended, that additional deployments would be made routinely from then on. There was no hint either that the decision was seen as an "initial phase" (the National Security Action Memorandum that stated the decision formally was entitled "First Phase of Vietnam Program").[17] And, perhaps most important, estimates of the level of involvement that might eventually be required were successfully kept secret. These were to prove spectacularly low: the Joint Chiefs estimated that 40,000 U.S. troops would be required to "clean up" the Vietcong, or 205,000 if North Vietnam and China intervened.[18] But they were high enough that if they had been publicly known the reaction to deepening U.S. involvement might have been very different.

Mixed Signals

"Fresh details are slowly emerging from reticent Administration sources about the expanded program of American participation in South Vietnam's anti-communist struggle," said a *Times* editorial on December 22, 1961.

> From now on Americans will be flying Vietnamese troops into battle and accompanying them in combat on the ground; Americans will help run the Vietnamese intelligence system, assist in military planning and have a voice in measures to improve social and economic conditions. If some of the more than 2,000 Americans now in South Vietnam get shot at in combat zones, they are authorized to shoot back. These new arrangements . . . represent a very extensive American commitment. Americans will certainly be shot at; some will almost certainly be killed.

The first U.S. combat death occurred that same day,[19] and the administration continued to be "reticent" about the extent of the U.S. commitment. New deployments were made quietly, and official figures on the size of the U.S. mission were not released; officially there were still only 685 U.S. advisors in Vietnam. Information about casualties was hard to get and often misleading.[20] Early in February 1962, after an army helicopter crashed and two were hit by ground fire, correspondents were banned from accompanying helicopter missions.[21] Later they would be banned from Bien Hoa airfield, from which air force pilots would soon be flying combat missions.[22]

In mid-February 1962, official secrecy became the focus of a small flurry of domestic controversy over Vietnam, one of only two such flurries before the Buddhist crisis of 1963. Kennedy's "No" to Tom Wicker's January 15 question about combat involvement, quoted at the beginning of this chapter, served its purpose for the moment. In such a brief denial, there was no news; the story did not make the *Times* the next day. (The official position was that since U.S. troops were not organized into combat units, and went into combat alongside the South Vietnamese, they were not "combat troops in the generally understood sense of the word."[23]) Over the next few weeks, however, Vietnam began increasingly to make headlines. The most significant story appeared on February 9, when it was announced that the Military Assistance Advisory Group for Vietnam would be absorbed by the newly created Military Assistance Command, Vietnam (MACV), which would be headed by a four-star general. This, as the *Times* observed, was unusual: not since the 1947 intervention in Greece had a U.S. aid mission been headed by a full general. On February 12, under the head "Fears on Vietnam Rising in Capitol," the *Times* ran a story on growing doubts in Washington.

The next day, February 13, The Republican National Committee, in a publication called *Battle Line*, called on the president to make a "full report to the American people" on Vietnam. The Republicans did exactly what Kennedy had feared. On the one hand they questioned whether the United States was "moving toward another Korea which might embroil the entire Far East"; on the other hand they stressed that the Republican party "always has been and still is firmly behind any policy which will block the Communist conquest of Southeast Asia."[24] Kennedy, asked about the criticism at a news conference the next day, responded by invoking the Cold War principle of bipartisanship, an important corollary of which was that foreign policy should not be publicly debated: "[M]y view has always been that the headquarters of both our parties should really attempt to leave these matters to be discussed by responsible leaders on both sides," Kennedy said. "In my opinion we have a very strong bipartisan consensus up to now, and I am hopeful that it will continue in regard to the action we are taking."[25]

Kennedy's appeal was not in vain; the bipartisan consensus continued. The Republicans, perhaps, merely wanted to go on record as having raised questions early about Vietnam in case they needed to distance themselves later from the president's policy. In any case, they did not follow up on their initial criticism, and the secrecy controversy quickly died out. (The *Times* supported the president editorially during this controversy: "Undue publicity might well inflate the American role beyond its true proportions, and this could compromise Washington's efforts to keep the South Vietnam struggle a limited war."[26]) The issue of U.S. troops in combat also faded; it was raised only once more in a Kennedy news conference. The next significant bit of domestic controversy over Vietnam did not occur until February 1963, when a Senate panel headed by Majority Leader Mike Mansfield expressed concern that Vietnam might become an American war.[27] This controversy, too, was news for only a few days.

Nevertheless, the administration was never again able to manage the news as successfully as it had in the fall of 1961, and relations with the press became increasingly strained. By mid-1963 Kennedy would be appealing directly to the publisher of the *Times* to remove its Saigon correspondent, David Halberstam; officials would be accusing the press of wrecking U.S. policy; and press coverage itself would become a major issue.[28] The administration's concern was clearly exaggerated. As we shall see, it retained a good deal of power to manage the news. The press, moreover, not only supported the basic outlines of U.S. policy, but was quite cautious in the "pessimism" it often opposed to the official "cautious optimism." Still, there is no doubt that Vietnam received far more coverage than the administration would have liked, and a good deal of this coverage contradicted what was being said by top officials in Washington and Saigon.

Officials and other critics of the Saigon press corps attributed the "press problems" to what we would call today the "adversary press." Joseph Alsop, writing at the height of the Buddhist crisis in 1963, called their reporting a "reportorial crusade against the government."[29] Marguerite Higgins, who had covered World War II and Korea, wrote, "Reporters here would like to see us lose the war to prove they're right."[30] This view of the Saigon press corps during the Kennedy years has become an important part of the mythology about Vietnam coverage, cited particularly by those who believe the press was decisive in the American defeat. "David Halberstam and successors played a key role in ridding Vietnam of the supposedly repressive Diem regime only to help usher in an even bloodier future," the *Wall Street Journal* wrote in a 1982 editorial on Central America coverage.[31] To some extent, this view has even been adopted by journalists themselves, who remember the period as one when a prescient crusading press exposed official deception. In 1964 the *Times* editorialized, "The harsh facts of the war in South Vietnam were only brought to public notice through the enterprise of American newspapermen on the spot."[32] And more recently David Halberstam has written, "What was to become a major foreign policy struggle . . . began as a press struggle, the White House version against the reporting of a small handful of newsmen."[33] The reality is less personal, less romantic—and more deeply rooted in the nature of the Vietnam War itself.

Two factors are crucial to understanding the problems Kennedy had with the press. And, as we shall see, the same factors would plague his successors, forcing the "credibility gap," as it would be called a few years later, wider and wider. The first had to do with the conflicting goals the administration pursued in its public relations efforts. Vietnam was a "public relations war," not merely in the sense that considerable effort was devoted to information policy, high-level "salesmanship," and so on, but in its basic strategic conception.[34] To some degree this is true of all wars and of all politics: politics has always involved managing appearances in order to influence decisions made by others. But this was particularly true of Vietnam. This had nothing to do with the absence of censorship or the presence of television cameras. It was rooted in the fact that Vietnam was a *limited* war. Top civilian policymakers did not conceive the use of American power in Vietnam in "strictly military" terms. The object, in theory, was not to destroy the enemy's capacity to make war, but to destroy their will: to convince them that they could not win at reasonable cost and should give up the struggle.[35] In part, this was why policymakers felt it made sense to escalate gradually, taking measures initially that were far short of what the military believed would be required to achieve "victory" in the conventional sense. Escalation was intended to "send a signal," to demonstrate American resolve; the assumption was that a political victory was possible at a level of military effort short of what would be required to destroy NLF and North Vietnamese forces, if the right "message" was conveyed clearly to Hanoi, Peking, and Moscow.

The problem was that the "enemy" was not the only audience to which the administration was sending signals. It was trying simultaneously, in shifting combinations, to convince the North Vietnamese that the United States was willing to persist in South Vietnam as long as it took to preserve a "pro-Western" government, to convince the South Vietnamese public that the Diem government was truly nationalist and American involvement not a new form of colonialism, and, especially later in the war, to convince Peking that the U.S. buildup did not threaten her security, and Moscow that U.S. "resolve" in Southeast Asia did not indicate inflexibility in other areas. And given the belief that American public opinion would not support a limited war in Southeast Asia, the administration had at the same time to convince the American public that war was not in the offing. To fight a limited war, in other words, the administration had to send contradictory signals: the North Vietnamese had to be convinced that the American commitment was in the end *unlimited*; the American public, that it was so limited it did not threaten war at all. Given this dilemma, it is hardly surprising that the administration relied heavily on deception and secrecy, nor that these were hard to maintain.

This dilemma was expressed, in somewhat confused form, in the February 12 "Fears on Vietnam Rising" story in the *Times*.

> The reluctance of the United States Government to divulge and explain publicly the extent and ramifications of its commitment in Southeast Asia is based on a possible enemy reaction.
>
> The heart of the problem, it is said, involves how to call attention to increased United States support for the South Vietnamese struggle against Soviet-supported Communist guerrillas without provoking the enemy into raising the ante.
>
> Tied to that problem is the fear that Americans are not ready to accept the idea of a long, drawn-out struggle. It is felt they might insist upon a quick, clean victory.
>
> Also linked to the public relations problem, officials say, is the increase in casualties in a guerrilla war that is being fought 7,000 miles away.
>
> Official sources say, nevertheless, that the White House has decided that it can help the South Vietnamese defeat the Viet Cong (Vietnamese Communists). The same sources concede that this decision, in fact, is a commitment to fight for victory over the Communists. The United States is said to be determined to put in what it takes to win.

"Possible enemy reaction" was a convenient rationale for secrecy. But the North Vietnamese and NLF were hardly likely to be affected by the official fiction that U.S. troops were not in combat, nor by the banning of correspondents from helicopter missions. Indeed, as officials told the *Times*, far from concealing American involvement from the North Vietnamese, the administration was trying very hard during this period to "call attention to increased United States support," to make clear to its adversaries that it was indeed "determined to put in what it takes to win."

And here lay the basic contradiction in the administration's public relations strategy: the measures it took to signal its determinaton to its adversaries contradicted its efforts to keep Vietnam off the domestic political agenda. The most important of these signals was the simple fact of sending U.S. troops into combat. But beyond that, the administration, at the same time it was trying to keep the lid on the issue domestically, made a series of other moves to dramatize its resolve, and these inevitably spilled over into the domestic arena. On January 14, for example, Secretary McNamara flew to Hawaii for a conference on the situation in Vietnam. "A Pentagon spokesman," the *Times* reported, "said the Secretary's unusually speedy mission was intended to underscore the administration's continuing and emphatic interest in assisting the South Vietnamese in their war against Communist guerrillas. The State Department [with an eye to the home front—DH] said no immediate crisis was involved."[36] The establishment on February 9 of MACV under a four-star general had similar purposes: "the command was established, as a Pentagon spokesman said today, to demonstrate that 'we're drawing a line here' and 'this is a war we can't afford to lose.' "[37] On February 16, "high officials . . . predicted the ultimate defeat of Communist guerrillas."[38] On February 17, Secretary McNamara, about to leave for Hawaii for talks on Vietnam, made a speech warning the Soviets that the United States was willing to fight limited wars.[39] On February 18, Attorney General Robert Kennedy said in Saigon that "United States troops would stay in South Vietnam until Communist aggression was defeated."[40] All of this was front page news, and intended to be so. Declaring a commitment publicly is important to establishing its credibility. But Vietnam had been placed on the news agenda, and the administration would thenceforth have to take the unintended consequences of publicity along with the intended, including the damage to its credibility that resulted from the mixed signals it sent.

The administration also faced a second dilemma: the very fact of sending U.S. forces into combat took the control of information and the power to make or not to make news to some extent out of its hands. The consequences, from the point of view of news and public opinion, of a decision to put "American boys" in the way of bullets are profound; and, as we shall see when we discuss the 1965–67 period, they are by no means all unfavorable to an administration. The commitment of Americans to battle makes the battle itself—Americans against "the enemy"—the story, upstaging the debate over policy options. It also introduces a powerful new justification for whatever policy the administration is pursuing: the vindication of American blood, the preservation of American honor. "Come what may," wrote columnist C. L. Sulzberger, "we cannot afford to be driven ignominiously from Vietnam, where we have committed so much prestige, interest and treasure and are beginning tangibly to commit our blood."[41]

But, once again, an administration must often take the bad with the good. Once it had moved from the stage of policy planning and actually created a large American military mission in Vietnam, the Kennedy administration could no longer manage the news as it had in 1961. Its control of the news agenda, its ability to emphasize or deemphasize the issue of Vietnam, became in part hostage to the fortunes of war: American combat deaths kept Vietnam in the news. It also lost the centralized control of information it had once held. The growing size of the American mission multiplied the number of sources available to journalists. In October 1961, when Taylor and Rostow were preparing their report, there were only a handful of officials, most of them in Washington and Saigon and most very high in the administration, whom journalists regarded as "authoritative." By the next spring the story could be covered from a very different level and perspective—from the perspective of the Americans in the field who were fighting and administering it.

The problem was exacerbated by two additional factors. The first was the fact that the administration was unable to limit significantly the flow of news from the field. In Korea, after an ambiguous period when reporters were not subject to censorship but could face court-martial for security breaches or "unwarranted criticism," censorship had been imposed. Censorship restricted, among other things, reports on "the effect of enemy fire" (i.e., casualties) and forbade "any derogatory comments" about U.N. troops or commanders.[42] These rules, combined with restrictions on transportation and communication, meant that from November 1950 on the war was largely reported from MacArthur's headquarters in Tokyo.[43] The administration (or, more correctly, MacArthur, whose goals were often very different from those of the administration itself) had thus been able to recentralize control of information. But here again the Kennedy administration was caught in a dilemma created by its own public relations strategy: it could not very well institute military censorship if it did not acknowledge that the country was at war. The South Vietnamese government, which was formally in control of all information policies, did make efforts to restrain the press. It restricted contacts between reporters and officials, including U.S. officials; restricted access to military transportation; expelled two reporters for American news organizations, François Sully of *Newsweek* and James Robinson of NBC; and, during the Buddhist crisis in 1963, directly censored some outgoing dispatches.[44] It also roughed up reporters on a number of occasions. And the U.S. command adopted restrictive press policies of its own. It was trying, as John Mecklin, public affairs officer for the U.S. mission, put it, "on the one hand to discourage publicity of any sort about our operations in Vietnam, and on the other hand to pamper the Diem regime."[45] And to accomplish these ends the U.S. mission not only released very little useful information, but made efforts to clamp down on officials who leaked "negative" information and to restrict reporters' access, in the words of a February 1962 State Department cable on press policy, to "military activities of the type that are likely to result in undesirable stories."[46] Judging from the final product, however, these measures served more as irritants than as means of real control over press coverage.

The second factor was the simple fact that the policy of the Kennedy period did not succeed. Americans in the field who became the source for so much of the "pessimistic" reporting from Vietnam in this period—the most important were middle-level officers, colonels and lieutenant colonels who served as key advisors to the South Vietnamese or as commanders of major American units[47]—were hardly dissenters from the basic policy of fighting an anti-Communist war in South Vietnam. They were, on the contrary, deeply committed to the success of that mission. If U.S. policy had been working to their satisfaction, they would simply have been another set of official voices serving to legitimate it. Much of the time they were precisely this. In 1962, when the U.S. buildup got under way, there was an initial flush of optimism in the U.S. mission. It began to erode later that year, however, as many field-level advisors became unhappy with the performance of the South Vietnamese army and impatient with the unwillingness of top American officials to pressure the South Vietnamese government more vigorously to follow American advice. This sentiment accelerated early in 1963 with a major South Vietnamese defeat at Ap Bac. Even so, American officials at all levels remained on balance happy with the progress of the war through the early months of 1963—or at least that is the impression one gets from the *Times*'s reporting. But the great political crisis that began in May 1963 finally shattered that optimism, eventually convincing most officials both in Washington and in Saigon that whatever progress had been made against the insurgency in the previous years had either been destroyed or had been illusory to begin with.[48] This was the period of the most bitter controversy over "pessimistic" reporting in the American media; but, as we shall see, this reporting came when those who made and carried out American policy were also bitterly at odds.

From 1962 on *New York Times* reporting from South Vietnam reflected very closely the views of Americans in the field. Objective reporting required, of course, that top officials in Saigon, both American and South Vietnamese, be given their due. But, for the most part, the *Times* reporters of this period focused on the views of field-level officers.

Their reporting was "pessimistic" where these officers were pessimistic, and enthusiastic where they were enthusiastic; it reflected their insights, which were many, and the limitations of their perspective, which were also many.

It is ironic that American soldiers, from officers down to enlisted men, now seem to regard the press as their enemy, on the basis of the precedent of Vietnam,[49] for the American war correspondent has typically served, among other roles, as an advocate for the soldier in the field, glorifying his exploits and also giving voice to his views and interests, which often conflict with those of the administration or the military command. Vietnam was no exception, and this was true not only in the early 1960s but throughout the war. The Kennedy administration, for instance, because it did not acknowledge that U.S. troops were in combat in Vietnam, initially refused to award the Purple Heart to soldiers wounded there. In April 1962, however, the *Times* ran a story on a wounded sergeant denied the medal. "The withholding of the medal rankled crewmen," Homer Bigart reported, "who believe the hazards of their operations . . . are getting no recognition in Washington."[50] The next day the White House rescinded the policy. Eventually U.S. troops in Vietnam were granted the right to receive other combat medals as well.[51] On January 19, 1963, David Halberstam reported on complaints of U.S. helicopter pilots about the quality of their equipment. Two months later he did a story on the frustration American officers felt about restrictions on operations into Cambodia, where NLF forces took refuge.[52]

The most important complaint of American officers though, and the most important theme in *Times* reporting from the field during this period, concerned their inability to get the South Vietnamese to follow their advice and adopt more aggressive tactics against the Vietcong, as well as some form of "pacification" program. Stories on these complaints became more frequent as time went on, and more explicit in counterposing the views of officers in the field with those of officials in Saigon. Here are some examples:

Homer Bigart, March 9, 1962. United States Army helicopters carried a Vietnamese battalion in a successful raid today against this Communist stronghold near the south tip of Vietnam. . . .

But as usual the main enemy force got away. . . . The Government troops failed to exploit the Viet Cong state of shock. They bunched up and dawdled in drainage ditches and under the shade of coconut trees until an American advisor cried out in exasperation, "Let's move the thing forward."

Bigart, May 9, 1962. Despite much top-level pressure, the Vietnamese Government is not moving fast [on plans for a pacification program for the Mekong Delta]. . . . President Ngo Dinh Diem has appointed Hoang Van Lac . . . as coordinator of Operation Delta. But the official has no organization. It is unclear to Americans how he can obtain the necessary support from the South Vietnamese Army and the provincial chiefs. This is a familiar American complaint here—no clear-cut chain of command.

Jacques Nevard, July 29, 1962. The Kennedy administration's cautious optimism on the progress of South Vietnam's war against the Communist insurgents is not widely reflected among Americans stationed here to help in that fight.

The furthest anyone in a position to know the situation is willing to go is to say that President Ngo Dinh Diem's regime has a 50-50 chance. . . .

Almost no one interviewed privately agreed with statements such as that made this week by Secretary of Defense Robert S. McNamara . . . that "the Vietnamese are beginning to hit the Viet Cong where it hurts most—in winning the people to the side of the government."

The consensus here is that political apathy or even hostility on the part of large segments of the population to the Saigon regime continues to be the Communists' biggest asset.

Divisions in the American mission, tensions between Americans and the South Vietnamese, and publicity about both of these began to become particularly severe after a major South Vietnamese defeat at Ap Bac in January 1963. This battle prompted the resignation of one of the journalists' favorite sources, Lieutenant Colonel John Paul Vann, advisor to a South Vietnamese division involved in the battle.

David Halberstam, January 7, 1963. The Battle of Ap Bac, in which attacking South Vietnamese troops were badly beaten by Communist guerrillas, had bewildered high United States officials in Saigon.

United States advisers in the field, however, have long felt that conditions here made a defeat like this virtually inevitable. . . .

American officers throughout the Mekong Delta feel that what happened at Ap Bac goes far deeper than one battle and is directly tied to the question—whether the Vietnamese are really interested in having American advisers and listening to them.

Halberstam, January, 11, 1963. Gen. Paul D. Harkins, commander of the United States forces in Vietnam, issued a strong statement today defending the courage of the Vietnamese soldier.

Sources said General Harkins' statement had come as a result of criticism in the United States following the defeat suffered by government troops in the recent battle of Ap Bac. . . .

Other sources said the problem of Ap Bac was not a question of the courage of the Vietnamese soldier. . . .

The advisers feel there is still too much political interference in the Vietnamese army and that promotion too often depends on political loyalty. . . .

Actually, most American field commanders believe the most helpful feature of the war here is the courage of the individual fighting man. Many who served earlier in Laos contrast this sharply with the record of the Laotian soldier, who they feel was not willing to help himself be saved.

This was critical reporting of course, and it angered both the U.S. administration and the South Vietnamese government. But the criticism, based as it was on the views of people firmly committed to the objectives of U.S. policy in Vietnam, was of the tactics of that policy, not its basic conception. By no means did all the *Times* reporting, moreover, focus on the negative. Where the war effort seemed to be going well, or where there seemed to be a story of heroism in the battle against Communism to report, *Times* reporters often wrote about it glowingly. On December 20, 1962, for instance, Halberstam reported from a Green Beret outpost:

Dak Pek is a far outpost of the non-Communist world, a small, knobby patch cut out of rugged mountains better suited for a tourist showplace than a military stronghold. . . .
Here a handful of tough United States Special Forces men day after day live a precarious existence training several hundred Montagnards, or mountain tribesmen. . . .
The Americans . . . know . . . that the Communists know and observe everything they do . . . yet they seem completely indifferent to danger.
"I am a fatalist about things like this," said Capt. George Gaspard of Orlando, Fla., leader of the team, a Marine veteran of Okinawa and Iwo Jima and a Silver Star winner during the Korean War. "We've got a job to do and we do it." According to Lieut. Pete Skamser of Covina, Calif., executive officer, every man on the team is willing to die for Dak Pek.[53]

A Halberstam piece in the Sunday Week in Review provides a good summary of *Times* coverage through the spring of 1963. The head read, "In Vietnam: 'Not Bad'; It's Still an Uphill Fight, but With Massive Aid From U.S., Results Are Now Visible." After reviewing the "stakes" in Vietnam, which he described as "sizable," Halberstam asked:

How is the war in Vietnam going? Fifteen months ago it was going badly. Now after a year of massive American aid it is not going badly and in some parts of the country it is going well, or as well as a war in jungled mountains can go. There is little danger of the Communists taking over any major city. . . . Now they hope to bog us down in a long unrewarding war which finally sends us to Geneva for a Laotian type settlement.
Fear of getting bogged down is still very real to Americans in the field who have both a healthy respect for the Vietcong and a healthy disrespect for American understanding of the length and depth of the struggle here. . . . Americans [in Saigon] talk of a great national movement moving irresistibly toward victory. Some of it is their own belief, some of it is done for local consumption, and some, according to sources here,

because of extreme pressures from the administration demanding positive results. . . .

[T]here is considerably more caution in the field. . . . These observers feel the war effort is generally going in the right direction, but they do not feel it is by any means a sure thing and they are worried over failure of Americans and Vietnamese to correct some basic problems. In the field there is a feeling that high American officials in Saigon, in a major effort to "get along" with the Vietnamese, are not employing enough leverage [i.e., not pressuring the South Vietnamese hard enough to change their ways].[54]

The Buddhist Crisis

The greatest controversy over press coverage developed in the summer of 1963, as the Buddhist crisis forced an American turnaround on support for Diem. Diem was a Catholic, drawing much of his political support from South Vietnam's Catholic minority, many of whom were refugees from the North. He had favored Catholics with choice government and military appointments and special property rights; he had also kept on the books a French statute relegating Buddhism to "private" status, while the Catholic church was considered a public institution. Tensions over these issues flared on May 8, when Buddhists in Hué gathered to celebrate the 2,527th birthday of Buddha.[55] The deputy province chief, a Catholic, decided to enforce a law prohibiting the flying of religious flags. That law had not been enforced the previous week, when Catholics had flown their own flags at a celebration of the 25th anniversary of the ordination of Ngo Dinh Thuc, Diem's brother, who was the archbishop of Hué. Angry Buddhists assembled outside a radio station to hear a speech by Tri Quang, a Buddhist leader, and government troops fired into the crowd. Nine people were killed either by gunfire or in the panic that ensued. The government, which claimed that the casualties had been caused by a Vietcong hand grenade thrown into the crowd, met subsequent protests with intransigence and repression, and the conflict escalated into a general political crisis, with the Buddhist "struggle movement" becoming the primary vehicle of opposition to the Diem regime.

It was during this period especially that the media were charged with shaping events rather than reporting them, wrecking American policy in the process. The argument generally had two parts, both reflected in a blast against the Saigon press corps printed in *Time* magazine's Press section in September. The first was that the reporting reflected the journalists' own animosity toward the Diem regime, reinforced to the point of dogma by the "camaraderie of Hotel Caravelle's eighth-floor bar—they pool their convictions, information, misinformation and grievances . . . [they] have tended to reach unanimous agreement on almost everything . . . suspect because it is so obviously inbred. The newsmen have themselves become a part of South Vietnam's confusion."[56] The second was that they were manipulated by the Buddhists. The *Time* piece featured a picture of a Buddhist press conference; accounts of the period almost always mention that the Buddhists were shrewd about cultivating contacts with Western reporters. (The right to hold press conferences is an important element of political legitimacy in the twentieth century, and when a new political force begins to hold them, there are always charges that the press is becoming "part of the story." They are always part of the story; they are part of modern politics. But their role is generally not noticed until it changes significantly. A good recent example is the 1985 Beirut hostage crisis, during which the Amal militia offered the media extensive access to the hostages.[57])

The Buddhists' contacts with the press were indeed an important element of the situation (though it should be added that they were used as sources less often in *Times* coverage than official representatives of the South Vietnamese government).[58] They tipped reporters in advance of several of the suicides by fire that dramatized their movement around the world. They carried signs in English for American television. While the Diem regime had been consistently hostile to the American press, the Buddhists were both friendly and open. They even relied to some degree on the Western press to publicize their cause within South Vietnam: the Vietnamese press was government controlled, and as the crisis deepened Vietnamese began increasingly to rely on the Voice of America, which provided a summary of the news Western audiences were receiving and thus sent back into Vietnam press reports that originated there, for news about their own country.[59]

It was also true that most of the Saigon press corps considered the Diem regime, as Halberstam would later put it, an "incompetent and hostile instrument of American policy."[60] This had not always been the case. Diem's press up to about the middle of 1962 was not particularly unfavorable.[61] But from mid-1962 until the end of his regime, there is no doubt that a strong hostility toward the Diem regime was building up among American journalists. On occasion, this hostility came out in their reporting. In July 1962, for instance, Homer Bigart, who had just finished his tour in Saigon, wrote of the Diem regime with a bluntness unusual in modern American journalism (or, to be precise, unusual when dealing with a controversial, rather than a consensus, issue; reports about the North Vietnamese, for instance, were always blunt):

[V]isions of ultimate victory are obscured by the image of a secretive, suspicious, dictatorial regime. American officers are frustrated and irritated by the constant whimsical meddling of the President and his brother, Ngo Dinh Nhu, in the military chain of command.[62]

But reporting of this sort was not at all the norm. For the most part, there was simply very little coverage of the character of the Diem regime or the opposition to it until these became the focus of a major debate among American officials. In the *Times*, reporting on the political weakness of the Diem regime rarely appeared except in two cases: as a side issue in reports focused primarily on military activity, when U.S. officers complained of command problems or government sluggishness in undertaking "civic action" programs; and when officials in Washington went public with complaints about the regime, as they did periodically, beginning in November 1961, in an effort to pressure Diem into instituting reforms.[63] Of thirty-three stories with Vietnam datelines appearing in the *Times* in the four months preceding the Buddhist crisis only three could be said to have dealt primarily with South Vietnamese politics.[64] None dealt with the non-Communist opposition to the Diem regime. These four months were typical. Aside from a brief flurry of reporting following an attack in February 1962 on the presidential palace by two South Vietnamese pilots opposed to Diem, the opposition to Diem was essentially invisible. *Times* reporting was preoccupied with American activities and dependent on American sources[65]—very few American reporters spoke Vietnamese. Until the Buddhist crisis focused the attention of American officials on the political weakness of the Saigon regime, therefore, coverage of South Vietnamese politics was inevitably very limited, despite the reporters' personal attitudes.

For the most part the dynamics of news coverage during the Buddhist crisis were familiar. The suicide on June 11 of Quang Duc, the first Buddhist priest to burn himself to death, did not make page 1 of the *Times*, nor did the *Times* run Malcolm Browne's famous photo of that event. The day before, however, when Halberstam reported from Saigon that "the conflict between the South Vietnamese government and Buddhist priests is sorely troubling American officials here," the story did make page 1. And it did again, more prominently, on June 14, when Max Frankel reported from Washington:

The United States has warned President Ngo Dinh Diem . . . that it will publicly condemn his treatment of the Buddhists unless he takes prompt action to meet their grievances. American diplomats in Saigon have told the Vietnamese in the bluntest terms that Buddhist disaffection could become politically disastrous and that Washington wishes to dissociate itself from President Ngo Dinh Diem's policies. . . .

> The feeling here has been that a disavowal by the United States, though addressed only to Saigon's handling of the dispute . . . could jeopardize cooperation . . . in the long war against the Communist guerrillas.
>
> For that reason, Washington has been reluctant to speak out. But it is losing faith in the effectiveness of quiet, backstage pressure.

Mecklin later wrote of Frankel's story that is "read as though the reporter . . . had been shown the file of classified cables from Saigon."[66] The journalists were doing more or less what they always do: reporting what "officials here believe." But the Buddhist crisis had thrown both Saigon and Washington officialdom into a state of emergency and disarray. It aggravated existing divisions in the administration, and officials increasingly began using the press as an instrument of bureaucratic conflict, attacking one another and making conflicting statements about the Diem regime and U.S. policy toward it.[67] And the crisis shifted the balance between factions: as it continued, opposition to the Diem regime, which had until then been a "maverick" view that could only be expressed anonymously, became the dominant position, both in Saigon and in Washington. As the administration moved toward a break with Diem, moreover, it faced a new version of the old problem of multiple audiences. Even if they preferred for domestic reasons to minimize publicity about the Buddhist crisis, officials feared that if they kept silent Diem would assume that it was business as usual. A public stance was considered essential to the administration's "leverage" over Diem, and the press was used repeatedly to signal to the Diem regime the administration's desire for "dramatic measures of redress," as the Frankel story put it.

From the beginning officials recognized the Buddhist crisis as a serious threat to the stability of the Diem government and thus to the war effort. "Unlike our attitude toward the state of the war," Mecklin wrote later, "there were no U.S. illusions about the Buddhist upheaval. The U.S. mission, like everyone else, was surprised by the crisis, but quickly recognized its gravity."[68] There were, however, disagreements over how the United States should respond. Until the Buddhist crisis the official position had been what Homer Bigart dubbed "sink or swim with Ngo Dinh Diem:" the view that Diem's rule was essential to political stability, and that the United States could therefore not afford to antagonize or undercut him. The stern warning to Diem reported in Frankel's story came at a time when Frederick Nolting, the U.S. ambassador and chief proponent of the "sink or swim" policy, was on vacation and the mission was under the direction of Chargé d' Affaires William Truehart, who favored a much harder line and interpreted his State Department inst: actions to pressure Diem in accord with that belief.[69] Nolting was furious when he returned to discover that the United States had come so close to a public break with Diem, and a major struggle followed within the mission. But Nolting's tour of duty was nearly up. He was replaced in August by Henry Cabot Lodge, who would quickly begin pushing for Diem's ouster; and in the interim he was increasingly undercut by other American officials who expressed their alarm over Diem's policies to reporters.

In Washington the pattern was similar: a period of caution following initial warnings to Diem, and then, after a political struggle, a decisive shift against him. In July, when a month-long government truce with the Buddhists began to break down, Kennedy sent a letter to Diem reaffirming U.S. support for his government, while Nolting told the Senate Foreign Committee that the Saigon government had a "winning program." "Officials are gravely concerned about the effect of Buddhist demonstrations on the war effort," Hedrick Smith reported—a statement that seemed to put the onus on the Buddhists. "Although officials here feel the Saigon government made some blunders . . . they see no alternative to working with President Ngo Dinh Diem."[70] Nolting, however, was sent back to Saigon with instructions to make one last attempt quietly to persuade Diem to conciliate the Buddhists. This he was not able to do, and by the middle of August officials in Washington were beginning to press publicly for conciliation once again.

The Diem government, however, did just the opposite. On August 21, police and soldiers raided the Buddhist pagodas in Saigon, arresting hundreds of priests. The *Times*'s lead ran under a four-column head, the largest yet used for a Vietnam story, and was, like most leads played with that prominence, from Washington: "Official reports reaching here," James Reston reported, "indicated this morning that the conflict between the government of President Ngo Dinh Diem and the Buddhists had created a situation that threatened the security of the Diem government and of the United States forces in Vietnam."[71] The administration denounced the attacks in strong terms the next day.[72] A debate then ensued within the administration over where to place the blame, on the president's brother, Ngo Dinh Nhu, or on the South Vietnamese army. The official position, initially, was that the army was to blame, and for several days there was an immense gulf between Washington reports and those from Saigon, where sources were telling reporters Nhu had been responsible.[73] On August 23 the *Times* ran two reports side by side, with an explanation that conflicting versions were being received. After a few days, however, Washington concluded that the

Ngo family had indeed acted without the army's knowledge, and by August 28 some officials would be talking to reporters about a search for "alternatives to the regime."[74]

A period of heavy "leaking" by contending factions ensued, and with administration policy unclear, Congress and also newspaper editorial writers began to become active; this is a pattern we will encounter many times in the history that follows—an upturn in journalistic and political activity when political divisions in the administration become acute.[75] By October, however, the administration had committed itself to the "search for alternatives," internal unity was for the most part restored, and both the leaking and domestic political controversy faded. The coup, when it came on November 1, was treated by the press as a positive development and was accompanied neither by publicity about American involvement nor by calls for a reexamination of the American role in Vietnam; a statement by Senate Majority Leader Mansfield calling for such a reexamination was played inside the *Times*, as it was in other papers.[76]

The Ideology of the Cold War

Despite the absence of an open public debate over Vietnam, the Kennedy period was one of bitter behind-the-scenes conflicts. There was the struggle within the administration over policy toward Diem; there was the struggle between the administration and the press; and there were conflicts within journalism. The *Time* Press piece criticizing the Saigon press corps, for instance, followed a period of growing tension between top *Time* editors in New York, who were strong supporters of Diem, and its reporters in Saigon, who felt their reporting was being distorted.[77] Those reporters, Charles Mohr and Mert Perry, resigned after the blast on their colleagues was printed. And the Saigon press corps was bitter at correspondents like Alsop and Higgins, quoted above, who flew into Vietnam and criticized their reporting. (The administration, incidently, which was carrying on a "press orientation program consisting of sponsored visits to Saigon by mature and responsible American correspondents and executives," encouraged such trips.[78])

As furious as these battles seemed to those involved, however, they all took place within the narrow confines of a tight consensus on the nature of world politics and the American role in it; none brought into question the premise that the preservation of an anti-Communist Vietnam was indeed a legitimate goal of American policy. The reporting of the 1962–63 period is generally described, both by its critics and its defenders, as a first step in the process of domestic polarization that eventually led to U.S. disengagement from Vietnam. And no doubt it was to some degree; no doubt the images of civil strife in South Vietnam (which shared the front pages with news of the conflict in the American South) and the contrasts that so often appeared between official optimism and reports from the field sowed the seeds of the "credibility gap" that would later emerge. But those seeds were still buried and dormant when Lyndon Johnson came to office in 1964. More immediately, the legacy left by the Vietnam reporting of the Kennedy years was an image of Vietnam as a vital though shaky outpost of the Free World, one that could not be abandoned without the gravest consequences.

"The tradition of the dead generations," Marx once wrote, "weighs like a nightmare on the minds of the living." And, to paraphrase him a little, just when people believe they are acting with hardheaded realism, facing directly the harsh realities of a changed world, shunning the temptation to live in the past that seduced the previous generation, just in such a period they "conjure up the spirits of the past to help them; they borrow their names, slogans and costumes so as to stage the new world-historical scene in this venerable disguise and borrowed language."[79] At the end of World War II, determined not to repeat the error they believed the nation had made in the 1930s, the foreign policy establishment acted to prevent a return to the prewar belief that American interests were best served by disengagement from international affairs.[80] They interpreted the world of 1947 by analogy to that of 1939: the democracies of the West confronted a totalitarian enemy dedicated to their destruction; it was essential, therefore, to think of American interests not merely in terms of defending the national borders, but in terms of global security; any political development that affected the balance of power between the Free World and Communism required an American response, and to rule out the use of force would encourage aggression.

As the world changed, new political phenomena were assimilated by this framework. "Her political techniques are self-confident, ruthless and capable of infinite variety, from military terror to humanitarian tracts," *Time* magazine wrote of the Soviet Union, in what was probably the first shot of the Cold War for the U.S. press, an April 1946 article based on George Kennan's "long telegram" on Soviet intentions, which policymakers had leaked to *Time*.[81] As new forms of political conflict arose—which occurred, above all, in the new nations that were becoming independent of colonial domination—they were interpreted as examples of the "infinite variety" of Communist tactics.[82] The World War II image of a vast, bipolar struggle between democracy and totalitarianism was thus carried over through the 1950s, and in the early 1960s, half a generation after the end of World War II, it was applied without question to the conflict in Indochina.

It was a popular view in the post–World War II period that the "age of ideology" had passed in America, replaced by the spirit of objective inquiry and political pluralism and pragmatism.[83] And it was true that no great philosophical debates over the direction of public policy were taking place. This silence, however, represented not the end of ideology, but the triumph of a single ideology over all competitors. It was an age of ideological consensus, and this was true above all in foreign policy. The world view of the Cold War dominated American thinking about international affairs so totally during these years that it became not merely dangerous but virtually impossible for most Americans to question or to step outside it. Americans simply knew no other language for thinking or for communicating about the world.

The journalists were no exception. American journalists like to think of themselves as particularly unideological; freedom from ideological bias is an essential principle of the ethic of the professional journalist. What this means in practice, however, is that journalists are loath to take sides when explicit political controversies develop (as we shall see, journalists kept their distance from the antiwar movement, even late in the war, when most were very critical of U.S. policy in Vietnam). Where consensus reigns, however, they rely as heavily as anyone else on the symbolic tools that make up the dominant ideology of their society.[84] Indeed, the nature of their work makes them particularly dependent on those tools, and this is especially true in the reporting of foreign affairs. The foreign affairs journalist must report events extremely distant from his or her personal experience, as well as from the experience of the audience. This must be done concisely, in the space of about two minutes on television or a thousand words in a newspaper. And the difficulty of the task is confounded by the immense complexity of international affairs in a century of world wars and an expanding and interdependent world system; in the 1961–63 period alone Vietnam shared the headlines with crises in Laos, the Congo, Berlin, and Cuba, to name only a few. The ideology of the Cold War was ideally suited to the reduction of this complexity: it related every crisis to a single, familiar axis of conflict; it enabled the journalist to explain to the news audience (and to him or herself), with minimum effort and, at least in appearance, great clarity, "what it all meant"— why South Vietnam, or Laos, or the Congo was worth reading about.

Ideological framing of events in the *New York Times* is done most explicitly in the Sunday Week in Review section, whose function is to put the week's news in context. In the Week in Review for February 18, 1962, for instance, Robert Trumbull reported:

THREE AREAS OF ASIA DISTURB THE FREE WORLD;
*U.S. Attempts to Stem Communist Aggression Are Hampered
by Weak Regimes on China's Fringes*

Domestic instability in key non-Communist nations fringing Communist China continues to hamper United States efforts to build up these lands against further Communist penetration into free Asia.

As the richest non-Communist power and the principal Western nation with a Pacific Ocean frontier, the United States has inherited the chief responsibility for confining Communist rule in Eastern Asia to its present boundaries. . . .

In none of these endangered nations [South Vietnam, Laos, and South Korea] can the United States rely upon internal stability as a source of strength in the free world's fight to contain aggressive Communism.

South Vietnam and South Korea are ruled by authoritarian regimes whose roots haven't sprung from the people.

This kind of reporting was a problem for the administration in that it focused on the political weakness of the Diem administration, but its message about why it mattered that South Vietnam was ruled by an authoritarian government remained firmly within the consensus journalists shared with officials. "Domestic instability" mattered because it stood in the way of U.S. efforts to contain Communism.

Trumbull's February 18 report was accompanied by a map of Southeast Asia, dividing the nations of the area into those that belonged to the Communist bloc, those allied with the West, and a no-man's-land in between, to which South Vietnam belonged. The heading was "Communist Pressure Points in Southeast Asia." These maps appeared in most Week in Review pieces on Southeast Asia, often spreading imposingly across eight columns above the article itself. They provide a good summary of the Cold War view of the world and of the conflict in Southeast Asia. Here are headings and descriptions of some of them:

October 15, 1961. "Laos and the Threat of Communist Expansion"

July 22, 1962. "The Warfare in South Vietnam—The History, Present Communist Pressure and the Threat to Southeast Asia"

The largest of three maps that appeared under this heading was titled "The Importance of South Vietnam to the Area"; it explained South Vietnam's importance in three boxes:

"It Holds Key to SEATO Security: The Government of South Vietnam falls within the protective sphere of the Southeast Asia Treaty Organization. Its loss to the Communists would be a fatal blow to the defense of the area."

"It Bars Chinese Expansion: The strategic location of South Vietnam on the Indochina peninsula is of vital importance to the West. The nation is the gateway to Malaya, Singapore and the islands to the south."

"It Protects Rice Bowl Nations: The free nations on the Indochina peninsula, South Vietnam, Laos and Cambodia, produced 7 million tons of rice in 1961. Peiping's control of rice would give it a major bargaining asset."

September 16, 1962. "Ten Major Areas of Conflict in the Struggle Between the United States and the Soviet Union"

In the box pointing to South Vietnam: "RUSSIA moves to aid Communist forces in bid to gain control of area; U.S. steps up aid to Diem Government to spur offensive against guerrillas."

October 21, 1962. "Communist Expansion in Asia Since the End of World War II—and the Military Situation in Southeast Asia"

What these articles said about the nature of the Diem government and the effectiveness of U.S. tactics varied a good deal. But what they said about the nature and significance of the conflict was consistent: it was a struggle against centrally directed Communist aggression, "an undeclared war," as Hanson W. Baldwin put it, "against the proxy armies of Soviet Russia—North and South Vietnamese guerrillas."[85] This view of the conflict explains in part why the strategy of limited war, introduced earlier, made sense both to policymakers and to journalists. If the Vietnamese guerrillas were indeed proxy armies of the Soviets (one cartoon the *Times* carried in the Week in Review shortly after the Cuban missile crisis showed Khrushchev as a football coach, injured "Cuba" being removed from the field, "Laos" and "Vietnam" on the bench, and "Berlin" asking, "Did you call me, Coach?"[86]), then Vietnam was a limited war for the Communists as well, one front among many in the global struggle, and they could reasonably be expected to back down if the United States raised the stakes. Given the strength of the "global" perspective of the Cold War, virtually no one, either in the administration or in the press, took seriously until much later the possibility that their Vietnamese adversaries might not only prove to be the key "players," but might turn out not to consider the struggle for control of their country a "limited war."[87] The Vietnamese Communists (as well as political forces allied with them) were almost totally absent from the news coverage of the early 1960s.

The same view of the conflict that was expressed explicitly in the analytic reporting of the Week in Review pervaded day-to-day news coverage as well. To some extent, of course, this was because the news columns were filled with the statements of U.S. officials. But the journalists themselves were as deeply steeped in the ideology of the Cold

War as those they wrote about. Its images pervaded their language; its assumptions guided their news judgments. Its power can be seen both in the "framing" of the events that were covered and, equally important, in the things that were *not* covered, that fell through the conceptual gaps of the world view the journalists accepted as common sense.

The most important element in the ideological framing of Vietnam news was the simple fact that the war was consistently described as a conflict between a "Western-backed" regime and "Communist guerrillas." This was essentially true; the National Liberation Front (whose name, incidentally, American reporters never used without quotation marks) included many non-Communist members but its leadership was overwhelmingly Communist and its coordination with the Communist Lao Dong party in Hanoi close; the great powers of the Cold War, moreover, had indeed chosen sides. But other things were equally true about the conflict in Vietnam: it was a war of peasant revolutionaries against a feudal social order. It was also a conflict born out of a nationalist struggle against colonial rule. The ideology of the Cold War directed attention almost exclusively to the first of these three facets. (A good illustration of the power of that ideology is the fact that it was able to assimilate even the French Indochina War, which one *Times* report described in 1961 as "a seven-and-a-half-year struggle between the French army and foreign-inspired and supplied Communists."[88])

Following are a few examples of daily news coverage in which the framing of the story in Cold War terms is clearly evident. Each is from the lead of a front page story. Notice that the phrases that identify the "problem" in Vietnam in Cold War terms are taken entirely for granted: throughout the *Times*'s coverage "the Communist threat" or the "Red advance" (sometimes more graphic phrases were used, e.g., "the swiftly encroaching Communist menace"[89]) is treated as a sort of baseline reality, which can be used to give meaning to day-to-day events. The reporter feels no need either to justify these phrases, to attribute them to any authority, or otherwise to signal that they involve an interpretation of reality.

E.W. Kenworthy, Washington, May 10, 1961. Vice President Johnson left today on a mission to reassure nations in Asia of U.S. support against Communist aggression.

Robert Trumbull, Dalat, South Vietnam, October 22, 1961. Gen. Maxwell D. Taylor and his chief aides made an extensive air and ground tour of actual fighting zones in South Vietnam today. They had a look at the enemy through binoculars where the Ben Het river separates the embattled South from Communist-ruled North Vietnam [note the imagery here of a conventional conflict between two states]. General Taylor heads a twelve-man group . . . assessing how Washington can best help stop the Red advance.

David Halberstam, Saigon, January 20, 1963. Communist guerrillas trying to subvert this country admit to having underestimated the depth of United States intentions, according to an important captured document, and have had to move back their timetable for victory.

Halberstam, Saigon, June 10, 1963. The conflict between the South Vietnamese Government and Buddhist priests is sorely troubling American officials here.

It has brought to the surface American frustrations of the apparently limited influence of the United States here despite its heavy investment in troops, economic aid and prestige to help South Vietnam block Communism.

An ideology defines not only what people see, but also what they do not see. What Americans saw in Vietnam was aggression; what they did not see and could not see, given the political concepts available to them, was revolution. This is not to say that they were unaware that the conflict in Vietnam had a political dimension which made it different from, say, the Korean War (though imagery of conventional military conflict was certainly used). On the contrary, after "the stakes are enormous," the next most common cliché, both in official discussion of Vietnam and in news coverage, surely was "this is as much a political as a military struggle." (Later, as the war escalated, it would increasingly become a conventional military conflict, but in the early 1960s it was still very much a political war.) The war in Vietnam was understood as a "new kind of aggression," carried on by "subversion" ("subversion" was the bridging concept that linked the phenomenon of revolution to the Cold War framework). The news audience was told repeatedly that the key to victory was the loyalty of the peasant, and the critical problem was the inability of the South Vietnamese government to secure it. Beyond this, however, the journalists could not go. Neither they nor their sources could explain why the peasants failed to rally to the anti-Communist government. No aspect of the *Times*'s reporting during this period was as fragmentary or as inaccurate as its reporting of what was going on in the South Vietnamese countryside.

The major U.S./South Vietnamese program designed to counter Communist influence in the countryside was the Strategic Hamlet program, under which peasants were removed to fortified villages, which would, in theory, deprive the guerrillas of access to them as a source of recruits, food, intelligence, and cover and simultaneously make it possible for the government to carry out its own activities to win them over. This was a high-priority program for the U.S. mission, and even though there was generally little coverage of the countryside, it was fairly heavily reported. In its initial stages, as "Operation Sunrise," the Strategic Hamlet program was described in the *Times* as a "harsh and drastic military measure" (most of the time, the peasants had to be rounded up into strategic hamlets by force), which was nevertheless necessary and was being "conducted as humanely as possible."[90] After a while, however, the emphasis on harshness faded. The typical description of the Strategic Hamlets portrayed them as a measure taken for the benefit of the peasant: "The Agrovilles [an earlier name for Strategic Hamlets], by concentrating the rural population, not only give better protection against the Communists but enable the government to provide health, education and other services."[91] Through most of the Kennedy period, moreover, the Strategic Hamlet program appeared in the *Times* as one of the most promising aspects of the war effort.[92] The precedent of the successful British counterinsurgency effort in Malaya in the 1950s was often invoked.

Peasants still generally had to be moved into the Strategic Hamlets by force, and correspondents were well aware that the Saigon government had little support in the countryside. They explained this in several ways. At times they blamed it on the "rigidity" of the Diem regime, which, among other things, meant that the government did not carry out aid programs in the villages as Americans had urged. At times they blamed it on inadequate propaganda ("failure to spread sufficiently information on the reasons for the removals"[93]). And at times—probably most often—they blamed it on "the reign of terror instituted by Communist guerrillas." "The Communists have had considerable success in cutting the contact between President Ngo Dinh Diem's government and the people," said one typical report. "Their activities have hampered almost every effort of the Saigon administration to improve the lives of the peasants and villagers."[94] As for the guerrillas, they were shadowy figures in the news; nothing was said about their history, organization, or politics. They were simply one manifestation of the generic Cold War threat: "militant Communists who seek to take over South Vietnam,"[95] terrorists who "lived here comfortably, dominating the countryside."[96]

What was missing from all of this was any conception of the social structure of rural Vietnam and the patterns of interest arising from it which enabled the revolutionary movement to prosper. There was, to be sure, another standard cliché of the period which held that "poverty" (a purely quantitative concept which requires no understanding of social structure) provided "fertile ground for social unrest." But the "unrest" was assumed to be either coerced or irrational: the peasants were assumed to be acting against their interests, either because they were forced to do so or because they were fooled by "clever Communist propaganda." (The peasants, one *Times* report explained, "remain in a degree of ignorance that the Communists exploit to debase them even further."[97]) In fact what the Communists "exploited," according to most who have studied the political economy of the Vietnamese revolution, was not so much the peasants' vulnerability or "ignorance" as their interests.[98] They provided a form of village government that radically redistributed political power and, along with it, economic and social privileges of many kinds, breaking or limiting the power of the old feudal elites—landlords and government officials—and favoring the interests, particularly, of the poorest peasants. They offered a route of social mobility not usually open: the ordinary peasant could rise up through the ranks of the NLF, which was not possible in the South Vietnamese army or government. They often protected villagers against corrupt or oppressive government officials; their terrorism was not directed against "defenseless peasants" in general, though they would sometimes take reprisals against ordinary peasants who cooperated with the government, for example, by giving information.[99] Most violence was directed against government officials, and its purpose was often not to terrorize the villagers but to win their support by killing particularly hated representatives of the government.[100] And the NLF distributed land, or prevented landlords from taking back land that had been distributed earlier by the Viet Minh (the guerrilla organization which had led the struggle against the French), and controlled rents and evictions. In the entire corpus of *New York Times* coverage from 1961 through September 1963 I was able to find only two references to land tenure. Both were extremely brief; the most substantial came in an article based on an interview with Colonel Pham Ngoc Thao, a South Vietnamese officer who had once served in the Viet Minh and who was, unbeknownst to the reporter or the South Vietnamese government, working for the NLF.[101]

As for the Strategic Hamlets, they probably did cause considerable difficulties for the NLF, at least initially; this at least is what NLF documents of the period suggest.[102] By early 1963, however, it was clear that the program was in trouble. In part this was because Ngo Dinh Nhu was pushing the program wildly forward with little sense of the kind of planning that would be necessary to make it work. The press, or at any rate the *Times*, had not really discovered Nhu at this point; hence the vague talk about "rigidity" as the reason for the government's failure to carry out the program as American advisors wished it carried out. But the Strategic Hamlet program also had more fundamental flaws, and these, deeply related to the dynamics of the insurgency, disappeared in the ideological blind spots of American journalism. The key assumption behind the program was that "security was the key" to political success in the countryside: that if one could only "protect" the rural population physically from the "terrorists" and "agitators," their loyalty could be won. The problem was that a large part of the rural population did not consider itself an object of attack by the guerrillas; for them, being forced off their land and into a government encampment where their movements were controlled was simply a hindrance to their ability to make a living, often one more reason to side with the "agitators," who, with the population sympathetic, could eventually repenetrate the physical defenses that were supposed to keep them out. The uncritical use of the analogy with Malaya suggests how little journalists—and many other Americans in Vietnam—knew about the Vietnamese countryside. In Malaya, unlike Vietnam, the insurgents were ethnically distinct from the villagers moved to the Strategic Hamlets, and hence were indeed perceived by the latter as outsiders. In Malaya, moreover, a different type of rural economy meant that peasants did not suffer economically from the removals as Vietnamese peasants did. The failure of the government to undertake civic action programs, finally, may not have been so much a matter of the "rigidity" or "mandarin style" of the Diem regime as it was a result of the fact that the South Vietnamese government was closely tied to the old elites, whose power the revolutionaries challenged. Its problem, in other words, may not have been primarily inefficiency or corruption, but being on the wrong side of class conflict in the countryside.[103] But Americans did not see revolution in terms of class interests.

To summarize the impact of the Cold War ideology, it will be useful to return to the maps that so dominated the *Times*'s Week in Review. The very fact that *maps* played such a prominent role in foreign affairs reporting reveals a good deal about the nature of the Cold War world view. This may seem an odd thing to say: maps are obviously a useful reporting tool, if only because the public's knowledge of geography is limited. But the maps the *Times* used in its Vietnam coverage were intended to do more than show where Vietnam was: they were intended to explain what the conflict there was about. That is why they were so large and prominent; it is rare today to find so dramatic a map in the Week in Review. The explanation for this emphasis on maps, and its implications, is easy to understand if one looks back at World War II. They were used very prominently then as well, both in news coverage and in propaganda. Frank Capra's *War Comes to America*, for instance, an Office of War Information film and a classic of wartime propaganda, used animated maps to drive home its central point: that Americans could not remain indifferent to events in distant parts of the globe. Like all tools of representation, the map has important limitations. It represents nations as geographical entities, but cannot easily represent them as political or socioeconomic or cultural ones, nor can it easily represent the divisions within them. But in the context of a world war in which the planet had become a vast battlefield, in which the intricacies of any nation's history and political economy could easily be rendered irrelevant by the force of an army marching across its border, these limitations seemed insignificant: "geopolitics" was the only reality that counted. It made perfect sense to think of, say, Indochina, as a "gateway" to the rest of Southeast Asia and a source of strategic materials (the Japanese appropriated massive quantities of rice from Indochina to feed their armies, causing a major famine there); the details of social stratification in the countryside seemed of little importance.

It was this geopolitical view, in its Cold War adaptation, that dominated American thinking in the early 1960s. For the journalists covering Vietnam it had two important consequences. First, it meant that they started out with a presumption that the "defense" of South Vietnam was vital to American interests, a presumption strong enough to stand up despite their considerable skepticism about the conduct of the war. Second, it meant that their coverage said little about those aspects of the conflict that might have provoked deeper doubts. The progress of military efforts to "block Communist expansion" was considered more important than the grievances of peasants against their landlords; if it was a question of putting the conflict in context, the latest speech by Khrushchev was considered far more relevant than, say, the history of Vietnamese anticolonialism. Thus for all the conflict over "negative" Vietnam coverage, the consensus that in 1961 had made escalation in Vietnam something "apparently taken for granted," as the *Pentagon Papers* put it, was intact when Lyndon Johnson came into office at the end of 1963.

3

"It Does Not Imply Any Change of Policy Whatever," 1964–1965

The President desires with respect to [these] actions . . . premature publicity be avoided by all possible precautions. The actions themselves should be taken as rapidly as practicable, but in ways that should minimize any appearance of sudden changes in policy, and official statements on troop movements will be made only with the direct approval of the Secretary of Defense. . . . [T]hese movements and changes should be understood as being gradual and wholly consistent with existing policy.

> (NSAM) 328, April 6, 1965, approving "a change of mission for all marine battalions deployed to Vietnam to permit their more active use under conditions to be established."[1]

PRESIDENT PLANS NO MAJOR CHANGE IN VIETNAM POLICY

He Is Adhering to Firm but Cautious Course,
With Talks With Reds a Main Goal

Parley Unlikely Soon

Raids on North Will Continue But American Combat
Role Is Still Being Avoided

> *New York Times* head, April 25, 1965

Let me make the news and you can write all the editorials you want against it.

> JAMES RESTON, on Franklin Roosevelt's view of news management[2]

In July 1962, with optimistic reports coming in from field commanders and a lingering concern that public support for U.S. military involvement could not be sustained indefinitely, the Kennedy administration began planning for a "phased withdrawal" of U.S. forces, which was expected to take about three years and to leave South Vietnamese government forces capable of dealing on their own with what remained of the insurgency. This policy was reaffirmed publicly in October 1963, when the White House announced that the "major part" of the U.S.

59

military task could be completed by the end of 1965. A first withdrawal of 1,000 men (which the Joint Chiefs wanted to make in four increments, to minimize the effect on military operations and provide "news prominence and coverage over an extended period of time"[3]) was planned for November–December 1963.

But by that time the Buddhist crisis had eroded the optimism of 1962, and the withdrawal actually carried out was little more than an accounting exercise. By March 1964 planning was in full swing for an escalation of U.S. involvement. That "escalation" (in 1965 the term was a bit of bureaucratese intended to lessen the symbolic impact of decisions to increase the scope and pace of the war; later, like many other such terms, its meaning turned around, and it became a symbolic weapon of the opposition) involved two major shifts in American strategy and commitment. The first was the initiation of "graduated military pressures" against the North, culminating in the onset of sustained bombing in February 1965. The second was the decision, made in March–July 1965, to commit U.S. combat units to the ground war in the South. The most important decision of the Johnson period came on July 17, when the president approved a request from the Joint Chiefs for the deployment of 100,000 troops to join the 75,000 already committed. This decision constituted approval of the first phase of a three-phase plan proposed by General Westmoreland. A decision on the second phase, which was estimated to require a troop level up to about 400,000, was deferred until the end of 1965, when Phase I was expected to be completed. But the fateful threshold had been crossed: American forces had been committed to a land war in Asia.

A Special National Security Estimate issued on July 23, as the administration was deliberating when and how to announce the decision on Phase I, recommended that "in order to mitigate somewhat the crisis atmosphere that would result from this major U.S. action . . . announcements about it be made piecemeal with no more high-level emphasis than necessary."[4] Johnson followed this recommendation. Announcing the decision in a July 28 press conference, he began dramatically, pledging the nation to stand firm against aggression:

> Nor would surrender in Vietnam bring peace, because we learned from Hitler at Munich that success only feeds the appetite of aggression. The battle would be renewed in one country and then another country, bringing with it perhaps even larger and crueler conflict, as we have learned from the lessons of history.

But when he turned from the lessons of history to the politics of the present, Johnson announced only a modest deployment of 50,000—

half of the increase he had decided upon. He then added, "Additional forces will be needed eventually, and they will be sent as requested."[5] He said nothing about the force levels his advisors had recommended for Phase II. And he was silent about the change of strategy that represented the real significance of the new troop deployment: the decision that U.S. forces would have to take over from South Vietnamese government troops the burden of defeating NLF and North Vietnamese forces in the South. "Mr. President," Johnson was asked after his formal statement, "does the fact that you are sending additional forces to Vietnam imply any change in the policy of relying mainly on the South Vietnamese to carry out offensive operations and using American forces to guard installations and to act as emergency backup?" And the president replied simply, "It does not imply any change of policy whatever. It does not imply any change of objective."[6]

It was true enough that the objective of U.S. policy in Vietnam had not changed; what had changed was the strategy. The same could be said of U.S. policy on the "home front," where the objectives also remained constant. For Johnson, as for Kennedy, the basic purpose of public and press relations policy on Vietnam was to keep the war off the political agenda.

Like its predecessor, the Johnson administration sought to accomplish this in part by appealing to the Cold War consensus and to its symbolic roots in the "lessons of history." And the continuing strength of the Cold War consensus is no doubt the most important reason the administration was able to contain the debate over Vietnam policy. The *New York Times* itself illustrates the position of the administration's critics, who as the war began to escalate were drawn increasingly from the liberal side of the American political spectrum. In its editorials and in the opinions of its major columnists the *Times* broke sharply with the administration early in 1965, calling for negotiation rather than escalation and decrying the secrecy that surrounded administration policy. But it never broke with the assumption that the cause of the war was Communist aggression and that—to quote Reston—"the political and strategic consequences of defeat would [be] serious for the free world all over Asia."[7] The debate of 1965, like that of 1963 over Diem, was a debate over tactics: there were some who favored escalation, some who favored negotiation, but very few in Congress, the press, the administration, and the "establishment" generally who doubted that the United States had, in one way or another, to preserve South Vietnam as an outpost of the Free World. So it is not surprising that when Congress voted in May 1965 on funding for the war, a vote the president had explicitly said should be considered a vote to "persist in our effort to halt Communist aggression," and not a routine appropriation, there were only a handful of votes in opposition.[8] The vote in the Senate was 88 to 3; the opposition had picked up only a single vote since the Gulf of Tonkin resolution the previous August.

Nevertheless, Johnson's administration was no more willing than Kennedy's to take its policy openly to the court of public opinion. It assumed consensus would not hold if the war seemed likely to take on Korea-like proportions; it also feared that opponents of the "Great Society" would use Vietnam as an opportunity to gut it, demanding cuts in domestic spending as the price for a wartime military budget. For Johnson, moreover, the problem of public opinion was far more severe than it had been for Kennedy. Kennedy had faced only one major decision involving an escalation of U.S. involvement; once that decision had been made and the initial controversy had passed, the issue largely faded from the news. As late as May 1964, 64% of the public acknowledged that they had given "little thought" to Vietnam.[9] Johnson, however, was faced with a situation in which the defeat of U.S. policy seemed imminent unless a series of new moves were taken, moves of such magnitude that they made Southeast Asia the primary point of conflict among the superpowers, the focus of a wide-ranging international debate, and the site of a war in which Americans would soon be dying in combat in the hundreds and thousands. There was no question, therefore, of keeping Vietnam off the front pages or of avoiding some degree of debate at home simply by sitting tight and keeping quiet, as the Kennedy administration had done during much of its tenure. Johnson thus found it necessary to engage in a continuous and often elaborate effort to manage the news, the purpose of which was to preserve an appearance of continuity and inevitability, to make each new step in the growing American involvement appear as though it constituted "no change of policy" and hence required no public discussion.

Ironically, the success of these efforts at news management depended to a large degree on the ability of the administration to manipulate the routines of what was known at the time as "objective journalism." The press neither cooperated directly with the administration, as it had done, for instance, during the Cuban missile crisis, nor—at least a good deal of the time—were the journalists really fooled by the euphemisms or the silences of the administration's public statements. "The time has come to call a spade a bloody shovel," James Reston wrote in February, as the bombing of North Vietnam was getting under way. "Our masters have a lot of long and fancy names for it, like escalation and retaliation, but it is war just the same."[10] But the routines of the profession of journalism—the very procedures that are intended, in theory, to maintain the political autonomy of the press—ensured that for the most part the long and fancy names of official discourse would dominate the headlines and news columns.

In a moment we will begin to analyze the *New York Times*'s coverage of the 1964–65 escalation, starting with the Gulf of Tonkin incident in August 1964 and ending with Johnson's decision on the ground war a bit less than a year later. The focus of this chapter will be on coverage of administration *policy-making*; coverage of the fighting and of the political situation in South Vietnam will not be included. It should be noted, though, that the 1964–65 escalation took place against a backdrop of chaotic political conflict in Saigon which was heavily reported in the *Times*. The relative lack of political controversy as Johnson stepped up the American commitment is all the more impressive given that background.

Before returning to August 1964, however, we need to take time out to look in some detail at the principle of "objectivity" which lies at the heart of the modern profession of journalism. The term *objective journalism* is not much used by reporters today, except in the past tense, to refer to the naiveté of the period we are now exploring. And it is true that the conventions of American journalism have changed a good deal, in part because of the events that began in August 1964. "I was brought up with the lessons of World War II," explains Tom Wicker, who covered the White House for the *Times* at the time of the Gulf of Tonkin incident. "We were being told that this was Communist aggression. . . . The Secretary of State tells me that, and who am I to argue with him . . . that's the view one had at the time. . . . We had not yet been taught to question the President. . . . We had not been taught by bitter experience that our government like any other *in extremis* will lie and cheat to protect itself."[11] We will see in later chapters that as consensus on foreign policy broke down, journalists began to reexamine the deference they showed to political authorities. Nevertheless, the conventions outlined in the pages that follow remain central to American journalism—"[they've] just been modified," to quote Wicker once again. So I shall refer to objective journalism most of the time in the present tense, as the professional ethic of American journalism in the late twentieth century.

Objective Journalism

"You must be very brave to go down the highway for no other reason than to get the truth. This is hard to believe."

"I went down the highway because it is the only way to find out what was really happening. How else can I find out?"

"You can listen to what the government says."

"The government gives its version, you give yours, so we must find out what is really happening. . . ."

"But this United Press, it is American?"

"Yes, American."

"So you work for the American government."

"No, I don't work for the American government. It's called United Press International. It is broadcast all over the world . . . and we write about what is happening, not our opinions."[12]

KATE WEBB, On the Other Side:
23 Days with the Viet Cong[12]

Nothing is more central to the self-conception of the American journalist than the conviction that the modern American news media are independent of state power. And in fact the political autonomy of twentieth-century American journalism is very great. Beyond the constitutional guarantee of freedom of the press, two characteristics of the modern media are central to the existence of that autonomy. The media, first of all, not only are privately owned but are large and profitable commercial institutions. They are therefore economically autonomous—free from the need for subsidies faced by the party press of the nineteenth century or by most Third World media today. Second, journalism has come to be regarded as a profession. Journalists are socialized to a professional ideology which makes political independence the premier journalistic virtue. We have already seen a number of examples of the difficulties this independent press can cause, under certain circumstances, to the administration in power. We will see many more as our exploration of Vietnam coverage continues. But this is only half the story. In many ways, the professionalization of journalism in the United States has *strengthened* rather than weakened the tie between press and state.

Objectivity has of course not always been held a virtue in American journalism. The main purpose of a newspaper in the eighteenth and early nineteenth centuries, when it dealt with public affairs, was to express a particular point of view as forcefully and eloquently as possible. By the early nineteenth century most papers were backed financially by parties and politicians whose politics they represented and whose followers they served to mobilize. No pretense was made of balance or objectivity. At the same time no automatic deference was accorded to political authority. Alexis de Tocqueville recalls in *Democracy in America* that the first American newspaper he encountered called the president, Andrew Jackson, "a heartless despot exclusively concerned with preserving his own power . . . a gambler without shame or restraint."[13] It was customary for the president to back one Washington paper as his official organ; otherwise there was no guarantee his politics would find a forum.

Strong partisanship continued into the late nineteenth century. When the *Washington Post* was launched at the end of 1877, for instance, it pledged itself to "do what it can to uphold the Democratic majority in the House and the majestic Democratic minority in the Senate."[14] The paper's politics were reflected both in editorials and in the news columns; the distinction between these is a twentieth-century development. "We do not recognize the [Republican] Hayes administration further than is absolutely necessary to insure peace and tranquility," said one editorial (Hayes had come to office following a bitter dispute over the outcome of the election of 1876).[15] And a news story about a presidential speech was headed, "TWADDLE OF THE FRAUD."[16]

The modern concept of objectivity developed in the period between the two world wars. It was, as Michael Schudson has pointed out, a response to two intertwined changes in culture and social structure: the simultaneous rise of cultural relativism and of corporate capitalism.[17] It can be seen both as a defense, on the part of journalists, against these developments, and as an adaptation to them: it protected the journalists against the most threatening consequences of change and at the same time integrated them into the new cultural and socioeconomic system.

Culturally, the roots of objectivity lay in the notion that fact and value are radically separate. It is interesting here to contrast Walter Lippmann, who championed the emerging notion of a profession of journalism, with Lincoln Steffens, Lippmann's first editor, who decried it. Both took "scientific method" as their model; but Steffens's idea of science was essentially an enlightenment idea, while Lippmann's was in line with the asceticism of Weber and the logical positivists. Steffens saw no conflict between the empirical spirit and a stance of political and moral commitment. "Our stated ideal for a murder story," he wrote of the *Commercial Advertiser* of the 1890s, "was that it should be so understood and told that the murderer would not be hanged, not by our readers. . . . [This] is scientifically and artistically the true ideal for an artist and for a newspaper: to get the news so completely and to report it so humanly that the reader will see himself in the other fellow's place."[18] For Steffens, reality was transparent to human reason and offered a firm guide to action: one had only to see the "shame of the cities" to understand the need for political reform.

For Lippmann, on the other hand, it was precisely the fact that reality was *not* transparent to human reason that made scientific method and the discipline of professionalism essential. The ideal of objectivity arose in the age of psychoanalysis, "crowd psychology," existentialism, and public relations. At a time when human reason was generally seen as frail, facts as relative and subject to manipulation, and values as purely subjective, the journalist's reaction was to embrace the "habit of disinterested realism." In a sense, this was a stance of political independence: the journalist was to stand apart from the "prejudices" of his age. Yet the journalist was at the same time enjoined from challenging those "prejudices"; the price of independence was to relinquish the right to put forward a truth claim of one's own. "Have you ever stopped to think what it means when a man acquires the scientific spirit?" Lippmann's "Socrates" asked in a 1928 dialogue. "It means that he is ready to let things be what they may be, whether or not he wants them to be that way. . . . It means that he has learned to live without the support of any creed."[19]

The interwar years were also a period when the country was adapting to the massive change in socioeconomic structure that had occurred since the 1830s, when the industrial revolution had begun to take root in America (the newspaper industry was among the first to adopt modern mass production methods). The decentralized market society of the preindustrial period had given way to a society dominated by great industrial organizations. The days when printer, writer, and proprietor were one had long ago passed, and the journalist had become an employee of a large bureaucracy. The rise of a profession of journalism can be seen as a sort of negotiated compromise that gave the journalist enough autonomy and prestige to be both content and credible and at the same time integrated him into the news organization. Most nineteenth-century reporters were employees pure and simple; the proprietor had absolute authority over the content of the paper. But the rise of the ideology of professionalism in the twentieth century gave the journalists grounds to claim their own authority, and the modern news organization has a kind of dual structure that gives journalists a bounded sphere within which they answer primarily to members of their own profession. There is still frequent conflict along the boundaries between the journalist's and, today, the corporation's authority. At the television networks, for instance, disputes erupt periodically over whether it is proper to have as president of a news division someone without a background in journalism. And one need only read the "Darts and Laurels" column in the *Columbia Journalism Review* to see that owners of news organizations frequently intervene in what journalists consider professional decisions.

Dart: to John Tarrant, publisher of John McGoff's News-Herald News-papers in Wyandotte, Michigan, for a March 26 [1982] memo on changes in editorial policy that, among other things, directed "all of our news-papers to begin immediately to deemphasize hard news copy"; the order further decreed that "plant closings, business failures and layoffs will not appear on the front page of any of our newspapers." *Laurel:* to editorial director John Cusumano who promptly resigned.[20]

Still, the trend over the course of the twentieth century has been toward substantially increased journalistic autonomy. The same is true of income and prestige. The average nineteenth-century journalist was poorly paid and invisible; the professionalization of journalism was accompanied by an increase both in salaries and prestige, the latter manifested in the use of by-lines, which began to become common roughly in the 1930s. The journalists, in return, submitted to the au-thority of a set of rules which required them to relinquish the right to use their newly won autonomy and prestige in pursuit of their own individual or collective political values. In the 1930s, for instance, pub-lishers appealed to the principle of objectivity in their struggle against the influence of the Newspaper Guild, which they feared would, among other things, slant the news toward the interests of labor.[21]

For both the journalists and the news organization the principle of objectivity serves an important legitimizing function.[22] In the nineteenth century, when newspapers were small and numerous, they could ade-quately defend their political role by appeal to the First Amendment and the notion of a free market in ideas. Concentration of the industry, however, undercut this basis of legitimacy and put the news organi-zation, and with it the journalist, in a delicate position. Modern news organizations clearly possess enormous power: they control the society's major channels of political communication. Yet they are privately owned and have virtually no direct accountability either to the public or to formally constituted political authority; as the phrase goes, "Nobody elected the press." The professionalization of journalism allows both the corporation and the journalist to respond to criticisms of their power with the claim that they have in effect placed it in "blind trust" to the principles of objective reporting.

Just what these principles are is not something about which journalists are entirely in agreement. The belief system that guides American journalism is complex, ambiguous, and often contradictory. Many jour-nalists, aware that objectivity is at best an ideal, would reject the term *objective journalism*; "mainstream" journalists of the Vietnam era often referred to their form of journalism in interviews as "straight" or "es-tablishment" journalism, distinguishing it from the "advocacy" or "new"

journalism that flourished in alternative media during the war.[23] The
ideology of objective journalism, moreover, coexists in an often ambiguous relationship with other ideals. The ideal of the muckraker
crusading against the "powers that be," for example, has persisted into
the age of professionalism. Even in the Cold War period we are dealing
with here, which was a low point for this view of the journalist's role,
Bernard Cohen found that most foreign affairs reporters accepted the
notion that journalists had a responsibility to serve as "critics of government" (Cohen did *not* find that they did this very often).[24] We shall
see, moreover, that the journalist will often set aside the "habit of
disinterested realism" to play the role of patroit, defender, and celebrant of national consensus. Correspondents reporting on World War
II were certainly not expected to be disinterested, and a good deal of
the patriotism of that era spilled over into the Vietnam period. Nevertheless, most journalists would acknowledge the following principles,
in one form or another, as central to modern American journalism.
These principles, which I have summarized under the headings "independence," "objectivity," and "balance," together—and, as we shall
see, this is significant—with a set of routines and assumptions which
allow them to be put into practice in concrete situations, form the core
of the ideological system that is referred to throughout this book as
"objective journalism."[25]

> *Independence.* Journalists should be independent of political commit-
> ments and free of "outside" pressures, including pressures from govern-
> ment and other political actors, advertisers, and the news organization
> itself as an institution with economic and political interests.
>
> *Objectivity.* The journalist's basic task is to present "the facts," to tell
> what happened, not to pass judgment on it. Opinion should be clearly
> separated from the presentation of news.
>
> *Balance.* News coverage of any political controversy should be inpartial,
> representing without favor the positions of all the contending parties.

These principles are deeply held by American journalists, and their
impact on the practice of journalism is profound. But they cannot guide
that practice by themselves. Their guidance is essentially negative: they
tell the journalist *not* to allow political pressures to interfere with "news
judgment," *not* to take sides in political controversy, *not* to let personal
opinions color the reporting of news. But they do not say how "news
judgment" should actually be exercised; they do not tell the journalist
how to make the series of positive choices the production of news
necessarily requires: which stories to cover—what, out of the seamless
flux of human activity, should be singled out as news—which "facts"

to include and which to emphasize, or how to present those facts in a way that will render them meaningful to the news audience. In part, these choices are guided by the cultural assumptions of the wider society; we have already seen the importance of the ideology of the Cold War in directing journalists' attention and guiding their presentation of "the facts." Later we shall explore the role of other aspects and other levels of American political culture. And in part they are guided by a set of routines (themselves rooted in the dominant political culture, though modified by the particular demands of the journalists' activity) which form the real working infrastructure of the institution of journalism.

The working routines of objective journalism establish a relation to political authority very different from what its explicit principles would seem to mandate. Simultaneous with the rise of the ethic of objectivity and the growing autonomy of the journalist within the news organization was another fundamental change in the nature of American journalism: a tightening of the bonds between journalism and the state, centered, above all, on the presidency. Edmund Burke had called the early press the "Fourth Estate," meaning that it stood as a force independent of all established social institutions. But what was true in the eighteenth century certainly was not true of the American press of the 1950s. By the second half of the twentieth century the American press had taken its place as an integral part of the governing process, and the new profession of journalism had come to be defined largely in terms of the "responsible" performance of media's new quasi-official function. Journalists were regularly taken into the confidence of government officials, for whom they were the primary means of communication with the public and often also with other officials, with foreign governments, and with a variety of other political audiences. And journalists, for their part, came to rely on those officials as their primary source of information, to focus on their activities as the basic subject matter of news, to share their perspectives, and often to cooperate with them, though the principles of objectivity limited this more direct kind of relationship.

There were certainly points of tension between these two developments, the rise of objective journalism and the tightening of the bond between the press and government. Journalists were aware of and often lamented the fact that objectivity, as it was practiced, frequently left them open to manipulation by government officials; officials often lamented their dependence on an institution they could not control directly and were often unsuccessful in manipulating. Both often described their mutual relations as adversarial. But these were not mutually opposed developments: journalists depended on their relation with the state to make objectivity work as a practical form of journalism, and objectivity, in turn, was essential to the new role the press was playing as a "fourth branch of government." Far from sundering the connection between press and state, objective journalism *rationalized* that connection, in the Weberian sense of the term: it put that relation on the firm footing of a set of abstract principles embodied in the "professional" standards of news judgment. It was no longer possible for a party or politician to control any news medium as an official organ; and it was no longer necessary for high officials of government to do so. Their views were guaranteed access to all the major media—and protected against "irresponsible" attack—by virtue of the authority of their position, not their particular party or politics.

Objectivity in Practice: The Gulf of Tonkin

Now we can return to the *Times*'s reporting of the Gulf of Tonkin incident, which we have already encountered in the introduction to Part I. Tom Wicker's right-hand lead on August 5 began:

> WASHINGTON, AUG. 4—President Johnson has ordered retaliatory action against gunboats and "certain supporting facilities in North Vietnam" after renewed attacks against American destroyers in the Gulf of Tonkin.
> In a television address tonight, Mr. Johnson said air attacks on the North Vietnamese ships and facilities were taking place as he spoke, shortly after 11:30 P.M. . . .
> This "positive reply," as the President called it, followed a naval battle in which a number of North Vietnamese PT boats attacked United States destroyers with torpedoes. Two of the boats were believed to have been sunk. The United States forces suffered no damage or loss of lives.
> Mr. Johnson termed the North Vietnamese attacks "open aggression on the high seas."
> Washington's response is "limited and fitting," the President said, and his administration seeks no general extension of the guerrilla war in Southeast Asia.

This was precisely how the administration wished its action to appear, as a "positive" but limited "reply" forced upon the president by the actions of the enemy, *not* related to any change in U.S. *policy* which might require public debate. This was also objective journalism: Wicker merely presented "the facts"—in this case primarily facts about what the president said in his television address; he took no position on the truth or falsity of the president's remarks or on the policy itself. A right-hand lead on a major event, Wicker explained looking back on this story, was "supposed to be almost dead-pan . . . as near absolutely—

'objective' is too strong—it's supposed to have no content other than what is documentable and quotable fact. No interpretation of any kind. If the president says, "Black is white," you write, "The president said black is white."[26] Of course, the reporter is doing more here than simply excluding interpretation. He is exercising "news judgment" according to several of the basic conventions of objective journalism, conventions which here make the *New York Times* essentially an instrument of the state. These conventions include the following:

1. *The use of official sources.* The injunction to present "just the facts" leaves the journalist in a difficult position, for in politics the facts are almost always to some degree in dispute. As many studies of news-making have shown, American journalism resolves the problem, most of the time, by taking its facts from official sources.[27] This was certainly the case on August 5, 1964. Wicker's story contained official sources exclusively. Most were administration officials; the only sources outside the administration were Senators Mike Mansfield, the majority leader, and Barry Goldwater, Johnson's opponent in the approaching 1964 election, both of whom supported his action. Indeed, every *Times* story on the Gulf of Tonkin incident that day was based on official U.S. sources exclusively, with the exception of a two-paragraph "shirttail" reporting Hanoi's contention that the naval battle of August 4 was "sheer fabrication" (as we have seen, there is strong evidence that in fact there was no battle that night). One study of the *Washington Post* and the *New York Times* found not only that most of the sources in the two papers were official, but that most stories were based on government/press contacts initiated by officials rather than journalists, especially press conferences and press releases. And, indeed, each of the *Times*'s three front page stories on the Tonkin Gulf incident on this day centered around officially initiated events: the right-hand lead, around the president's address; the other two stories, around two Defense Department press conferences.

The use of official sources, as many have pointed out, is convenient for reporters. The government is organized to provide a timely flow of information, geared to the demands of daily journalism; it is extremely efficient for news organizations to locate their personnel at the channels provided by government. But the use of official sources also fulfills another, perhaps more important function for the media: it fills a vacuum of authority left by the rise of "disinterested realism." Journalists cannot, without stepping outside the role of disinterested observer, decide on their own authority to favor one version of the facts over another because it seems to them, for instance, closer to the truth or more desirable in terms of its effect on public opinion. The principle of balance is no solution. The decision to weight equally conflicting accounts of political reality is no less a political act than the decision to report only one. For the *Times* to have given prominent play to Hanoi's version of the Tonkin Gulf incident would, in the political context of the time, have been a significant and highly controversial political statement, a challenge to the structure of political authority. The solution American journalism has adopted is to defer to authority, justifying that choice as a decision to "let things be what they are," and hence a choice compatible with objectivity. Whether they are true or not, statements by top administration officials are unquestionably "newsworthy" because they come from people of power and authority.

2. *Focus on the president.* Whenever the president acts publicly, he is the focus of coverage; his "newsworthiness" overrides all other priorities. On the day of the Tonkin raids the right-hand lead was constructed around Johnson's address, the address itself was printed next to it, and above the address, beside the headline on the right-hand lead, was a photograph of the president speaking behind the presidential seal, with the caption, "DECISION: President Johnson, in a nationwide broadcast, tells of action he ordered taken against North Vietnam." The personal leadership of the president occupied the foreground of the coverage. Judging from what we know about public response to international events, this is probably very significant. People generally know little about policy, and their attitudes on foreign policy options tend to be ambivalent and unstable. But when a president appeals for unity in a crisis situation, popular support is generally forthcoming.[28]

3. *Absence of interpretation or analysis.* The principles of objectivity forbid editorializing in the news columns. But the status of interpretation, what journalists call news analysis, has been ambiguous since the rise of the ethic of objectivity.[29] Its role was particularly circumscribed during the early 1960s.

Here we encounter another important dilemma which the principle of objectivity creates for the journalist. Journalists are supposed to report the news "straight"—"just give the facts." At the same time they are inevitably teachers and storytellers: they must place events in some kind of framework that will make them meaningful to the news audience. Journalists have generally resolved this dilemma by focusing on the only sort of fact which really does "speak for itself"—facts about what people—in the case of political reporting, generally official people—*say*. Wicker's Tonkin story is a perfect example. All he does is to report what the president said. The president's words, however, are more than mere data being transmitted to the audience: they serve to place the day's events within a context the public can easily understand.

American ships were attacked on the high seas; the president, as commander in chief, responded to the Communist challenge with military force; the United States seeks no wider war. Good and evil and cause and effect are clear—yet the journalist has remained strictly objective. Here again official sources fill an important void left by the ethic of objectivity: they fill the vacuum of meaning left by the journalist's renunciation of the role of intepreting reality.

This renunciation of the role of interpretation is not, of course, required of all journalists all of the time. Coverage of a major story like the Tonkin Gulf incident would normally include a number of "news analysis" pieces, though these were less common, less extensive, and less prominently played in the early 1960s than they are today. And none had more prestige in American journalism in the 1950s and early 1960s than the columnists whose job it was, much more exclusively at that time than now, to put the news in perspective—Alsop, Reston, Krock, Lippmann, Sulzberger, and others. But the line between analysis and "straight" reporting was drawn so rigidly in this period that, as we shall see, even at times when the columnists and editorial writers were all but screaming that things were not as they appeared, the front pages continued to report as fact official assurances of "no change in policy." And there is good reason to believe that front page reporting, not the views of columnists or editorialists, is the most important influence, at least on mass public opinion.[30]

In many ways, moreover, analytic journalism was not so different from "straight" journalism. It was, after all, the Alsops, two of the most prominent columnists of the time, who quipped, "His feet are a much more important part of a reporter's body than his head."[31] The columnists, too, were above all gatherers of facts. And what gave them their prestige was primarily their "access": they were not less, but more closely tied than the average journalist to the highest policymakers, though the range of their contacts often made them more independent in relation to any given official or branch of the bureaucracy than reporters who covered only a single beat, at the State Department, for instance, or the White House. Their reputation for influence derived in large part from the fact that they were seen as a kind of semiofficial voice, reflecting the private thinking of the very highest levels of government.

In foreign affairs coverage during this period, a "news analysis" was generally a story based on background briefings or other not-for-attribution contacts with officials, rather than public press conferences, in which the reporter would present, either in the officials' words or in his or her own, the rationale behind the policies announced in public.

When officials were unified, therefore, as they were at the time of the Tonkin Gulf incident, analytic reporting generally served as one more channel for the transmission of the official view. Thus Reston reported in one *Times* analysis:

> Had Washington hesitated, or left the retaliation to the South Vietnamese, the President is understood to have felt, the North Vietnamese might then have been encouraged to believe that they could commit their main forces to the war and win a military victory without United States intervention. . . . The objective of his policy is not to widen the war but to convince the communists that they cannot win the war, and that their sensible course is to negotiate an honorable peace.[32]

4. *Focus on immediate events.* Closely related to the low priority American journalism places on analysis and interpretation is a strong tendency to focus on immediate events. The definition of *news*, as the term implies, involves a time dimension. In principle, journalists could report on phenomena of any duration, as long as demographic changes unfolding over decades or as instantaneous as individual deaths in battle. In practice, news is normally defined in terms of discrete "events" which unfold over the course of a day or less[33]—the period of time between one broadcast or issue of a newspaper and the next—and the historical or structural context of these events, unless it is made an issue by the newsmakers themselves, is relegated to the ambiguous realm of analysis—and generally to the back pages. A presidential speech or press conference is news; a gradual change in policy is not. A clash between Buddhists and the South Vietnamese government is news; the power relations or cultural tensions that lie behind it are not.

The news on August 5, 1964, was the president's address and the raids on North Vietnam, which were described in great detail in the *Times*—the nature of the targets, the damage to them, and so on. Officials had described those raids as a response to the North Vietnamese attacks on U.S. destroyers, and those events were mentioned prominently in the *Times*. Beyond that, the *Times* contained only the slightest fragments of historical context. And this was true not only on the day of the event, but in the days that followed as well, as attention first turned to the passage of the Gulf of Tonkin resolution and then fell off. The *Times* contained, for example, only a few brief and ambiguous allusions to the intensification of covert operations against North Vietnam which had preceded the previous clash in the Gulf of Tonkin, the North Vietnamese attack—this one acknowledged by North Vietnam—of August 2. Little was said either about the implications the incident might have for the future, aside from the official statement that the United States sought no wider war. The closest thing to an independent assessment of the significance of the event was an ambiguous comment buried deep in Wicker's August 5 story, and stated virtually without elaboration: ". . . despite Mr. Johnson's assurances that the U.S. sought no 'wider war,' it was plain that the situation in South Vietnam and the surrounding area had reached new gravity." The absence of these elements of historical context cannot be explained by simple lack of information. The *Times* had reported in some detail on the covert operations against the North as recently as July 23;[34] and although the administration was giving out little information about its policy deliberations, it had, as we shall see, frequently gone public in the months preceding Tonkin with warnings to Hanoi that it might well expand its involvement—among other things by air action against the North—if North Vietnam did not cease its "aggression." By the conventions of objective journalism, however, none of this was news in August 1964.

"We Aren't Going North"

Before the Gulf of Tonkin incident the Johnson administration had been in an awkward position on Vietnam. Johnson's campaign strategy depended in large part on portraying Goldwater as a man likely to involve the United States in a major war. And in fact Goldwater and other Republican politicians had spoken out in favor of more vigorous U.S. action against North Vietnam. But the administration itself was already moving along the very road Goldwater was advocating—the road North.

The Johnson administration, moreover, like the Kennedy administration before it, was trying simultaneously to signal to Hanoi its threat of escalation and to reassure the American public that the war would be contained, and these contradictory messages had caused some embarrassment.[35] Late in May Secretary of State Rusk warned in Saigon that the war might be expanded if North Vietnamese "aggression" persisted. Shortly thereafter Republican Congressman Melvin Laird said in a radio interview that the administration had prepared plans for air strikes against North Vietnam. Then, in a June 2 press conference, Johnson played down the warning, asserting that he "knew of no plans to carry the anti-Communist struggle in South Vietnam to the North."[36] A similar shifting of ground occurred after another Rusk warning to North Vietnam and China, delivered at a June 19 background luncheon with reporters.[37] That warning was followed by a shift of military equipment to Thailand, which, the administration made clear to reporters, was to be taken as a warning to the Communists.

> In informal talks with newsmen and diplomats and pointed references to
> United States military power [reported the *Times*], the Administration
> has undertaken to publicize warnings that a major war in Asia will surely
> result if the Communists do not desist in their aggressive actions in Laos
> and South Vietnam.
>
> President Johnson called attention to the United States military strength
> in a speech in California yesterday. Newsmen in Washington were infor-
> mally advised to convey the word that the United States commitment in
> Southeast Asia was unlimited, comparable to the stand in defense of West
> Berlin.
>
> These warnings were echoed publicly today by Adm. Harry D. Felt,
> Commander in Chief of the United States Pacific Command, at a news
> conference in Thailand.[38]

A few days later, on July 1, Rusk held a news conference to say that
peace "ought to be possible without any extension of the fighting," and
that any appearance of "blowing hot and cold" resulted from "changing
trends in the way in which speeches are reported."[39]

But the Tonkin incident defused Vietnam as a campaign issue for at
least a few weeks. And after Tonkin, with his right flank protected by
the use of force against the North, the president took aim more vigorously on Goldwater's hawkish policy. "I want to be very cautious
and careful and use it only as a last resort," Johnson said in an address
in New Hampshire at the end of September, "when I start dropping
bombs that are likely to involve American boys in a war in Asia with
700 million Chinese. So for the moment I have not thought we were
ready for American boys to do the fighting for Asian boys. . . . So we
are not going north and drop bombs at this stage of the game, and
we're not going south and run out and let the Communists take over."[40]

"We aren't going north at this stage" continued to be the administration's public stance right up to the onset of bombing the following
February. It was a half-truth. For several reasons the administration
was not ready until February to make a final decision on bombing. The
political situation in Saigon, where a series of coups had begun, was
judged too unfavorable. The White House was "not certain . . . how
public opinion could be handled."[41] And, probably most important,
the administration was still deeply divided over how exactly the bombing should be implemented—how rapidly it should be escalated, for
instance. Nevertheless the policy process was moving, as one account
puts it, "inexorably" toward bombing.[42] "By early September," according to the *Pentagon Papers*, "a general consensus had developed
among high-level administration officials that some form of additional
and continuous pressure should be exerted against North Vietnam."[43]
And in November, when a major policy review was undertaken, the

range of options considered was limited to the following: A—to continue the existing policy, B—to escalate rapidly against the North, and C—to escalate gradually. The available record is ambiguous as to the decision actually taken following the November policy review. But according to most accounts Johnson decided to stick with Option A for the moment, with the assumption that some form of Option C would be implemented in the near future.[44] Option A by itself was considered inadequate to arrest a rapidly deteriorating situation in South Vietnam.[45] When the December 1 decision to defer escalation was announced, reporters were admitted briefly to the Cabinet Room, where before being shooed out they overheard Robert McNamara say softly to the president, "It would be impossible for Max [Maxwell Taylor, then ambassador to Saigon] to talk with these people without giving the impression the situation is going to hell."[46]

The administration released little information about the policy debate, and would have preferred to keep it out of the news altogether. But the dispute was too large for that; too many officials were talking to the press, and reporters could not help but learn the broad outlines. How much did the public learn? This is a kind of question that cannot be answered with any certainty. It depends in part on how the public (which is of course itself a complex entity, as is the press) reads newspapers; and that is something about which we know very little. What can be said is this. A faithful reader of the *New York Times*—someone who read it thoroughly every day—would certainly have obtained enough information about the policy debate to be able, with a little imagination, to see that a major escalation of the war was imminent. Very few of the basic facts about the policy debate were missing. Only one really important piece of information remained literally a secret during this period, and this was something that was probably known only to a handful even within the administration: in December, after the decision to defer bombing, Johnson had begun pressing Taylor about a request for American *ground* troops to be sent to the *South*.[47] About the bombing, however, journalists knew what was being discussed and reported it. Yet "the facts" about the Vietnam policy debate emerged in the news in such fragmentary form that it is hard to see how the average member of the public—who did not read political news thoroughly and faithfully, whose own paper may have contained less inside information than the *Times*, and who did not have the sophistication to put the information together for him or herself—could have had more than a hazy awareness of the momentous decision the administration was making. Perhaps even the average member of Congress had little more than that.

On the day Johnson spoke in New Hampshire the *Times* had four significant stories on Vietnam policy. It led—following the normal procedure of focusing on the president—with Johnson's address, played on the front page under the head "President Wary of G.I.'s Fighting China's Millions." In Japan, meanwhile, another administration official had delivered a somewhat different message, and his remarks were reported in a shirttail to the Johnson story, under the head "U.S. Warns on Wider War."

> Increased pressure by the Communists could force an expansion of the war in South Vietnam outside the boundaries of that country, William P. Bundy, Assistant Secretary of State for Far Eastern Affairs, said today.
> "Expansion of the war outside South Vietnam, while not a course we want or seek, could be forced upon us by increased external pressures of the Communists, including a rising scale of infiltration," Mr. Bundy declared.

Farther down, after reporting Bundy's comments at length, the report quoted a "high United States source" as saying that the United States had "contingency plans" for action against infiltration routes.

Following the Bundy story was yet another shirttail, this one only three paragraphs long, under the head "Many Factors Involved." "Secretary of State Dean Rusk and others," the story ran, "have expressed confidence that South Vietnam could be pacified if North Vietnam and Communist China were to 'leave their neighbors alone.' Few officials, however, have read that literally, and no one here has predicted a rapid end to the guerilla war." The Communists, the report said, had been quite successful recruiting manpower and capturing weapons *within* South Vietnam.

Finally, on page 4, there was a news analysis by military correspondent Hanson W. Baldwin. "The situation in South Vietnam appears to have reached the most critical stage since the United States began its massive military support there three years ago," Baldwin wrote. "The concern centers not so much on the military situation . . . as on the apparently increasing weakness of the government in facing a rise in religious, labor, tribal and army dissidence." Baldwin went on to report that the administration, its options narrowing, was looking at proposals for action against the North with "greater urgency."

The *Times*'s coverage thus took the form of an "inverted pyramid"— in a sense ironically different from the way the term is used in journalism textbooks. Instead of leading with the most important fact and moving to less important ones, the *Times* did essentially the reverse. It led with the statement least revealing of the actual course of the policy debate, and moved on, as coverage trailed off into the back pages, to information that progressively undermined the lead—and moved closer to the truth. The lead article said, "We aren't going north." The shirttail on Bundy's address said, "We're reluctant to go north, but might have to if the Communists force us." The "Several Factors" shirttail suggested that infiltration from the North was not all there was to the crisis (from which one might have inferred that perhaps action against the North would not be the last step in the widening of the war). Finally, Baldwin's analysis revealed that the administration was actively and urgently considering action against the North, not to meet the "contingency" of a possible increase in infiltration, but to deal with a crisis in the South that already existed.

Again objective journalism protected the administration: the lead stories focused on the public statements of top officials and were written "straight," as though the reporters knew nothing of the information printed inside the paper. Unlike in the Tonkin incident, the information contradicting the official version was there, as it usually is when a major policy debate is under way. And no doubt politically sophisticated readers were able to put it together to see that something important was going on behind the scenes. Indeed, a brief flap erupted early in October over whether the administration was concealing its plans in Vietnam for political reasons (the administration's denial appeared as the right-hand lead in the *Times* on October 9, but the *Times* never had any substantial coverage of the charge itself).[48] If one assumes, however, that the general public is familiar with little more than front page news, the administration was not suffering greatly at this point from its inability to keep the debate over escalation really secret. On the front pages, an expansion of the war still seemed like something that was, as Rusk would often put it throughout this period, up to the Communists rather than Washington, which was committed to keeping it limited.

From the end of September through the end of January 1965, news analyses continued to appear inside the paper, reporting correctly that the administration's options seemed to be narrowing and that action against the North was being very seriously considered.[49] One of these analyses, an October 2 column by James Reston, criticized the administration for its secrecy and conflicting signals about U.S. policy.[50] On the front pages, meanwhile, what appeared was precisely those conflicting signals. The most extensive publicity came after the election, at the end of November, and bore considerable similarity to the reporting of the Taylor-Rostow mission in 1961. Taylor was once again returning to Washington for a policy review, and this time had made his views known to reporters. On November 23, the *Times* story on

Taylor's visit ran under the head "Taylor Expected to Ask Expansion of Vietnam War." Officials in Washington began immediately, as they had in 1961, to deny that any such decision was imminent. The next front page story on Vietnam policy was on November 28, under the head "U.S. Discourages Talk of Widening Vietnamese War." That same day the president himself, in a news conference, indicated that no change in policy was imminent.[51] After December 1, when the decision was postponed, Vietnam decision making essentially faded from the news until February.

Retaliation and the "Eerie Silence"

The Tonkin Gulf incident drove home to officials the utility of retaliation as a cover for escalation. In September the Joint Chiefs and other officials proposed actions "to provoke a military DRV response [which] should be likely to provide good grounds for us to escalate if we wished."[52] This proposal met with general approval in principle, according to the *Pentagon Papers*, though officials had concluded that the time was not yet ripe. In October one policy paper said of a decision to "go north:" "An attempt to legitimize such actions in general terms, and in advance of an emergency situation, would not only be likely to fail, but might well evoke public expression of domestic and allied opposition . . . from opponents that would make it much *more* difficult for the President to contemplate this approach when an occasion actually arose."[53]

The time never really ripened: the political situation in Saigon, which officials had hoped would stabilize, still had not done so. But in January the policy process finally moved to a decision. Taylor pressed the president in a series of cables early in the year to "look for an occasion to begin air operations just as soon as we have satisfactorily compromised the current political situation in Saigon."[54] Some officials, including Rusk, were apparently still hesitant,[55] but Johnson himself seemed convinced. On the fourteenth, the president cabled to Taylor that "immediately following the occurrence of a spectacular enemy action you would propose to us what reprisal action you considered desirable."[56] Late in the month, a DESOTO patrol was authorized for early February, with the expectation that a North Vietnamese response was likely (they had been suspended for the second time in September, after another ambiguous incident in the Tonkin Gulf, which the administration had kept quiet at the time). At the same time Operational Order FLAMING DART, providing for a number of alternative "reprisal" actions, was issued by the Pacific Command and three aircraft carriers were positioned off the North Vietnamese coast to assist in carrying it out. The planned resumption of the DESOTO patrols turned out to coincide with a visit to Hanoi by Soviet Premier Aleksei Kosygin, and they were postponed. But on February 7 a Vietcong company attacked a U.S. advisors' billet in Pleiku in South Vietnam's central highlands, killing eight and wounding over a hundred. The next day FLAMING DART was put into action.

The reporting followed the pattern of the previous August, with the right-hand lead again reported from the White House:

> United States aircraft struck at North Vietnam early today in response to what President Johnson called "provocations ordered and directed by the Hanoi regime."
>
> Mr. Johnson made it clear, however, that the air strike was a limited response rather than a signal for a general expansion of the guerrilla warfare in South Vietnam.[57]

Next to the lead was a story by Max Frankel giving the official rationale for the air strikes, as it had been explained to reporters in background briefings:

> The Administration ordered the strike against North Vietnam today in the belief that it faced the most serious test so far of its will to help resist aggression in South Vietnam.
>
> Informed sources said the United States had acted on the assumption that North Vietnam's Communist government had organized the test without warning Soviet premier Aleksei N. Kosygin, its guest in Hanoi. . . .
>
> Sensing that the Soviet leader might find himself in an awkward position, the administration sent a special message to Moscow to explain its raid as an act of retaliation rather than a move to expand the war in Southeast Asia.

This time, in contrast to the Tonkin incident, there were expressions of skepticism at certain points in the *Times*'s coverage. There was, in particular, a news analysis by Charles Mohr, a young reporter who had recently moved from Saigon to Washington and whose reporting throughout this period was distinctly more skeptical than the rest of the *Times*'s Washington coverage. Mohr, among other things, observed that the attack at Pleiku was not unusually large or intense, questioned the administration contention that Hanoi had specifically ordered and "made possible" this particular attack as a test of U.S. will, and noted the unusual presence of three carriers off the North Vietnamese coast.[58] On the editorial page, while the *Times* accepted the administration's statement that it "could not fail to respond" and did "not strive to expand the war," it also argued that a process of inevitable escalation seemed to be under way, as each side responded to the other, and called on the administration to "explain . . . where we go from here."[59] But Mohr's story appeared on page 14, and none of the questions that it or the editorial page raised were reflected in the rest of the *Times* coverage. (News reporters do not normally see editorials until they are published and of course are not supposed to be influenced by them. But editorials speak to questions being discussed behind the scenes in Washington, and it can be assumed that all journalists dealing with Vietnam were aware of the issues they raised.)

The administration had thus succeeded once again in bombing North Vietnam without appearing to have expanded the scope of American involvement. But it had also created a dilemma for itself. It had described the raid as a response to a particular North Vietnamese action, but it had done so for the purpose of initiating sustained bombing of the North and had now to face the problem of what it would say about subsequent raids. As usual, the problem of multiple audiences complicated things further: it had to be made clear to Hanoi that the administration was indeed expanding the U.S. commitment. Immediately after Pleiku, therefore, the administration began to broaden the concept of retaliation. On February 9, officials revealed to reporters, on a not-for-attribution basis, that future air strikes might be ordered in retaliation for attacks on South Vietnamese as well as U.S. forces.[60] Two days later, following an attack on another U.S. advisor's barracks, at Qui Nhon, another set of air strikes was carried out. This time the raids were described as a "response" not to a particular incident, but to "continued acts of aggression." "The change in terminology," according to the *Pentagon Papers*, ". . . was clearly deliberate . . . [and] reflected a . . . decision to broaden the reprisal concept as gradually and as imperceptibly as possible to accommodate a much wider policy of sustained, steadily intensifying air attacks against North Vietnam."[61]

At the same time the administration continued to maintain that its action should be interpreted as nothing more than retaliation. It also became unusually silent: Johnson did not go on television after the Qui Nhon attack, as he had after Pleiku, and the administration made no major public statement on Vietnam policy until the end of February, despite intense activity in Washington and attention worldwide. The silence was due primarily to confusion and division within the administration, which had initiated the bombing without a consensus about its scope, its purpose (was it, for instance, to "signal" U.S. resolve to Hanoi or to destroy North Vietnam's war-making capacity?), or about what would be done if, as many officials expected, it failed to alleviate the crisis in South Vietnam.

Two things are notable about the *Times*'s reporting during this period.

First, the paper began to take a more active and independent role than it had in the past. Its editorials and some columns—Reston's especially—began to question administration policy more and more sharply. Coverage in the Week in Review also diverged from the official line more substantially than it had in the past. At the same time the paper made an unusual effort during this period to justify the American commitment in South Vietnam—for as much as they doubted the wisdom of escalation, journalists were still deeply committed to the anti-Communist cause in Southeast Asia. This upsurge in journalistic independence was a response to lack of leadership from the White House; as we shall see, the "eerie silence" that followed Pleiku disturbed journalists greatly. It might, in fact, be considered a general law of American politics that once an issue is on the political agenda, the activity of the press on that issue varies inversely with that of the administration, receding when the administration speaks—especially in the person of the president—and expanding to fill the vacuum of leadership when it is silent.

At the same time, however, the "schizophrenia" of the previous summer and fall continued: while the editorials and columns diverged increasingly from the official line, the news columns and espcially the front page continued to reflect it—in all its ambiguity—more or less at face value.

Here is partial chronology of *Times* coverage following Pleiku:

February 8. On page 1, Max Frankel reported, "President Johnson and his advisors refused to rule out further retaliatory raids or to define the circumstances under which they might be resumed. In a brief public comment Mr. Johnson expressed hope that no one would misjudge the character, strength and fortitude of the United States. . . . McGeorge Bundy, the President's special assistant for security affairs, voiced optimism on South Vietnamese efforts to form a stable government."[62] (Shortly before, Bundy had cabled from Saigon, "The situation in South Vietnam is deteriorating, and without new U.S. action defeat appears inevitable."[63]) Inside, a Reston news analysis was reassuring: "Both Sides' Tactics in Vietnam Crisis Aimed to Avert Major Conflict."[64]

February 10. Officials announced the widening of the basis for retaliation. But they downplayed the significance of the bombing: "Officials said that the weekend raids should not be construed as precedents that might indicate what future course of action the United States might take. . . . The officials said that the policy that went into effect last weekend was designed to serve primarily as a deterrent, and to make Hanoi reconsider its active support of the Vietcong. . . . The present judgment is that there is no immediate danger of an expansion of the

Vietnamese conflict."[65] And in this context the *Times* played the story inside. Also inside: a news analysis by Hanson W. Baldwin, based on military sources, arguing that "one-shot" air strikes would not affect the military course of the war and reporting that the military favored heavy sustained bombing.[66]

February 11. The page 1 story gave details from official briefings on the second of two sets of raids that followed Pleiku; it also mentioned "tight security" surrounding consultations in Washington. Inside was a news analysis by Tom Wicker:

> On the surface, then, Mr. Johnson appeared to have taken a significant decision to step up resistance to Vietcong infiltration in South Vietnam, and to carry the war by airpower and seapower to North Vietnam whenever it seemed "justified." One informed view expressed now [this was noted, without comment, deep in one of the page 1 stories] was that the President's aim was not just to deter the Vietcong from further attacks like the one at Pleiku, but to hurt the North Vietnamese government enough to bring Hanoi into serious negotiations. . . . [This] kind of leapfrog can lead to exactly what the President said on Sunday he did not seek—"a wider war."[67]

February 12. Another set of raids was reported under a four-column head on page 1: "160 U.S. and Vietnamese Planes Attack Military Bases in the North; Washington Seeks to Limit War." "The action," reported Seymour Topping, "was a swift reprisal for Vietcong thrusts, including the terrorist attack last night on a United States army barracks. . . . In a communiqué, the United States and South Vietnam asserted that air strikes had been carried out in response to 'continued acts of aggression by Communist Vietcong under the direction and with the support of the Hanoi regime.' " None of the *Times*'s reporting that day commented on the change in wording on retaliation. But some of the reporters' frustration at the administration's vagueness did spill over into the news columns. Accompanying the lead was a report by Charles Mohr, giving the view from the White House (which wasn't the lead story, because the president hadn't spoken personally):

> Administration officials insisted today that there remained in their own minds a distinction between outright war against North Vietnam and retaliatory air strikes of the kind they ordered three times in five days this week.
>
> The latest attacks this morning, the White House said in a formal statement, were ordered "in response to further provocations by the Hanoi regime." . . .
>
> Administration sources added, however, that they still hoped to prevent the "spreading" of the war. There was said to be considerable pressure

from military leaders to continue the raids, with or even without the pretext of retaliation.

President Johnson was said to have resisted that advice. . . .

Officials acknowledged [when this was suggested by reporters at the daily press briefing] that their unwillingness to define precisely the circumstances under which they would retaliate in the future might have blurred definitions and given the impression that virtually any kind of setback in South Vietnam would henceforth draw a reprisal against North Vietnam. They refused, however, to commit themselves to any set course.

Mohr's shifting of the emphasis from the formal statement to the issue raised by reporters was highly unusual in foreign affairs coverage in this period and illustrates the degree to which Vietnam was beginning to strain the routines of objective journalism. The editors, however, pushed the tone of Mohr's reporting back toward the official emphasis in their selection of headlines. Mohr's story ran under the head "LIMIT ON CONFLICT STRESSED BY U.S.; Officials Point to Distinction Between Retaliatory Raids and Outright Hostilities"; and on the jump, running across six columns: "Washington Seeks to Limit Vietnam Conflict to Retaliation; U.S. Stresses Aim to Curb Conflict." There was, finally, another story on the front page of the *Times* that day which, like Mohr's, probably reflected the journalists' concern about the administration's silence, but showed a different side of their response: an exceptionally long news analysis by Max Frankel giving a history of American involvement in Vietnam and explaining why that involvement was necessary. Since the president was failing to explain to the public why the United States was going to war in Vietnam, the journalists were beginning to do it for him.

February 13. "The Administration left undefined today its intentions about further air attacks," Frankel reported, ". . . but they were the subject of a continuing debate behind the scenes. . . . [Some policymakers] believe the time has come to use American air and sea power more extensively. . . ."[68] On this day, in fact, the administration gave the go-ahead for Operation ROLLING THUNDER, the sustained bombing of North Vietnam.

February 14, Sunday. On page 1, John W. Finney reported that the administration was considering sending "a small number of additional troops to South Vietnam" for base security. Again, however, officials downplayed the significance of the move. This was the first report on the buildup of ground forces, which would begin in March but, as we shall see, it took the press a long time to catch on to the significance of that buildup. The Week in Review, meanwhile, did capture the significance of the new policy on retaliation. If the administration meant

that it would bomb North Vietnam in response to Vietcong attacks on
South Vietnamese forces—which of course occurred daily—it would
represent a major change in policy, the *Times* noted; and the Week in
Review piece closed with the comment that the nation seemed to be
at a point of choice, to escalate or to negotiate. Also in the Week in
Review, Frankel again wrote about the "global stakes" in Southeast
Asia: "The crisis over Vietnam, in which the desperate Washington
now finds itself pitted against the stoically confident Peking, can be
understood only through an appreciation of the slow but steady sub-
surface gains made by China in the larger contest throughout Asia."[69]
On the editorial page, finally, it was clear that the *Times* editorial board
was worried, and its best-known columnist upset. "The two actions—
the assault on a United States military installation . . . and the American
decision to [bomb] North Vietnam—vastly increased the perils to world
peace," said the editorial, which concluded with a call for negotiation.
And it was on this day that Reston called on Johnson to "call a spade
a bloody shovel."

Initiation of ROLLING THUNDER was postponed first by another
coup in Saigon, then by weather. So there were no further air strikes
until early March. There were also few policy statements until late
February, so Vietnam policy for the most part faded from the front
page, though the *Times* continued to emphasize it in editorials and the
Week in Review. The administration's public relations strategy for the
new policy of sustained bombing was laid out in a February 18 cable
to U.S. embassies in the Far East:

> Careful public statements of USG, combined with the fact of continuing
> air action, are expected to make it clear that military action will continue
> while aggression continues. But focus of public attention will be kept as
> far as possible on DRV aggression, not on joint GVN/US military op-
> erations. There will be no comment of any sort on future actions except
> that all such actions will be adequate and measured and fitting to aggres-
> sion.[70]

The main vehicle for focusing attention on "DRV aggression" was
a State Department white paper, released to the press at the end of
February. The reporting of the white paper suggests the importance of
the background briefings and public statements an administration normally uses to shape coverage of a major story. The white paper was
scheduled for release late on Saturday, February 27, for use in the
Sunday papers. McGeorge Bundy, however, showed the document to
Max Frankel before its release, on the understanding that Frankel would
not use it early.[71] That is not unusual, particularly at a time when
reporters are clamoring for proof of claims an administration is making.

What was unusual was that Frankel decided to go ahead and use the story. This meant, however, that the various glosses on the meaning of the white paper, which officials would deliver the next day, were not there to be reported. So the story emerged with Frankel's spin: it mentioned prominently that "in policy terms, [the white paper] represented a clear departure from the United States position . . . that the 'main problem' [lay] inside South Vietnam."[72] The subheads, under the three-column banner, read, "POLICY IS ALTERED; Washington Now Feels Military Effort Must Go Beyond South." This was the most prominent statement in front page reporting that U.S. policy was changing in all the *Times*'s coverage of the 1964–65 escalation. It should quickly be added that most of Frankel's story was a summary of the charges the administration was making against North Vietnam, and that the possibility of a major escalation was suggested only subtly. "It stops just short of predicting further air strikes against North Vietnam," Frankel wrote of the white paper, "but it invites Hanoi . . . to choose between peace and an 'increasingly destructive' conflict."

The next day, after the white paper had been officially released, the emphasis was back on "DRV aggression." Again the right-hand lead and the editorial differed radically in their emphasis. The lead story began:

> The United States issued today a detailed, documented indictment charging North Vietnam with flagrant and increasing aggression against South Vietnam.
> The charge was accompanied by a warning that the United States might be compelled to abandon its present policy of "restraint" and to expand the war in Vietnam if the Communist aggression from the North did not cease.[73]

(Farther down the report noted, "State Department officials . . . insisted [the white paper] did not deal with questions of policy.") The editorial, meanwhile, said, "The Johnson administration seems to be conditioning the American people for a drastic expansion of our involvement in Vietnam."[74]

Interlude: The Great Debate that Wasn't

"A great debate on the Vietnamese conflict is now raging all over the United States," said the *Times* on February 21. "It goes from the White House, Congress and the Pentagon to every home, office, factory and farm." But there was little evidence of such a debate in the columns of the *Times* at any time during the 1964–65 escalation. The reason was simple: the "objective journalist" would not report on criticism of administration policy unless it came from "responsible sources"—which meant, in effect, from within the government itself. And the president's control over the political process was still strong enough that, although there continued to be leaks about the policy process, very little open controversy emerged, either within the administration or in Congress. As U.S. allies and major neutral nations began to criticize U.S. policy, the *Times* did give substantial coverage to the international debate. But at home it was different. Despite substantial divisions over strategy, dissent within the administration was tightly contained throughout the first half of 1965. There was some criticism from the military, and this appeared (at the liberal *Times*, usually in the back pages) in the columns of Baldwin and other journalists close to the military and its backers in Congress. The few within the administration who opposed escalation, on the other hand, felt they had to keep their views strictly private in order to preserve some measure of influence in the policy process.[75] In Congress there was great unease over the war, but the principle of presidential prerogative in foreign policy was still strong enough that few legislators were willing to oppose the adminstration publicly.[76] Only a handful of major stories on congressional discussion of Vietnam appeared in the *Times* in the first half of 1965.

There were, of course, other actors speaking out on the war, especially in the academic community. But because they had no official standing, their views were not newsworthy by the standards of the "fourth branch of government." "[O]ne of the many paradoxes about the event," Frankel wrote about the first national "Teach-In" in May, "is that McGeorge Bundy, Walt W. Rostow and a few other intellectuals in Government were chiefly responsible for its success and public notice."[77] Frankel was correct, though the phenomenon he was describing with such detachment was primarily the behavior of journalists. The teach-ins of May and June 1965 made the front page of the *Times* on three occasions, and in each case the focus was on McGeorge Bundy, who canceled his appearance at the first debate but appeared at the second. On June 21, for example, the story ran under the head "Bundy Says U.S. Must Block Reds"; in each story the first several paragraphs were devoted to Bundy and his remarks.[78]

It is now a widely accepted view that the government's decision-making on Vietnam suffered from an extreme narrowness of discussion: decisions were made incrementally, often through a process of bureaucratic compromise; basic assumptions about the nature of the conflict and the wisdom of U.S. objectives, derived mainly from the ideology of the Cold War, were unexamined; a very narrow range of policy options was given serious consideration.[79] The same could be said of the process of public discussion, as it was carried on through the press. The 1964–65 escalation took place without any substantial reexamination in the press of the assumptions that had guided both U.S. policy and news coverage since 1961 and before: no second look at the roots of the conflict, no debate over whether the security of the Free World indeed required that South Vietnam remain an independent state with an anti-Communist government.

This is not to say that the prospect of a major war, and the debates that did take place during this period, provoked no questioning at all among journalists of the views that had dominated American thinking up to that point. It is clear that some such thinking was going on. While in 1961–64, for example, the Communists of Vietnam, North and South, had been treated almost exclusively as an arm of international Communism, in 1965 the history of the Vietnamese revolution began to creep occasionally into the news, and references to its nationalist roots became more common.[80] The term *civil war* began to be used in 1965; and the term *aggression* began to appear sometimes in quotation marks, as a contention of the administration rather than a self-evident fact. But these were subtle signs of change scattered through the mass of day-to-day news coverage, mostly deep inside the paper, they were not a subject for extended or prominent discussion. News, to the American journalist, is above all about official Washington, and official Washington was debating whether to maintain the bombing, pause it, or step it up, not whether the doctrine of containment should continue to guide U.S. policy in Southeast Asia. News, moreover, is about events and actions, not about ideas. (It is easier to judge with an attitude of detached realism the significance of an event than an idea, just as it is easier to judge power than wisdom.) When Lyndon Johnson "signals" to Hanoi and the Communist powers what he may do in Vietnam, that is news. But when George Kennan, establishment figure though he is, gives a speech urging a "readiness to relax" American policy toward China (as he did at the end of February 1965), he can at best expect to make an inside page in the *Times* and a few other elite papers.[81] It might be added that the modern op-ed page, with its fairly wide range of political opinions, did not exist in the mid-1960s. It was a product of the Vietnam-Watergate era.

"It Does Not Imply Any Change of Policy Whatever"

It is difficult to say to what extent officials believed, when ROLLING THUNDER began, that it would succeed in accomplishing American objectives in Vietnam. McGeorge Bundy, in an important memo written just after the Pleiku incident, estimated the probability of success at "somewhere between 25 and 75 percent," and predicted that "at best" the war would be long.[82] Robert Galluci, reviewing the record of pessimism expressed from various quarters about the sufficiency of the bombing, suggests that many officials may have seen it as a necessary political prelude to the introduction of U.S. ground forces, necessary because the administration would have to demonstrate that the war could not be won "on the cheap" with air power in order to get public and congressional support for a war involving large numbers of U.S. casualties.[83] We have seen that Lyndon Johnson himself was already pressing Taylor on the issue of ground combat before the bombing was started.

At any rate, most policymakers quickly became convinced, once the bombing was under way, that it would not turn the tide by itself. As long as the North Vietnamese and the NLF were winning in the South— which at this stage they clearly were—they were not going to back down. And intelligence reports held out little prospect that the bombing would dramatically affect the course of the battle in the South: North Vietnam was clearly capable not only of maintaining but of increasing the flow of supplies and reinforcements.[84] So by mid-March the policy process was moving rapidly toward the decision to have U.S. forces take over the primary burden of the fighting in the South.

The first decision on ground combat troops had come on February 21, when the administration approved a Westmoreland request for 3,500 marines to provide security at the U.S. air base at Da Nang. That request, as we have seen, was reported as early as February 14, but it was presented, by officials and by the press, as a strictly limited move, both in February and on March 6, when it was formally announced by the Pentagon. "At this point," the *Times* reported, "the Administration is not considering any sizeable increase in American military missions. . . . [I]f South Vietnam goes through with plans to increase the size of its forces, additional Americans are likely to be sent as advisors, officials say."[85]

By March 8, when the Third Marine Amphibious Force—the first organized combat unit to be committed—landed near Da Nang, the possibility of a major escalation of U.S. involvement on the ground had hardly been mentioned, even in the most speculative way, in the *Times*. That this possibility was not raised in front page coverage should come as no surprise, familiar as we are now with the routines of objective journalism; officials were not yet talking even on a "background" basis about ground combat troops. This time, however, the editorial page and the Week in Review were little different. The "drastic expansion" the *Times* had written about at the end of February was the beginning of sustained bombing. The possibility of a "land war in Asia" was discussed at this point only by analogy to Chinese intervention in Korea. The danger, as the *Times* presented it in February, was that the bombing might provoke a Chinese or Soviet response, which would in turn require the commitment of U.S. combat troops. Despite considerable skepticism about whether bombing the North would change things in the South—the *Times* had observed in a March 7 editorial that "there really is a species of civil war in South Vietnam"[86]—few journalists seemed to have grasped the possibility that the Johnson administration, faced with a further narrowing of its options, might *choose* to fight a major land war in Vietnam. Perhaps one side effect of the concentration of American journalism on day-to-day events is a dulling of historical imagination.

With the onset of ROLLING THUNDER, the administration dropped retaliation as a rationale for increased military action. But its public relations strategy continued to follow the principle of keeping public attention on North Vietnamese "aggression," and later on U.S. peace initiatives, while presenting increases in the U.S. military role in as undramatic a way as it could. Its tactics became increasingly complex as time went on, but the basic approach is summarized in an April 6 National Security Action Memorandum (NSAM) and in a cable from Taylor to Rusk. In the National Security Council Meetings of April 1 and 2, the administration made a series of decisions on U.S. involvement in the South, the most important of which was a "change of mission for all Marine battalions deployed to Vietnam to permit their more active use under conditions to be established." This resulted in a shift in the marines' role from base security to offensive operations against the Vietcong. NSAM 328 said about press policy:

> The President desires with respect to [these] actions . . . premature publicity be avoided by all possible precautions. The actions themselves should be taken as rapidly as practicable, but in ways that should minimize any appearance of sudden changes in policy, and official statements on troop movements will be made only with the direct approval of the Secretary of Defense. [T]hese movements and changes should be understood as being gradual and wholly consistent with existing policy.[87]

Taylor's cable to Rusk outlined the U.S. mission's application of this policy.

> Under the circumstances we believe that the most useful approach to press problems is to make no, repeat, no special public announcement to the effect that U.S. ground troops are now engaged in offensive combat operations, but to announce such actions routinely as they occur. As the

marines move from their present posture of securing the Da Nang airbase "in depth" to actions which can be related only indirectly to Da Nang, military spokesmen will be queried about whether the marine mission has changed and will answer that, while we never discuss the future, current operations speak for themselves. Eventually, of course, the fact that the marines or other ground troops are engaged in offensive combat will be officially confirmed. This low-key treatment will not obviate [all] political and psychological problems . . . but will allow us to handle them undramatically, as a natural consequence of our determination to meet commitments here.[88]

From March through July the administration released information about increases in American involvement piecemeal, often on a not-for-attribution basis, presenting each additional step in the narrowest possible terms and refusing to comment on "future operations." "Special public statements," meanwhile—and there were many of these, as the administration ended its silence and took the political offensive—were concerned with justifying the American commitment, defending its effectiveness, and focusing attention on peace efforts. This approach took good advantage of the routines of objective journalism, capitalizing above all on the journalists' focus on day-to-day events and policy statements.

Here are highlights of *New York Times* coverage from March through July.

March 13. U.S. officials in Saigon revealed that they had recommended the deployment of an army division for security of U.S. bases, which would increase U.S. forces in South Vietnam from 27,000 to about 47,000.[89] But the *Times* was still preoccupied with the bombing, and did not attribute much significance to this report. "The prospect," the Week in Review said the next day, "seemed to be for a gradual increase in American military pressure on North Vietnam coupled with constant diplomatic soundings."

April 2. "President Johnson said today," Tad Szulc reported, "that no new 'far-reaching strategy' for Vietnam was being promulgated in this week's conferences" (these were the meetings that produced the decision on offensive combat operations). "Instead, Mr. Johnson said, the aim of discussions is to consider 'improved efficiency' in United States efforts to assist South Vietnam. . . . At the same time, the President indicated that the United States had no information or evidence that North Vietnam was 'ready and willing' to negotiate under 'productive' conditions."[90] The next day the administration released information that it had decided, among other things, to send several thousand additional troops for base security and training of South Vietnamese forces. It did not announce the change of mission, and the story was again not treated as particularly significant.

April 7. Two months had now passed since the start of the bombing. Criticism of that policy had been substantial, both internationally, where U.S. allies and neutrals had been urging negotiations (The *Times* gave this diplomatic activity extensive coverage), and on the domestic front. In response, the administration was engaged in a major effort both to defend the bombing and to defuse the impression that it was not doing enough on the political front. On March 26 it had released a statement by the president suggesting that the United States would initiate a "Marshall Plan" for Southeast Asia in which North Vietnam would be able to participate after a settlement. It had also begun a series of statements intended to convince the public that the bombing was effective and the war generally going well. This produced the following page 1 headlines in the *Times* in late March and early April:

March 28. "Taylor to Begin U.S. Visit Today; Sees Gain in War"

March 29. "Taylor, Arriving in U.S., Says Raids on North Lift Saigon's Morale"

April 5. "U.S. Says Bombing Cut Vital Route"

April 6. "Air Strikes Spur Saigon's Morale"

On April 7, at Johns Hopkins University, Johnson gave a nationally televised speech offering to engage in talks with North Vietnam "without preconditions" (the United States had previously said it would talk only after North Vietnam gave some sign of "ceasing its aggression") and proposing once again an enormous development project to provide a "carrot" for a settlement. The story ran under a four-column head in the *Times*: "PRESIDENT MAKES OFFER TO START VIETNAM TALKS UNCONDITIONALLY; PROPOSES ONE BILLION AID FOR ASIA." The usual Frankel "backgrounder" bore the head "Washington is Reported Shifting Stand in Effort to Tempt North Vietnam Away from Aggressive Course." The purpose of the president's address was to defuse liberal criticism, which was coming not least from a large segment of the American press; the editorial page of the *Times* had been in the forefront of the call for negotiations. And it was an extremely successful move. On the front pages, the phrase "unconditional negotiations" would appear again and again over the following weeks, as the administration continued to emphasize its peace initiative. On April 17, for instance, the *Times* carried, under a two-column head, another Johnson statement emphasizing the peace offer, this one read to reporters who had been summoned to the LBJ ranch in Johnson City, Texas.[91] On

April 27 at the televised news conference, Johnson again read a statement on the war, and the *Times* right-hand lead began:

> President Johnson renewed today his offer to talk with any government,
> without any conditions, about ways of ending the war in Vietnam.
> Emphasizing the "utmost restraint" of his administration in the war,
> the President defended the bombing. . . . The bombing will continue, he
> said . . . as long as North Vietnam's aggression continues.[92]

In mid-May a five-day halt in the bombing of the North dominated the
headlines.

Hanoi, meanwhile, had proposed a "four-point" plan as a "basis"
for talks. But this story, not surprisingly, received much less dramatic
coverage, running under a one-column head on the left-hand side of
the paper.[93] It was, more important, a one-shot story: Ho Chi Minh
could not invite reporters to the ranch to keep in the news as Johnson
could. So a powerful image emerged in the headlines over the next
weeks of American flexibility contrasting with North Vietnamese intransigence. The summary in the Week in Review the day the bombing
halt ended gives a good sense of the tone of coverage in this period:

> The bombing pause was the latest of a number of efforts to see if the
> Communists could be brought to the negotiating table. Since President
> Johnson made his "unconditional discussions" offer nearly seven weeks
> ago, North Vietnam and Communist China have rejected not only all
> American peace overtures, but also all intercessions by other countries
> as well.[94]

At times information was reported in the back pages which cast doubt
on the impression that the administration had shifted from a military
approach to the crisis to a vigorous search for a political solution. On
April 15, for example, near the end of a story on Washington's reaction
to the four-point plan (the subhead read, "Washington Officials Warn
it Would Bring Communist Rule in South Vietnam"), Frankel reported:

> Despite the President's offer, there has been no sign of eagerness for talks
> here.
> The Government of South Vietnam is still considered insufficiently
> stable to survive the pressures of diplomatic bargaining. The military
> situation in South Vietnam is still considered too poor to sustain a strong
> bargaining position, and North Vietnam's interest in serious talks is still
> doubted.[95]

In fact, while the administration's military policy was evolving rapidly
at this point (on that very day a Pentagon cable to the U.S. mission
noted that "highest authority believes the situation in South Vietnam
is deteriorating rapidly and that in addition to actions in the North,

something new must be added in the South to achieve victory"),[96] its
political policy was more or less unchanged. The peace initiatives were
seen as providing an opportunity either for Hanoi to give in to previously stated U.S. terms or, more likely, for the United States to demonstrate that Hanoi was not interested in negotiation, in order to "clear
the decks" politically for escalation.[97] Neither side had any serious
incentive to negotiate at this point: the U.S. position was too weak,
the North Vietnamese/NLF position too strong, and both sides too
confident of eventual victory. The bombing pause illustrates well the
continuity in the administration's political policy. Though the accent
publicly was on getting "unconditional discussions started," in contrast
to the previous U.S. position that it would talk only when Hanoi had
given an "indication" that it was prepared to stop the war in the South,
the bombing halt was still aimed at obtaining such an indication. The
message delivered to Hanoi at the time was, as Foy Kohler, the U.S.
ambassador in Moscow put it, "strenuous": it advised Hanoi that the
United States would be watching for reductions in Communist activity
in the South and warned of escalation if they were not forthcoming.[98]

Journalists certainly knew, and reported, that the peace initiative was
directed in part at public opinion; the bombing halt was described on
the day it ended as "partly aimed at demonstrating that Hanoi has no
intention of entering negotiations."[99] But they continued to assume that
the administration did not want escalation,[100] and therefore did not
suggest that the peace initiatives might be intended to pave the way
for it. They were not inclined, moreover, to question the U.S. objective
in Vietnam—which was the preservation of the existing anti-Communist
political order in South Vietnam, and hence meant, in effect, complete
defeat of the NLF—even to the point of asking whether that objective
was compatible with anything other than a policy of military victory.
The assumption within the liberal press seems to have been that the
American goal was eminently reasonable and should be achieved without compromise,[101] but that this could somehow be done short of full-
scale war if diplomatic channels were pursued. Perhaps the model for
this kind of resolution was the Cuban missile crisis; behind the analogy
lay the assumption discussed in Chapter 2, that Vietnam was simply
one front in the global struggle of the Cold War, and hence a limited
war for the Communists as it was for the United States. The administration's announced policy at this point coincided closely enough with
the liberal views of the *Times* that the usual split between the front
pages and the editorial page more or less disappeared, and the peace
initiatives of April and May produced a major change in the *Time*'s
editorial position: the *Times* strongly supported the administration dur-

ing those initiatives, and though it sometimes gave its support grudgingly as the ground war wound up, it avoided direct criticism of Johnson's Vietnam policy through the July troop decision. So in contrast to the escalation of the air war in February and March, there was little critical interpretation of administration actions anywhere in the *Times* during the escalation of the ground war in April–June.

April 21. Again, the "inverted pyramid." Officials had been meeting in Honolulu for a policy review. McNamara announced at a press conference a step-up in U.S. aid to South Vietnam, but told reporters that "the number of additional United States servicemen would not be large." The story ran on page 1 under an innocuous one-column head: "U.S. to Intensify Sea Surveillance on Vietnam Coast." On the jump, however, was a report by Baldwin, based on military sources, that the president had "already approved in principle" plans for "a major build-up of United States forces in South Vietnam and an intensification of the bombing." These plans included, according to Baldwin, "a possible build-up of United States ground combat troops . . . to several divisions" and a shift, "if necessary," from passive defense to offensive operations. In fact, the Honolulu conference did reach a consensus, approved by the president, that an additional 40,000 U.S. combat troops would be required (they apparently did not decide to step up the bombing).[102]

The next day sources in Washington told reporters that the administration would "shift its concentration to a greater effort to win the ground war in South Vietnam." About the possibility of additional U.S. troops being sent, however, the *Times* only quoted McNamara as saying that the level of American forces was "presently adequate."[103] And on Saturday, "high Government sources" told reporters the following, as reported in Tom Wicker's lead:

> President Johnson does not now intend either to halt the United States air attacks on North Vietnam or to move American combat troops into the forefront of a stepped-up antiguerrilla war in South Vietnam.
> Mr. Johnson does intend to keep open his offer to enter into "unconditional discussions." . . .
> Despite widespread speculation [Wicker continued, farther down] that many more American soldiers would soon be shipped to Vietnam, high officials here insist that no decision along those lines has been made.

Wicker said nothing about the basis for the widespread "speculation." This story, the right-hand lead on Sunday, April 25, ran under the head quoted at the beginning of this chapter. In the Week in Review that day, Baldwin's information was mentioned briefly. On Monday McNamara held a press conference, and the focus was once again on "DRV aggression": "M'NAMARA CALLS HANOI AGGRESSION 'MORE

FLAGRANT.' " This was the last major burst of publicity before Johnson went to Congress, obtaining an overwhelming vote in favor of funding for the war.

Mid-May. The first revelation from administration sources about the possibility of a major change in U.S. commitment on the ground—and the first discussion of this possibility in the *Times* outside of Baldwin's military reporting—coincided with the end of the bombing pause. On the seventeenth, officials in Saigon told the *Times*'s Jack Langguth that they did not expect meaningful talks with the North Vietnamese until after an expected Communist offensive in the South had been halted, which would require the use of U.S. troops in offensive operations. The story ran on page 1 under the head "FULL COMBAT ROLE FOR G.I.'S IS LIKELY IN VIETNAM SOON."[104] The next day the right-hand lead, under a three-column head, was about the resumption of bombing: "U.S. RAIDS NORTH VIETNAM AFTER 6-DAY LULL BRINGS NO OVERTURE FROM HANOI." Below that story, on the bottom of page 1, was another report by Hanson W. Baldwin, under the head "U.S. MAY MODIFY VIETNAM TACTICS." Based as usual on military sources, this was the only report during the first seven months of 1965 to predict accurately the actual scope of the Vietnam War. Baldwin reported that military officers were talking about moving U.S. troops out of their existing enclaves and using them for offensive operations across wider and wider areas. "It is estimated," Baldwin went on, "that a total of about 500,000 Americans might be needed, and years of fighting might be required."

Whether the timing was calculated or not, the impending decision to fight a major ground war surfaced at a very good moment for the administration. It was, in the first place, partially eclipsed by the news of the bombing halt (the Week in Review of May 19 devoted only one undramatic paragraph to the ground combat story). And it appeared in the most favorable possible context: as a response to Communist determination to press on to a military victory despite U.S. willingness to look for a political settlement.

June–July. Early in June, the administration began deliberating what was known as the 44 battalion request, which would increase U.S. troop strength in South Vietnam from the 70,000 approved by June 1 to almost 200,000 and give Westmoreland authority to use those troops to take the offensive against the guerrillas. As a decision on this move grew closer, the administration's public stance became increasingly complex. It could no longer simply deny that the country was becoming involved in a major war. On the contrary, the public had to be prepared for such a war, and officials gave both the war and the decision-making process a far higher profile that it had previously. In mid-July, for example, when McNamara visited South Vietnam prior to the final set of meetings on the 44 battalion request, the U.S. mission took the unusual step of announcing in a public press conference that the Saigon government had requested and the U.S. military had recommended substantial increases in U.S. ground combat troops.[105] The secretary also provided a wartime "photo opportunity," posing on a carrier to personally "launch" an air strike against North Vietnam.[106]

It is a common conception that the Johnson administration promised the American public a short and easy war, but that is not entirely accurate.[107] Beginning in June 1965, the administration relied heavily on the rhetoric of national self-sacrifice, avoiding optimistic predictions and warning that the war would be long and difficult. The public was never promised that any given escalation would be the last; officials, in fact, would consistently say that additional forces would be needed eventually. At the same time, however, the administration wished to maintain the impression that the war was limited and under control. So the rhetoric of national self-sacrifice was combined with a great reluctance to discuss specific facts and figures, especially about future deployments and the possible length of the war, and to take certain actions which would make the sacrifice more dramatic and tangible, notably a tax increase and a call-up of the reserves.

At the beginning of June the administration had an awkward incident with the press. On the fifth, the State Department's press officer, Robert McClosky, who had been questioned about reports from the field that U.S. troops were engaging in offensive operations, acknowledged for the first time the April 1 change in mission.[108] The State Department confirmed his statement four days later, but the White House immediately issued an ambiguous denial.[109] This shifting of ground was treated skeptically by the press and produced the first critical editorial in the *Times* since April.

After this, however, the administration had little trouble with the press, despite the complex balancing act it was performing, trying to bring both the Left and the Right on board for a great, but limited, national commitment. While the beginning of the bombing in February had produced visible alarm and skepticism, expressed strongly on the editorial page, and spilling at times into the news columns, there was little of this in June and July when the ground war escalated so dramatically. The news columns were extremely "straight"; editorially the *Times*—and apparently most other papers[110]—supported the administration strongly. Why was this much more significant escalation so much easier for the administration?

In the first place there was no vacuum of leadership for the journalists to fill—no "eerie silence" as there had been in February. The administration was much more certain of its course and was providing a large volume of public comments, which essentially filled up the news space.

The liberal press, moreover, given the nature of the American political spectrum and its acceptance of the limits of that spectrum, found itself in the summer of 1965 with nowhere to go politically except to follow Lyndon Johnson into the "big muddy." This is one of the most important consequences of the close connection between the modern media and government: the range of political discussion in the press is usually restricted to the policy alternatives being debated in Washington. In February most criticism of Vietnam policy had come from liberal Democrats. In June, however, many Republicans, seeing a potential Korea in the making, began to distance themselves from Johnson's policy, arguing that ground troops should not be sent unless Johnson was willing to relax limitations on the air war (these limitations were motivated mainly by fear of provoking Chinese intervenion). As pressure from the Right increased, liberals, including columnists and editorial writers for papers like the *Times*, closed ranks behind their president, and no voice remained to question the Americanization of the war.

Johnson, for his part, encouraged the perception that he was the man of moderation who could control the Right. In mid-June, for example, after news of the impending decision had first surfaced, Foreign Relations Committee Chairman J. William Fulbright gave an address calling for the United States to undertake a "resolute but restrained" holding action over the summer, while seeking a negotiated settlement. Fulbright had met with the president before speaking, and his remarks were widely interpreted as a statement of Johnson's views. E. W. Kenworthy reported:

> The Senator was said to be considerably heartened by what Mr. Johnson told him about the resistance he and Secretary of Defense Robert S. McNamara were putting up to pressures from the Pentagon and parts of the State Department for expanding the war.
> The President, according to informed sources, told Mr. Fulbright that it would be helpful if he made a speech emphasizing that the administration was committed to the goal of ending the war as soon as possible by negotiations without preconditions.[111]

The importance of the definition of political lines that occurred in this period can be seen in Reston's column. On June 11, in the wake of the flap over the administration's shifting statements about the change of mission, Reston had written a very critical column—the most critical piece of reporting in the *Times* since February—arguing, among other things, that the administration's objectives were vastly disproportionate to the level of power it was willing to speak publicly about committing. Five days later, referring to Fulbright's address, Reston wrote:

> On the one side, some Republican leaders are reverting to the Goldwater objective of total victory over the Communists, with main reliance on aerial bombardment. . . .
>
> On the other, the Administration is hoping to bring about a negotiated settlement by limited bombardment . . . and a holding action on the ground.[112]

On the editorial page the *Times* had been calling in the middle of June (without criticizing the administration directly) for further efforts at diplomacy. By early July, however, it was defending the administration against the Right: " . . . some [Republicans] in Congress have made it clear that they will be doing their best to embarrass and harrass the President in his effort to prevent the war from escalating too dangerously."[113]

Finally, by the time the decision on the 44 battalion request was announced, the involvement of American combat troops was essentially a fait accompli. While the bombing had escalated suddenly and dramatically, the ground war, which the administration had escalated bit by bit with few public announcements, had grown slowly, and news coverage about it had been muted and fragmented. Between the first bombing raid in February and the beginning of ROLLING THUNDER early in March, the *Times* had six lead stories on the bombing that ran under multicolumn heads. Not until Johnson's July 28 speech did the ground war rate a multicolumn head. But from March through July, as U.S. troop strength slowly grew and combat operations became more common, the ground war had crept almost imperceptibly into the news, until by July front page stories about American troops in action against the Vietcong were routine. It is impossible to say with any precision what effect this had on the Congress or the public, or even the press itself, but one can detect in the press a sense of resignation: "It is obviously futile to bemoan the past miscalculations that have contributed to making the present options so somber," said one *Times* editorial in July. "The immediate problem is to make sure that new investment in men and materiel is made on terms that offer maximum hope for effectiveness at minimum cost . . . and risk."[114] It seems not unreasonable to believe that to most of the public the decision the president announced on July 28 appeared, as Taylor had said in his cable on press policy, both "undramatic" and a "natural consequence" of the commitment already made.

When Johnson finally announced his decision, it appeared, like Kennedy's decision of November 1961, deceptively anticlimactic. A great deal of drama had surrounded the final stages of the decision-making process. The president had spoken of "new and serious decisions."[115] It had been widely reported that the administration was considering a troop level of up to 200,000 and a call-up of the reserves. The final meetings at the White House had taken place in an atmosphere of "semi-publicity," with "private meetings about which public announcements were made; high officials [slipping] furtively into the White House, only to have their names revealed by the Press Office."[116] (We now know, as much of the press apparently suspected at the time, that the president had already made his decision when these meetings took place.[117]) Johnson's address was taken as a kind of ceremonial recognition that the country was at war; the *Times* editorial was entitled " 'This Is Really War.' " But with the president announcing only an increase of 50,000 troops and no reserve call-up, the news was greeted with relief. The day Johnson spoke, Baldwin reported on an inside page that the troop level was likely to reach 200,000 by the year's end, and that even then the military saw the July deployment as a stopgap.[118] On the front page, however, nothing was said about the future except what Johnson had said, that more troops would be sent "as needed." On the editorial page, the *Times* called the president's address "measured," and continued, "The President made it very clear . . . that he intends a controlled and severely limited operation." In Congress, E. W. Kenworthy reported that "most members . . . received President Johnson's statement . . . with a sense of relief."[119]

II
THE WAR
ON TELEVISION,
1965–1973

As I sat in my office last evening, waiting to speak, I thought of the many times each week when television brings the war into the American home. No one can say exactly what effect those vivid scenes have on American opinion. Historians must only guess at the effect that television would have had during earlier conflicts on the future of this Nation: during the Korean war, for example, at that time when our forces were pushed back there to Pusan; or World War II, the Battle of the Bulge, or when our men were slugging it out in Europe or when most of our Air Force was shot down that day in June 1942 off Australia.

LYNDON JOHNSON, before the National Association of Broadcasters, April 1, 1968[1]

I can't say I completely agree with people who think that when battle scenes are brought into the living room the hazards of war are necessarily made "real" to the civilian audience. It seems to me that by the same process they are also made less "real"—diminished, in part, by the physical size of the television screen, which, for all the industry's advances, still shows a picture of men three inches tall shooting at other men three inches tall, trivialized, or at least tamed, by the enveloping cozy alarums of the household.

MICHAEL ARLEN[2]

Television news came of age on the eve of Vietnam. The CBS and NBC evening news broadcasts took their present form in September 1963, expanding from fifteen minutes to half an hour. As it happened, the pagoda raids at the end of August had just pushed the Buddhist crisis onto the front pages. So the first exclusive stories the expanded shows were able to broadcast had to do with Vietnam: Kennedy granted interviews to Cronkite and Huntley-Brinkley in which he tried, somewhat ambiguously, to clarify U.S. policy toward Diem. (Already there was controversy. Kennedy was unhappy about the way CBS had edited his thirty-minute interview with Cronkite, and insisted that NBC grant him the right to review the editing, which NBC did. Many in the print media criticized Kennedy for making show business of diplomacy.[3]) Two years later American troops went to war under the glare of the television spotlight.

Vietnam was America's first true televised war, television having been in its infancy, and not yet a major source of news, at the time of Korea. It was also the country's most divisive and least successful foreign war. And it is hardly surprising, as Michael Mandelbaum has put it, that many should suspect there might be some connection between these two facts.[4] Lyndon Johnson and Richard Nixon both believed there was. So did the British government when it made the decision in 1982 to restrict severely television coverage of the Falkland Islands campaign.[5] Those who have argued that the media played a decisive role in the defeat of American aims in Vietnam almost invariably focus on television as the principal cause of what they see as a national failure of will.[6] And the view that, for better or for worse, television turned the American public against the war is accepted so widely across the

105

American political spectrum that it probably comes as close as anything to being conventional wisdom about a war that still splits the American public.[7]

Television Power

Why should television be singled out as the decisive influence on the "first domino" of American public opinion? The most elementary reason is the assumption, almost universally shared, that by the mid-1960s television had become the most important source of news for most of the American public, and beyond that, perhaps, the most powerful single influence on the public. Whether this was true or not we cannot know for certain. But, for the sake of perspective, it is worth examining the few fragments of evidence that exist. The evidence most often cited for the preeminent power of television is a series of surveys conducted by the Roper Organization for the Television Information Office.[8] The first was taken in 1964 and showed newspapers and television running about even in the number of people saying they "got most of their news" from each medium. With multiple responses permitted, 58% said television; 56%, newspapers; 26%, radio; and 8%, magazines. Since then the balance has shifted in favor of television; in 1972, the last year Vietnam was a major news story, TV led newspapers by 64% to 50%. A survey by Louis Harris, commissioned by the U.S. Senate in 1973, produced nearly identical figures.[9] The Roper surveys also asked respondents which medium they would be most inclined to believe if the media gave conflicting accounts, and here television came out even more clearly on top. In 1972, 48% said television, 21%, newspapers. There is evidence that this trust is due primarily to two factors: the personal nature of the medium (Walter Cronkite was the "most trusted man in America") and the presence of pictures (the audience can "see it happen.")[10] There is, moreover, some evidence that the public relied on television for news about the war even more than about other subjects. One survey which, in contrast to the Roper studies, found newspapers generally rated more highly than television nevertheless found television preferred for news about the war.[11] On the other side, it should be noted that a series of Harris surveys shows public confidence in both television news and the press at a lower level than confidence in major governmental institutions, including the military and the executive branch, during the Vietnam period, and declining substantially from 1966 to 1972, spurting upward only the following year, presumably as a result of Watergate.[12]

There is, moreover, a significant problem with all these studies: they accept at face value what people say about television's impact on themselves. But objective data do not always bear them out. According to recent data, for example, only about a third of the U.S. public watches any television news, national or local, on any given evening (about two-thirds read a newspaper on any given day). A little more than half of the public will watch at least one network evening news broadcast in a month. "But only *one percent* of all 78.3 million American TV households," reports Lawrence W. Lichty, "watches CBS's Dan Rather as often as four or five nights a week, and Rather presides over the nation's most popular network evening news show. . . . The widely accepted notion that Mr. Rather and his followers each command a vast, devoted nightly following seems far-fetched."[13]

Even when people do watch, it is not clear how much, or in what way, the news will affect their opinions. One of the traditional findings of research on the effects of mass communication, for instance, is that because of selective perception, the media will often tend merely to reinforce people's existing attitudes. And there is evidence that this process was at work in the case of television coverage of Vietnam: a 1968 study found that 75% of respondents who considered themselves "hawks" on the war thought Walter Cronkite was also a "hawk." Somewhat more thought Huntley and Brinkley were "hawks." But a majority of "doves" thought each of the three anchors was a "dove."[14] As we shall see, Vietnam news was ambiguous and contradictory enough, especially after the beginning of 1968, that both hawks and doves could easily have found material to support their own views of the war.

People also do not remember what they see on television news very well, at least at a conscious level. W. Russell Neuman found in the mid-1970s that about 50% of viewers, asked if they could recall any stories from a news broadcast they had just watched, could recall none.[15] The average number remembered was 1.2. (Neuman's study contained some evidence that Vietnam news was more interesting or more vivid to the public: people recalled more Vietnam stories without prompting, 9.9% of all stories in that category, than in any other subject area. But there was also evidence that the details of Vietnam news didn't get across very well. When people were helped out with a list of stories, they could supply details for 19.2% of Vietnam stories, fewer than for any other category except commentaries.) It is possible, of course, that people do not need to remember the specific content of the news to be affected by it; there is evidence from a variety of studies that television may affect people's perceptions or attitudes even if they retain very few of the facts or arguments presented.[16] But we know relatively little about what aspects of the television message might have this sort of effect.

This is not to say that television should be assumed *not* to be a significant force in the shaping of public opinion. Very few media researchers today accept the "minimal effects" view that dominated academic media research in the 1950s and early 1960s. A growing number of studies confirm the commonsense idea that television—and other media—can indeed, in certain circumstances and in certain ways, shape political perceptions very powerfully.[17] But sweeping statements about the power of television, which have been a staple of most discussion of televison and Vietnam, clearly need to be taken with a grain of salt. And the reader should remember, as we look at television's presentation of the war, that it is impossible to be certain how the news affected the audience.

Another kind of argument about the power of television is worth a few words here. Perhaps it doesn't matter whether television really has the immense impact on public opinion so many attribute to it; perhaps the reputation is enough. If politicians believe television shapes public opinion, and respond to the news as an indicator of public sentiment, then the news might shape the course of politics regardless of its actual impact on the public. This is not an implausible argument, and there is even a bit of evidence that something like this happened at a crucial point in the war in Vietnam: in 1968, when Walter Cronkite concluded a personal report on the Tet offensive with the comment that the war had become a "bloody stalemate" and the time had perhaps come to get out, Lyndon Johnson is said to have turned to his aides and said, "It's all over."[18] Johnson had three television sets in the Oval Office, and no doubt he was not the only politician paying close attention in that sensitive political year to the images of Vietnam the public was seeing on its television screens. But, again, it is important to keep this fact in perspective. Truman, after all, lost his job over the indecisive war in Korea, where television was not a factor. And in 1968, as we shall see in Chapter 5, there were many influences, besides Walter Cronkite, on Johnson's decision to begin deescalating the war. We cannot be sure how much impact television had on the shift in U.S. policy in 1969, any more than we can be sure what role it played in the decline of public support for the war.

The Medium Is the Message?

The other reason many have singled out television's portrayal of Vietnam is that television coverage of a war is seen as very different from print coverage. Many arguments have been made about the distinctiveness of television coverage of Vietnam, but they can be boiled down without too much loss to two.

1. Because it is a visual medium, television shows the raw horror of war in a way print cannot. Often this agrument is coupled with its corollary, that a visual medium, while it can portray violence and suffering very effectively, cannot deal as effectively with politics or strategy, with the result that war necessarily appears on television as senseless killing. (Those who make this argument generally believe that this was a false appearance in the case of Vietnam.)

2. Television focuses on the negative—especially on conflict—more than print. Different explanations have been given for this. Sometimes it is seen as a result of the entertainment character of television news. Because American television is essentially a dramatic medium, the argument goes, and intensely concerned with ratings in a way that a newspaper is not (most American newspapers do not compete head-to-head with other newspapers for circulation, nor does their readership fluctuate from day to day as television viewership does), it is constantly searching for sensation, which is supplied largely by negative stories—conflict and scandal.[19] The other explanation is ideological: it is that television, perhaps because of recruitment patterns in a high-paying medium, embodies in particularly strong form a kind of oppositional culture common among intellectuals in contemporary American society. (Some, of course, argue this of journalism in general, without singling out television.) This was the argument Spiro Agnew put forward in 1969, when he launched his attack on the "liberal establishment" in the networks and the "prestige press." It has been taken up since by many media commentators close to the neoconservative movement of the 1970s and 1980s.

In the two chapters that follow, we shall examine television's coverage of Vietnam, from August 20, 1965—which, for reasons discussed in Chapter 1, is the earliest date for which sufficient television material is available—through January 1973. Chapter 4 will deal primarily with the period before the Tet offensive of January–February, 1968, Chapter 5 primarily with the period from Tet through the cease-fire.

We shall see that television's coverage was indeed distinctive in many ways. But it is far from true that television presented the war "literally." A television report is as much a cultural artifact as is a newspaper story; the television camera "sees" with human eyes, its use as much determined by political, economic, and cultural forces as the use of a typewriter. Nor was television's coverage particularly negative. In Part I we explored two powerful forces which most of the time kept newspaper coverage from straying very far from the official line on Vietnam: the routines of objective journalism, which tied the news closely to official sources and the Washington agenda, and the ideology of the Cold War, which locked events in a framework of understanding that made fundamental questioning of American policy essentially unthinkable. In different ways, we will see these same two factors at work in television coverage from 1965 to 1973. Television coverage was highly dependent both on official sources in Washington and, probably even more important in the early years of the war, on military sources in Vietnam. As for ideology, television reporting contained little of the articulated geopolitical world view that the *Times* had invoked to explain American intervention in its early phases. Ideology appeared instead in a complex set of conventions for talking about war, conventions which, like the more articulate level of ideology employed by the *Times*, had the effect of putting the war beyond what I shall refer to as the "Sphere of Legitimate Controversy." In the early years of the war, roughly up to the Tet offensive, these forces were powerful enough that television coverage was lopsidedly favorable to American policy in Vietnam, often so explicitly favorable, in fact, that we will have to rethink the role of the professional ideology of objective journalism discussed in Chapter 3.

Later television's portrayal of the war changed dramatically, and there seems little doubt that it must have contributed to the growing feeling of war-weariness in the later years of the war. But television's turnaround on the war was part of a larger change, a response to as well as a cause of the unhappiness with the war that was developing at many levels, from the halls of the Pentagon, to Main Street, U.S.A. and the fire bases of Quang Tri province. And the change in television coverage was also limited. We shall see, for example, that Richard Nixon did remarkably well, under the circumstances, at managing Vietnam news during his first term.

The Content Analysis

The discussion of *New York Times* coverage in Part I was based on a reading of all the paper's coverage from 1960 through the middle of 1965. After the middle of 1965, however, Vietnam became an almost daily story, and with a period of nearly seven and a half years to cover, it was impossible to deal with all the coverage. The analysis of Part II is therefore based on a sample of television coverage, 8 to 12 network evening news broadcasts selected randomly from each month, 779 broadcasts altogether, of which all but 56 had some Vietnam news.[20] The three networks were sampled with equal probability, although

ABC, because its broadcast was not expanded to thirty minutes until January 1967, contributed fewer stories to the sample. The networks did differ some in their coverage. In the pre-Tet period, CBS reports were somewhat less enthusiastic, or less consistently so, than those of NBC or ABC; after Tet, differences among the networks were less clear-cut, though ABC's commentaries continued to be more supportive of administration policy than those of the other networks. I am not particularly interested in differences among the networks, however, and will almost always combine them in the discussion that follows.

Besides this sample, which was subjected to quantitative content analysis, I also watched a great deal of other television coverage of the war. This was done unsystematically (in a statistical sense, anyway), over a period of many years, as I repeatedly went back to the archives to examine specific periods in detail, or to refresh my memory after months of dealing primarily with numbers, or to check the plausibility of new arguments I found myself making. Eventually I lost track of how much coverage I had seen, and all I can say now is that I am fairly certain I watched and took notes on the Vietnam coverage from somewhere between a thousand and fifteen hundred evening news broadcasts, plus some network documentaries. So, although the quantitative content analysis is based on the 779 broadcasts formally sampled, the discussion in Part II draws on a much wider body of material.

There is one serious problem with the data base for this analysis. For the period before August 5, 1968, when the Vanderbilt Television News Archive was started, I relied on the collection usually known as the Defense Department Kinescopes, now housed in the National Archives. This includes weekday evening news coverage of military affairs (the Vanderbilt Archive includes weekend coverage during parts of the period of this study) recorded by the U.S. Army Photographic Agency beginning after the first great controversy had erupted over television coverage of the war, when American troops were filmed burning the village of Cam Ne. But this collection does not include all the relevant news, even when one puts aside such problems as material not recorded on holidays, or occasional omissions that seem simply random.[21] Only news considered relevant to the Defense Department was recorded, and the standards of relevance were vague and inconsistent.

Fortunately, because "rundown" sheets for the *CBS Evening News* (that is, lists of the stories shown each evening) are available for this period, it is possible to determine what kinds of stories tended to be excluded. One hundred twelve of the 114 CBS broadcasts in the sample from the DOD Kinescopes could be matched with rundowns or transcripts in the CBS archives. Table 1 shows the results of this comparison,

Table 1 Comparison of *CBS Evening News* Rundowns with
Defense Department Kinescopes,
August 20, 1965, through August 4, 1968

Subject	Number and Percent of Film Reports Included	Number and Percent of Film Reports Not Included	Total Number of Film Reports and Percent of Coverage
Military activity	84 (90.3%)	9 (9.7)	93 (52.0)
Debate in U.S.	5 (15.2)	28 (84.8)	33 (18.4)
Administration policy-making	10 (50.0)	10 (50.0)	20 (11.2)
South Vietnamese politics	4 (25.0)	12 (75.0)	16 (8.9)
Diplomatic activity	2 (22.2)	7 (77.7)	9 (5.0)
Other	3 (37.5)	5 (62.5)	8 (4.5)
Total	108 (60.3)	71 (39.7)	179 (100.0)

for film reports and voice-over stories. (The pattern is similar for stories read by the anchor.) Television coverage in this period dealt primarily with day-to-day military operations—a very significant fact, as we shall see in the following chapter. This part of the coverage, amounting to more than half the total, is very well represented in the DOD Kinescopes. But in other areas—coverage of domestic debate and administration policy-making, the diplomatic side of the war, and the political situation in South Vietnam—the kinescopes include only a small part of the total. In some cases it was possible to supplement the kinescopes with transcripts from the CBS archives, but these are only available for limited periods. The discussion of pre-1968 coverage of the nonmilitary side of the war, therefore, is necessarily based on a fragmentary record.

Finally, a word about the technique of quantitative content analysis, which will play a limited but important role in the discussion that follows. Content analysis lends an aura of scientific authority to media research. And in fact quantification does, if done properly, impose a useful measure of discipline. It requires the analyst to define clearly the criteria for assigning stories or other units of content to the different categories of the analysis. And it requires dealing with all the content sampled, not just those parts of it that fit the story line the analyst starts out with. Nevertheless, at the risk of undermining scientific authority, it is important to point out that the data produced by content analysis are always the result of many choices and sometimes conceal a good deal of ambiguity or subjectivity in coding procedures. Many of the measures used in this study can be defined precisely enough that the numbers can be taken more or less at face value. This is the case, for instance, with counts of how often different kinds of people appeared on television—officials, soldiers, antiwar activists, and so on—or of how often the news showed civilian casualties, or of how many battles were presented as victories and how many as defeats—though even in these cases the definitions of coding categories can be surprisingly complex, as the reader can see by looking at the Code Book for the analysis, reproduced in Appendix B. Other measures are extremely difficult to define precisely, including, for example, one designed to measure the frequency and direction of journalists' interpretive comments in the news; content analysis does not deal easily with subtlety or complexity of meaning, which is why its role in this study is as limited as it is. Coding of this sort of measure involves considerable personal judgment that cannot fully be spelled out.[22] Whenever data of this sort are presented, they will be accompanied by a note about coding criteria.

4

The "Uncensored War," 1965–1967

As we shift from print to television, the mode of exposition of this study must change: rather than following Vietnam coverge in detail day by day, as we did in examining print coverage, we will push chronology into the background for most of the present chapter, and examine themes which persisted in television coverage thoughout the period from the deployment of large-scale ground forces in the summer of 1965 until the Tet offensive in January 1968. In part, this change of style is necessary because of the sheer volume of coverage during this period, compared with 1961–65, when Vietnam was in the news more sporadically. But it is also appropriate to the nature of television coverage, which was less the "first draft of history" that the press is supposed to provide than a series of more or less timeless images of men— or, more precisely, of Americans—at war.

More than half of television's coverage in these early years was concerned with military operations, the rest being divided among various forms of politics—the policy debate in Washington, the development of the antiwar movement, the political conflicts that continued to rock South Vietnam, and diplomatic activity.[1] So this chapter will focus primarily on the "uncensored war" that Americans saw so often on their television screens. We will begin, however, where we left off in Part I, with the policy debate in Washington, where we can start to get a sense of how network television coverage might differ from the "prestige press" coverage we have examined to this point.

Unfortunately, Washington coverage is one of the areas for which the Defense Department Kinescopes are incomplete. It will be impossible, therefore, to provide a fully representative picture of the networks' Washington coverage throughout the 1965–67 period. There is, however, one important episode for which the kinescopes do contain extensive Washington coverage: the "peace offensive" which began on

December 24, 1965, intended by the administration to prepare public opinion for an expansion of the war. The reporting of the peace offensive cannot be taken as typical of television's Washington reporting throughout 1965–67; on the contrary, as we explore television's response to the growing conflict over the war in Chapter 5, we shall see that there is good reason to assume that the networks moved gradually away from the kind of "patriotic" journalism we are about to encounter. But the peace offensive will show us where television stood in relation to official policy at the war's beginning, and provide us with a model of journalism very different from anything we have seen in our reading of the *New York Times*.

After considering the Washington beat, we will move on to the heart of television's coverage, the story of "American boys in action." Finally, this chapter will close with a look at the way the "bad guys" were portrayed in television's melodrama of war—coverage of the North Vietnamese and Vietcong. The portrayal of two other major actors—the domestic opposition to the war and America's South Vietnamese allies—will be taken up in Chapter 5.

The Peace Offensive and the Boundaries of Objectivity

The decision of July 1965 to raise the level of American troops in Vietnam to 175,000 was intended as the first of two phases, with approval of the second phase expected early in 1966. Phase II was originally planned to involve 112,000 additional U.S. troops. But the North Vietnamese were matching U.S. escalation. By November 1965, it had become clear that infiltration from North Vietnam had increased substantially, and Phase II had to be revised upward. By December, force levels of up to about 400,000 were being discussed for the end of 1966. Vietnam was going to be a big war. Political support would be a problem, and there was considerable sentiment in the administration that an escalation of this magnitude should not be undertaken without some major new peace effort which would, if nothing else, convince world and American public opinion that diplomatic channels had been fully explored. At the end of November, Secretary McNamara wrote to the president:

> It is my belief that there should be a three- or four-week pause in the program of bombing the North before we either greatly increase our troop deployments to Vietnam or intensify our strikes against the North. The reasons for this belief are, first, that we must lay a foundation in the mind of the American public and in world opinion for such an enlarged phase

of the war, and, second, we should give North Vietnam a face-saving chance to stop the aggression.[2]

So on Christmas Eve 1965, a thirty-seven-day pause in the bombing of North Vietnam began. It was accompanied by a moderately serious, secret contact with the North Vietnamese through their mission in Rangoon, Burma, which was broken off for reasons we will examine later. It was also accompanied by a massive public peace offensive, aimed at both U.S. and world opinion. W. Averill Harriman, Vice President Humphrey, and other officials were dispatched to various capitals to carry the messge of American willingness to negotiate; Arthur Goldberg did this at the United Nations; Secretary Rusk released the first formal statement of American peace proposals, known as the Fourteen Points. Not everyone was convinced by the peace offensive. Perhaps most important, J. William Fulbright, chairman of the Senate Foreign Relations Committee and at one time the president's key Capitol Hill supporter on foreign policy, went public with his opposition to U.S. policy in Vietnam, holding hearings in February which could be considered the first major congressional debate on the war. But on television, the peace offensive was an unqualified success.

In order to understand television's reporting from Washington during this period, we need to consider a more complex view of American journalism. The model of objective journalism introduced in the preceding chapter does not apply: the television journalist presented himself, in this case, not as a disinterested observer, but as a patriot, a partisan of what he frequently referred to as "our" peace offensive. It is useful to imagine the journalist's world as divided into three regions, each of which is governed by different journalistic standards.[3] These regions can be represented by the concentric circles shown in Figure 1. The province of objectivity is the middle region, which can be called the Sphere of Legitimate Controversy. This is the region of electoral contests and legislative debates, of issues recognized as such by the major established actors of the American political process. The limits of this sphere are defined primarily by the two-party system—by the parameters of debate between and within the Democratic and Republican parties—as well as by the decision-making process in the bureaucracies of the executive branch. Within this region, objectivity and balance reign as the supreme journalistic virtues.

Bounding the Sphere of Legitimate Controversy on one side is what can be called the Sphere of Consensus. This is the region of "motherhood and apple pie"; it encompasses those social objects not regarded by the journalists and most of the society as controversial. Within this

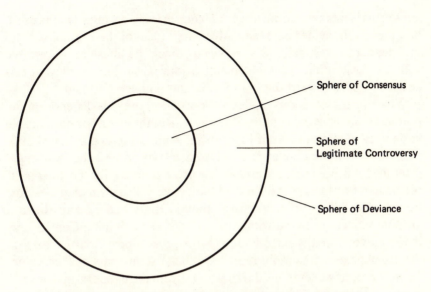

Figure 1 Spheres of consensus, controversy, and deviance.

region journalists do not feel compelled either to present opposing views or to remain disinterested observers. On the contrary, the journalist's role is to serve as an advocate or celebrant of consensus values.

And beyond the Sphere of Legitimate Controversy lies the Sphere of Deviance, the realm of those political actors and views which journalists and the political mainstream of the society reject as unworthy of being heard. It is, for example, written into the FCC's guidelines for application of the Fairness Doctrine that "it is not the Commission's intention to make time available to Communists or to the Communist viewpoints."[4] Here neutrality once again falls away, and journalism becomes, to borrow a phrase from Talcott Parsons, a "boundary-maintaining mechanism":[5] it plays the role of exposing, condemning, or excluding from the public agenda those who violate or challenge the political consensus. It marks out and defends the limits of acceptable political conflict.

It should be added that each "sphere" has internal gradations, and the boundaries between them are often fuzzy. Within the Sphere of Legitimate Controversy, for example, the practice of objective journalism varies considerably. Near the border of the Sphere of Consensus, journalists practice the kind of objective journalism we encountered in the previous chapter, where objectivity involves a straight recitation of official statements. Farther out, as the news deals with issues on which consensus is weaker, the principle of balance is increasingly emphasized, and then, still farther out, the "adversary" ideal of the journalist as an independent investigator who serves to check the abuse of power. We will see these other faces of objective journalism increasingly as this account moves toward the era of polarization over Vietnam.

Which of these various models of journalism prevails depends on the political climate in the country as a whole. But there is also considerable variability within American journalism. And at the beginning of 1966 there was a dramatic contrast between television and the "prestige" print media in Vietnam coverage. The prestige press, for the most part, continued to practice the kind of objective journalism that lies just outside the Sphere of Consensus, though there had perhaps been a little movement outward within the Sphere of Legitimate Controversy in the eleven months since Pleiku. Most press reports, particularly on the front page, still simply reported official statements at face value. There were, however, considerably more front page reports on congressional criticism of administration policy. There were more stories in which a number of different sources, some from inside the administration and some from outside (almost always in Congress), were used more or less coequally, with the journalist constructing a synthesis. And nonelite opposition was beginning to be reported in a "straight" way, that is, stories on opposition figures, like those on the administration, would be centered around the sources' own statements.[6]

On television, on the other hand, the peace offensive appeared as a kind of morality play: while the coverage of a paper like the *Times* had a dry and detached tone, television coverage presented a dramatic contrast between good, represented by the American peace offensive, and evil, represented by Hanoi. In part, the effectiveness of the peace offensive in creating a powerful television image of American virtue might be considered a result of the familiar ironies of objective journalism, somewhat modified by the nature of television presentation. It has often been observed that American television coverage is more "thematic" than print reporting.[7] Because television news is organized in time rather than space, the television audience must be "carried along" from the beginning of the story to the end. It cannot be allowed—as a newspaper audience can—to shift its attention from story to story. A definite theme or story line is therefore essential to a television report (or even, at times, will structure a whole broadcast) in a way it is not for a newspaper article.

Some recent critics have described the thematic quality of television news as a factor that pushes it toward a more openly "adversarial" stance vis-à-vis political authority.[8] And under certain conditions that can be true. A good example, if the reader will permit a digression a decade and half past 1965, would be the reporting of the Gulf of Sidra incident early in the Reagan administration, in 1981. Two Libyan jets had attacked U.S. planes off the Libyan coast, during exercises described by the administration as "routine," and were shot down. Information was available to reporters, however, that the maneuvers were not routine at all, but were considered likely—if not actually intended— to produce some sort of response from Libya. The parallel with the Gulf of Tonkin incident was so clear, and contrasting information had so recently come out, that many press reports were quite skeptical. In the *Washington Post*, for example, the lead story (which was generally an "objective" presentation of the various official statements) was accompanied by a long news analysis which was—if one put together the various facts it presented—quite damning to the official version of events.[9] The *Post*'s analysis, however, was presented simply as a discussion of the background to the conflict and did not focus explicitly on the contrast between official statements and background information. In television reports, by contrast, information that in the *Post* was dispersed was joined together into a single package of stories, and the contrast between the administration's public statements and what reporters knew (mostly from officials speaking off the record) jumped to the foreground. CBS, for example, cut directly from a statement by presidential aide Edwin Meese denying that the United States had been challenging Libya to correspondent Leslie Stahl, who reported:

> However, *Newsweek* magazine ran an item before the incident [video: still of *Newsweek* article] that the Reagan administration was choosing the Gulf of Sidra for the exercises specifically to challenge Qaddafi as a way of "neutralizing" him. And CBS News has been told that the engagement was—quote—"not unanticipated . . . it did not come out of the blue."[10]

In 1966, however, when contrasting interpretations were rarely being reported, what jumped to the foreground in television's simple, thematic presentation was the administration's own rhetoric. Television's version of objective reporting looked something like this:

> *David Brinkley.* President Johnson's peace campaign continues, and there has been no bombing of North Vietnam for more than ten days now. But radio Hanoi called the whole campaign a swindle and there is no public sign of any peace talks. [Hubert Humphrey is then shown speaking at a news conference, after which Brinkley "wraps up."] What Humphrey did was to deliver a brief, simple list of this country's efforts to end the war and a quick explanation of what the United States is after in Vietnam. It says among other things: the U.S. wants no bases there, will happily pull

out its troops, will give economic aid to all sides, will accept a neutral Vietnam if that is what the people there freely decide they want. In short, Humphrey said, we have offered to put everything into the basket of peace except the surrender of South Vietnam. As yet, again, there has been no favorable response from the North.[11]

What Brinkley does here is not so different from what a newspaper reporter might do: he structures the story around the vice president's remarks. The difference is that on television the story is boiled down to a single image, the contrast between the American peace offensive— "everything in the basket of peace except surrender"—and North Vietnamese failure to respond, an image sharpened by Brinkley's simple, expressive language.

Television, moreover, tends to "thematize"—that is, to simplify and unify—not only within a particular story or broadcast, but over time as well. Television tends, in other words, to pick out a limited number of ongoing stories and cover them day in and day out. This may in part explain (I will offer some other possible explanations, or parts of the explanation, below) why television focused much more heavily on the peace offensive than did the press. In the major papers, coverage of Vietnam policy shifted among a number of subjects, including the administration's developing plans for further increases in the U.S. commitment and the growing debate in Congress over the prospect of escalation. On television, however, the peace offensive was the single major theme of Vietnam coverage as long as it went on, and was in the foreground of coverage on most days. CBS used daily graphics showing how long the bombing pause had lasted.

But in drawing the contrast between America and its enemies— between good and evil—television journalists did not always confine themselves to reporting the official proceedings of the peace offensive. Their role was much more active: they moved back and forth between "straight" reporting and commentary; their language was peppered with phrases strongly charged with moral and ideological significance. Television treated the peace offensive largely as a matter of consensus, to which the injunctions of objective journalism did not apply. Here are a few excerpts.

ABC, January 4, 1966, Peter Jennings. Hanoi, commenting for the first time on the halt in U.S. bombing of North Vietnam, snapped that the U.S. had no right to make any conditions for ending the war except on Hanoi's terms. Ambassador Goldberg talked again of negotiating peace.

NBC, January 21, 1966, David Brinkley. As for the peace campaign, the Communist side has repeatedly called it a sham. If it is, they could come to the bargaining table and expose it. But they haven't.

Chet Huntley. The Communists in Vietnam demonstrated today that they attach no more solemnity to a truce than to their politics. [Huntley then reported on charges of violations of the Tet truce, which received prominent and dramatic coverage on all three networks that day. On the cease-fire, the *New York Times* reported, "Most cease-fire violations have been of 'minor significance,' a United States military communiqué said, and casualties suffered by allied forces have been light."[12]]

ABC, February 1, 1966, Jennings (making a transition between a report from the U.N. and another from Paris.) The uncompromising position of North Vietnam was also made clear today in a different quarter. . . .

Following the February 1 report from Paris, Jennings continued, "The stubborn defiance of the North Vietnamese leadership in Hanoi is often evident in the Communist prisoners captured in the South." Jennings then reported on North Vietnamese prisoners, being returned to the North in an exchange, who had thrown into the river packages given them as a "goodwill" gesture by the South Vietnamese. This kind of connection between different stories usually does not exist in newspaper coverage. It is one of the things that makes television a more ideological medium than the newspaper: television forces much more of the news into the unity of a story line—and therefore of a world view.

Why should television have been more inclined than major newspapers to stick to consensus journalism on Vietnam, or to the narrowest kind of objective journalism? In part, it may simply have been the immaturity of a medium that was just beginning to be taken seriously, and to take itself seriously, as a major part of the journalistic profession. Most of television's Washington coverage during the peace offensive was not reported by correspondents with regular beats in the State Department, White House, and so on.[13] The typical report on Vietnam policy would consist of lengthy film clips of public statements by officials, introduced and wrapped up by the anchor, who relied primarily on wire service material. Perhaps this is one reason television tended to take official rhetoric so often at face value, and to fall back on stereotypes: a great deal of the news was put together by anchors, producers, and newswriters in the New York office, people who did not have the familiarity with particular areas of policy that reporters covering a beat normally will have. There is a "gee whiz" quality to much television coverage that suggests very limited awareness of the background to official rhetoric. This lack of background knowledge can be seen in reports of January 4 and 5 on NBC and CBS, respectively. On January 4 David Brinkley reported, "So the United States is willing to go anywhere, anytime and negotiate anything." In fact, the United States was not willing to negotiate the one thing that mattered to the North Vietnamese and the NLF: political power in the South. Debate in Congress was beginning to broach the issue of what the U.S. attitude should be toward Vietcong participation both in peace talks and in the future government in Vietnam, and this issue received some attention in the press;[14] it received almost none on television. As it turned out, it was probably the central issue of the negotiating process. The North Vietnamese broke off the Rangoon contact early in February, in response, U.S. analysts believed, not to the resumption of bombing that occurred then, but to the Honolulu Declaration issued after a meeting between U.S. and South Vietnamese officials, which reaffirmed that the United States considered the GVN the "sole legitimate representative" of the South Vietnamese people.[15] The following day Walter Cronkite began dramatically, "Good evening. The United States is offering to decelerate the pace of the Vietnam War as a prelude to peace talks." The following Sunday, January 9, the *Times*'s Week in Review closed its discussion of Vietnam by quoting the Senate majority and minority leaders, each of whom said the possibility of negotiations was remote and a decision on escalation would have to be made soon.

One of the most striking differences between television and prestige press coverage of Vietnam policy early in 1966 is that television reporting centered around public press conferences while newspaper reporting was based primarily on background contacts with officials. A difference in focus naturally accompanied the difference in sources. When major officials spoke publicly, they focused on the peace offensive. Privately the talk of Washington was the growing debate about what to do when, as expected, it did not lead to promising diplomatic results. Among the *Times*'s headlines during peace offensive:

Jan. 5.   "$12 Billion More Sought by Johnson for Vietnam"
Jan. 13.   "Army Due to Gain Up to 50,000 Men"
Jan. 18.   "McNamara to Ask 113,000 More Men for the Military"
Jan. 22.   "Vietnam Buildup to 400,000 Troops Expected in Year"
Jan. 30.   "U.S. Aides Said to Feel War May Last 6 or 7 Years"

Little of this talk of escalation was covered on television.

But I do not think the immaturity of television news in the mid-1960s is adequate by itself to explain the more "patriotic" character of its Vietnam coverage. Television news has "grown up" a great deal since 1966. Its Washington coverage is no longer a mere summary of wire reports, backed by film of press conferences. The reporter, with his or her established beat and inside contacts, now provides most of television's coverage of national politics. Yet TV journalism is still often moralizing journalism, either of the condemnatory or the celebrating variety. Two good recent examples would be the Korean airliner incident and the invasion of Grenada. I will suggest here two possible explanations.

It may be, in the first place, that television's very power—or reputation for power—has the ironic consequence of making the medium particularly sensitive about the boundaries of legitimate controversy. Television seems to generate much more intense political reactions than other media. In part this may be because of its reputation for immense influence over the public. In part I suspect it is because of the nature of television's presentation, which is both unsubtle, because of its thematic simplicity, and very personal. When the invisible—and in this case anonymous—writer of the *Times* Week in Review notes in the middle of a long article that "the weakness of the [peace] offensive seemed to be . . . in the nature of the message conveyed. . . . Official sources gradually made clear that the message contained no new substantive offer,"[16] the *Times* need not worry terribly about charges it is aiding and abetting the enemy. If Cronkite had come on and said, "Good evening. The United States has offered a new plan for peace in Vietnam. But CBS has learned the proposal contains little that is new," the reaction might have been quite strong. By the time of the progress offensive television had already been "burned" once on Vietnam, the previous August when Morley Safer's report from Cam Ne (discussed below) had generated a major public controversy; events like Cam Ne were reported routinely in the newspapers without any significant reaction.[17] Later, when boundaries of the Sphere of Legitimate Controversy began to shift and become themselves a subject of debate, so that it was no longer clear where they lay, the networks would have such problems often, as they did, for instance, with their portrayal of the police at the Democratic National Convention in 1968.[18] So perhaps television people, consciously or not, were particularly wary of treating as controversial things many people might regard as belonging properly to the Sphere of Consensus.

Television, moreover, seems to have a positive attraction to the role of moralist. This I believe is true for two interrelated reasons, the first having to do with television's audience, the other with its presentation. The papers we have been comparing with television news, particularly the *Times* and *Post*, are written for an audience most of which follows politics relatively closely. Television's audience is diverse, but compared with elite newspapers it is a long way "down-market": older, less educated, much more heavily a working-class audience. And television people often say that they assume the audience to be uninformed about and uninterested in politics. As for presentation, television merges information and entertainment far more than an elite newspaper does. This is related to the nature of the audience: readers of the *Times* are assumed to want the news for information, television viewers, for entertainment. (Newspapers with audiences similar to television's also merge the functions of entertainment and news reporting. Vietnam coverage in the New York *Daily News* was much more like television coverage than like the reporting of the *Times*.) And it is also related to the "time-embeddedness" of television's presentation: the evening news is an integral part of the "audience flow" which builds up to the real heart of television's product, prime-time entertainment. Television cannot separate its entertainment and information-providing functions as easily as a newspaper can, with its spatial dispersion of separate stories and sections.

The argument is often made that because television news is inescapably also entertainment, and therefore takes the form of *drama*, television is constantly searching for conflict and controversy, with the result that it portrays social and political institutions in a particularly negative light.[19] But that is much too glib. Television does love drama, on the news as well as in prime time, and drama does require conflict, but what that conflict will be about, what characters will be the "good guys" and "bad guys," what kind of resolutions and morals will be deemed appropriate— none of this is determined by the dramatic nature of the medium itself. It depends on the prevailing ideology of the society as well as on the particular historical conjuncture, which brings certain elements of that ideology to the fore and pushes others into the background.

American political ideology is deeply ambivalent about politics and authority (perhaps this is true, in different ways, about the political culture of any society). Americans have always had a suspicion of power and those who seek and wield it; power is often portrayed in American popular culture as the enemy of the Individual, who is of course the basic American hero. Exposés of abuse of power and tales of individuals who resist oppression by it are indeed a favored source of drama for American journalism and in particular for television. But there is also in American political culture a deep desire for order and unity. The institution that represents Community in its "good" form, in most popular culture, and which makes the Individual a part of society and therefore not a threat, not "evil" in his or her individualism, is the Family. Almost all prime-time TV entertainment sets its characters within a family or (especially in the late 1970s and early 1980s) a substitute family of some sort. In politics, the Nation tends to be treated as a Family writ large; suspicion of power therefore coexists with a deep belief in loyalty to the political family and harmony within it. And those who hold political authority, though they can be treated as seekers of power, that is, Individuals breaking the limits of Community or usurping its functions, can also be treated as paternal representatives of Community itself.

It is by no means always true that the dramas of television news focus on disharmony or place established institutions or authorities in a negative light. Television loves, in fact, to find stories that allow it to celebrate the unity of the National Family. These are essential to the dramatic structure of the news: Evil must stand in contrast to Good, disharmony to the ideal of harmony. And the medium not surprisingly likes to identify itself with Good. It is interesting here to think what kinds of stories television has dignified and identified itself with by sending the anchor to cover them in person. Until a recent move to make the anchor a reporter as well, almost all were in some sense ceremonies of national unity. They included national political conventions and elections, which involve conflict, but of an especially controlled and sanctified kind; space shots, which are symbolic of national accomplishment; presidential trips abroad, in which the Nation, in its dealings with other countries, becomes personified; and the Kennedy funeral. In only a single case, so far as I know, had an anchor covered personally a story that lacked this ceremonial quality. This case we will look at in the following chapter: Cronkite's trip to Vietnam during the Tet offensive. As for stories of conflict, those that are the best material for television drama are the ones in which Good and Evil can be represented as clear and separate, where the source of conflict can be located outside the National Family.

Because of their different audiences, then, and because of television's special need for drama, TV and the prestige press perform very different political functions. The prestige press provides information to a politically interested audience; it therefore deals with *issues*. Television provides not just "headlines," as television people often say, nor just entertainment, but ideological guidance and reassurance for the mass public. It therefore deals not so much with issues as with symbols that represent the basic values of the established political culture. This difference is certainly not absolute. Newpapers too can play the role of moralist; much of the *Times*'s coverage of Vietnam in the early 1960s, before Vietnam had moved into the Sphere of Legitimate Controversy, did this, albeit in a more sophisticated way for its more sophisticated audience. And television has always been torn between a desire to belong to the inner circle of serious journalism and its other identity

as storyteller-moralist. Since the mid-1960s the balance in television
has shifted considerably toward "serious journalism," and the contrast
between television and the press has narrowed. But in 1966 it was still
very great, and it was therefore natural for television to focus on the
good moral tale of the peace offensive, while the elite papers gave their
attention to the growing policy debate.

The "Uncensored War"

In mid-1965, as troopships and, later, commercial airliners began pour-
ing young Americans into Vietnam, the ranks of the media swelled.
On the eve of the Tet offensive, in January 1968 there were 179 American journalists accredited by the military command in Saigon, and the
number swelled still further with the Tet offensive itself.[20] There was
nothing new about this. About 500 correspondents had covered the
Civil War for northern newspapers.[21] In World War II a similar number
of American reporters had assembled in England to cover the invasion
of Europe.[22] Over 100 British correspondents had covered the Boer
War, which involved only 31,000 troops on both sides.[23] But in other
ways Vietnam did represent a real change in the intensity of news
coverage.

There was, in the first place, no military censorship—a situation
which, while by no means new in itself, had never before been combined
with routine official accreditation of war correspondents. The modern
system of accreditation and censorship, like many of the public relations
techniques of modern warfare, developed during World War I. There
had been fledgling systems of accreditation before—in the American
Civil War, for instance—but for the most part few established rules
had governed the correspondent's relation to the military organization.
Some reporters, usually taken on at the discretion of particular commanders, would be regarded as official; others would simply make their
own way to the front and, unless they were arrested by military authorities, which frequently happened, were free to report whatever they
could find out and transmit.

In World War I, after considerable controversy over lack of press
access to the front and many arrests of unaccredited correspondents,
the modern precedent was established: the right of the press to
be granted access to the front on a routine basis was accepted,
on the condition that the press submit to censorship by military
or political authorities. Frederick Palmer of the New York *Herald*
wrote:

There was not the freedom of the old days, but there never can be again for the correspondent. We lived in a mess with our conducting officers, paying for our quarters, food and automobiles. I do not recall ever having asked to go anyplace without receiving consent. Day after day we sallied forth from our chateau to different headquarters and billets for our grist, and having written our dispatches, turned them over to the officers for censorship. We rarely had our copy cut. We had learned too well where the line was drawn on military secrecy. The important items were those we left out; and these made us public liars.[24]

The purpose of this system was, from the beginning, at least as much political as military. The mobilization of public opinion was increasingly seen as something that needed to be organized systematically, and the press was naturally considered central to that effort. This meant that governments had an incentive to offer the press access and to give it adequate information and freedom to insure its credibility.[25] (In World War II, newspaper reporting was considered "essential service," grounds for the same kind of draft exemption given to workers in defense plants.[26]) It also meant that censorship and other controls would be used to prevent damage to morale on the home front as well as to deny to the other side information about military operations and capabilities. Correspondents with U.N. forces in Korea, for example, were forbidden to make "any derogatory comments" about U.N. troops.[27]

At one point, it looked as though Vietnam might follow the familiar pattern. As the 1965 buildup began, the American command tightened restrictions on the media, particularly on access to American air bases. This produced a wave of protests from news organizations, and the possibility of the old bargain of submitting to censorship in return for access was raised. Wes Gallagher, general manager of the Associated Press, said in New York, "So far as the Associated Press is concerned, our correspondents are prepared to submit air base copy to formal censorship if the United States Army installs it. But correspondents should be free to see and cover all aspects of the war as was done in World War II."[28] The military did consider the feasibility of formal censorship, but decided that it would not be practical. Officials felt, for one thing, that censorship in the field would be of limited use in an undeclared war in which it could not be imposed in the United States as well. Reporters could always get around the rules by filing from Hong Kong or Tokyo, and many of the leaks were likely to come from Washington rather than Saigon. There was also a problem of legal jurisdiction in a war where U.S. forces were fighting as guests of a foreign government. Effective censorship would have required U.S. court-martial jurisdiction to be extended not only to American civilians in South Vietnam, but also to third-country nationals—reporters from Asia and Western Europe. And this would have created political difficulties both with the Saigon government and with U.S. allies.[29]

American officials also seem to have felt that the voluntary guidelines which substituted for formal censorship served adequately to protect military security. Correspondents accredited to U.S. forces agreed to a set of rules outlining fifteen categories of information which they were not allowed to report without authorization. They were forbidden, for example, to report troop movements or casualty figures until these were officially announced in Saigon. Violation of these rules could result in revocation or suspension of a reporter's accreditation. "The MACV information officer had to impose that penalty only a few times in the four years I was in Vietnam," Westmoreland says in his memoirs, "which, in view of the hundreds of newsmen involved, is a distinct credit to the press corps."[30] In 1969 Gen. Winant Sidle, then the top press officer for the U.S. Mission, told the *New York Times* that "an awful lot of odds and ends get out that are helpful to the enemy," but that the voluntary guidelines generally worked well; and he noted that accreditation cards had been suspended only four times since 1966.[31] More recently, Sidle headed a Pentagon panel set up after the controversy over the exclusion of the media from the invasion of Grenada, to recommend procedures for coverage of military operations. The report of that panel cites the experience of Vietnam as evidence for the effectiveness of voluntary guidelines.[32]

At any rate, censorship was not instituted, and Vietnam became the first war in which journalists were routinely accredited to accompany military forces, but not subject to formal censorship. There were many times, to be sure, when journalists felt the military was interfering with their ability to report the war. Information was often withheld. The military did not, to take just one of many examples, release total U.S. casualty figures until 1967 (journalists kept their own unofficial figures before that). From time to time there were embargoes on information or restrictions on access to the "front"—which was generally accessible only by military transportation—which were ostensibly intended to protect military security, but which journalists believed were politically motivated. In 1968, for example, John Carrol of the *Baltimore Sun* had his credentials suspended for reporting on preparations for U.S. withdrawal from Khe Sanh. Technically it was a violation of the rule forbidding reports on future military operations without authorization. But many journalists believed the North Vietnamese could see for themselves that the marines were preparing to leave, and that the embargo was enforced to minimize publicity, since defense of Khe Sanh had been controversial (see Chapter 5), and withdrawal from the base was potentially embarrassing.[33] But for the most part journalists in Vietnam were free to go where they pleased and report what they wished.[34] Vietnam was in this sense genuinely an uncensored war. It represented a further step in the "rationalization" of media-government relations discussed in Chapter 3: the integration of the media into the political establishment was assumed to be secure enough that the last major vestige of direct government control—military censorship in war-time—could be lifted.

The second change in the intensity of coverage was of course television itself. World War II had its newsreels, but with Vietnam, for the first time, film from the front could become a regular part of daily news coverage. A number of technological changes facilitated television's coverage of Vietnam, including the development of a new, lightweight sound camera and the increasing speed of transportation and communication. With the coming first of jet air transportation and then the satellite, it became possible to transmit images as fast as words.

What did television show of this war? Let us begin by considering some of the contradictory conventional wisdom about television and Vietnam. Probably the most common notion about TV and Vietnam is that television brought the American public graphic scenes of death and destruction on a more or less daily basis. It is, on the other hand, frequently argued that television reporters clung to the safety of Saigon and rarely ventured into the countryside, where the war was actually being fought. Neither view is accurate. Television certainly did not cover the war from the Caravelle Hotel in Saigon. As soon as American troops were committed to combat in large numbers, television coverage focused overwhelmingly on one central story: American boys in action. And television (perhaps even more than print, because of its need for pictures) could only cover this story from the field. Most television stories from Vietnam were reported by crews traveling with American troops in "the bush"; nine network employees—correspondents, cameramen, and sound men—were eventually killed in Indochina and many more wounded.[35]

But this does not mean most film reports were graphic depictions of the horror of war. In fact, only about 22% of all film reports from Southeast Asia in the period before the Tet offensive showed actual combat, and often this was minimal—a few incoming mortar rounds or a crackle of sniper fire (perhaps followed by distant film of air strikes called in to "take out" the unseen enemy). A similar percentage, about 24%, showed film of the dead or wounded, and again this might be no more than a brief shot of a wounded soldier being lifted onto a helicopter. Of 167 film reports and voice-over stories in the sample for the period before the Tet offensive, only 16 had more than one video shot of the dead or wounded.

Why so little blood on television, despite the emphasis on military "action"? In part this may have resulted from choices the networks made not to use certain pieces of film. It was network policy, for one thing, not to show film of identifiable American casualties unless their families had been notified by the Defense Department. More generally there was concern about offending the families of killed or wounded soldiers if coverage was too graphic. Francis Faulkner quotes a CBS directive on combat film as saying:

> Producers and editors must exercise great caution before permitting pictures of casualties to be shown. This also applies to pictures of soldiers in a state of shock. Obviously, good taste and consideration for families of deceased, wounded or shocked takes precedence. Shots can be selected that are not grisly, the purpose being not to avoid showing the ugly side of war, but rather to avoid offending families of war victims.[36]

But the major reason for the limited amount of bloody film was probably the simple fact that this was how the war was: most operations in Vietnam involved little contact with the enemy; for the average combat unit a bloody firefight was not an everyday occurrence.

This is not to say that television represented fully the experiences of its major characters, the Americans fighting in Vietnam (let alone those of any of the others involved in the war). If one looks, for example, at the way veterans have portrayed the war in novels and memoirs, there is a visceral grimness and a sense of psychological damage done by the war that are rarely reflected in television coverage, even late in the war (these coexist in soldiers' memoirs with a sense of pride in their ability to survive and to master the strange art of war that they must suddenly become expert in). Anyone who thinks the television camera necessarily shows war more graphically than print should look at these accounts, or at Michael Herr's *Dispatches*.[37] Television crews, after all, would stay with any given unit for only a brief period, and no doubt could elicit from soldiers only guarded statements about their experience.

But there is another kind of question that needs to be addressed: not *what* or *how much* television showed of the war, but *how* it showed it: the point of view it employed and the framework of meaning into which it fit the incidents and images it reported. Violence is nothing new in war reporting. World War II reporting was sometimes graphic as well in its description of the results of violence,[38] but in World War

II violence and suffering were represented within a framework highly supportive of the overall war effort. Did such a framework exist in Vietnam coverage? The conventional wisdom is that it did not, that the media's coverage of Vietnam either showed literally the destructiveness and frustration of the war or—again the conventional wisdom is contradictory—presented it from a critical rather than a supportive perspective. Once more the conventional wisdom is off the mark.

One element of this conventional wisdom is the notion that because of the camera, television shows war in a particularly literal and unmediated way—from which it is sometimes concluded that any war covered by television, regardless of the political context, would lose public support. But this argument ignores the elementary facts of selection and editing. It also ignores—and this may be even more important—the fact that television's visual images are extremely *ambiguous*. This is true for a number of reasons. Television images, for one thing, are tiny fragments torn out of streams of experience and causation unknown and, in the case of a war in a distant culture, extremely unfamiliar to the audience. They leave out one dimension of the visual and three of the sensory field and they contain nothing of the historical, social, or cultural context of the events they show. Television images, moreover, pass very quickly, leaving the audience little time to reflect on their meaning, and are accompanied by nearly continuous voice-over narration, which they are edited to illustrate. We know very little about how television audiences construct the meaning of what they see and hear. It is possible that at times the visual images have independent impact, but it seems a reasonable hypothesis that most of the time the audience sees what it is told it is seeing.[39]

Television people themselves are too much aware of the selection involved in constructing a television story to take seriously the notion that the camera presents reality literally. But they have their own version of the "mirror of reality" argument: like all American journalists, they believe that what they do most of the time is simply to tell "what happened." This is of course the professional ideology of objective journalism, which we will have an opportunity to examine here in a setting very different from the Washington setting examined in Chapter 3.

Journalists are in fact sincerely committed to the—somewhat ambiguous—ideal of telling "what happened," regardless of the political consequences. And it was true that when they let loose on the battlefield of Vietnam without censorship, and in a war less firmly planted in the Sphere of Consensus than, say, World War II, a good many "negative" stories were reported that could never have been reported in other twentieth-century wars. The most famous of these in the early years of Vietnam was Morley Safer's August 1965 report which showed marines burning the village of Cam Ne, setting fire to some of its thatched roofs with Zippo lighters. Safer clearly was shocked by what he saw in Cam Ne. "During the operation," he reported in his initial cable to CBS, "the marines were telling the people in English to get out of their underground bunkers before they burned the houses. The people therefore stayed put, causing several close shaves, until pleas from this reporter that our Vietnamese cameraman should be allowed to speak to them in the Vietnamese language."[40] Back in New York, according to David Halberstam's account, Safer's story was greeted both with shock at its substance and considerable concern at the political reaction, which in fact did turn out to be substantial.[41] Lyndon Johnson is said to have made a scatological phone call to his friend Frank Stanton, president of CBS News;[42] and, probably more important, the report has been a subject of public political controversy on and off for two decades. But after a high-level meeting and numerous calls to Saigon to see whether Safer was certain of his facts, political caution was set aside and Safer's report was aired. Indeed, it led the evening news twice, once when Safer's original cable came in—it was read verbatim on the air—and again when the film arrived. In each case "balance" was provided: Safer's reports were followed by reports on the administration's reactions to them, read by the anchor. But the reports themselves were highly critical:

> The day's operation burned down 150 houses, wounded three women, killed one baby, wounded one marine and netted these four prisoners. Four old men who could not answer questions put to them in English. Four old men who had no idea what an I.D. card was. Today's operation is the frustration of Vietnam in miniature. There is little doubt that American firepower can win a military victory here. But to a Vietnamese peasant whose home is a—means a lifetime of backbreaking labor—it will take more than presidential promises to convince him that we are on his side.[43]

This is the stuff of which the myths about Vietnam reporting are made—the crusading reporter or "adversary journalist" exposing what the government refuses to admit about the war; the news organization upholding journalistic autonomy by standing by its reporter, despite the political consequences. In every American war, World War II not excepted, there has been recurring tension between military and political authorities, worried about public opinion as a resource of war, and reporters wishing to tell "what really happened" or to expose what they saw as abuse or stupidity of one sort or another (in practice, the line between simply reporting the facts and taking a stand on them is very fuzzy, especially in a situation that stirs the emotions as deeply as war). And in Vietnam, for the first time in the era of modern warfare, they were free to do so, and even to back up their reports with pictures.

As a result, from the beginning of its sustained coverage of Vietnam, television periodically reported critical stories very different from anything Americans had encountered in the reporting of previous wars. These fell into four major categories. Most common in 1965–66 were reports like Safer's from Cam Ne on civilian casualties caused by American action, some of which—though, as we shall see, by no means all— had a muckraking tone and presented events like Cam Ne as representative of "this dirty little war," to use a phrase from one report by Safer's colleague, Dan Rather.[44] There were also occasional exposés of corruption in the South Vietnamese regime, usually involving the theft of American aid. There were reports on Americans or South Vietnamese killed by "friendly fire." And finally, beginning in 1967, an increasing number of reports dealt with the frustration of fighting the war of attrition that Vietnam had become. (The development of the frustration theme will be taken up in detail in Chapter 5.)

But these "negative" stories were by no means typical of television coverage in the period before the Tet offensive. They were minor currents in a general flow of reporting that was strongly supportive of American actions in Vietnam. Even the Cam Ne episode itself can be taken as representative of two contrasting sides of American journalism. On the one hand it shows that the commitment to "objectivity," combined with the tradition of the reporter as crusading reformer, which continues to coexist in an ambiguous relationship with the principle of objectivity, is strong enough that it can force the reporting of stories that run sharply counter to the political assumptions of the day. On the other hand it shows how strongly those assumptions affect the practice of journalism. There was no need for high-level meetings of network executives when it was a question of reporting a claim of victory from an official briefing in Saigon or a story of American heroism. In 1965 official statements about the war or positive images of the American role flew through the gates of journalism unimpeded. Images of Americans destroying peasant homes had to have their credentials carefully examined before they were allowed to pass.

The absence of censorship did not mean the absence of restrictions on the flow of information that might have damaged public support for American policy in Vietnam. But the system of "control" that kept the media "in line" with the war effort was impersonal. It rested on the same two factors we saw at work in Part I in the relation between the *New York Times* and the Kennedy and Johnson administrations: the routines of journalism, and the ideological assumptions journalists shared with officials, as part of the political mainstream in the early to middle 1960s. But in the case of television coverage, most of which was from the field rather than from the briefing rooms of Washington, these factors worked somewhat differently. While the *Times* had reported the war, in the years we looked at, largely on the basis of high-level official sources in Washington and Saigon, television's most important sources in 1965–67 were American soldiers in the field; television reported the war from their point of view, and as long as they remained supportive of it, there would be strong tendency for television to be so as well. As for ideology, what was important in the case of television was not primarily the articulate Cold War perspective that dominated the *Times*'s interpretation of the war in 1961–65, but a mainly subconscious level of ideology, composed of dramatic images of war that could be "pulled off the shelf" to make this confusing conflict more familiar.

The "Good Guys": American Boys in Action

On September 1, 1965, CBS ran a commentary on the war by Charles Collingwood. Many Americans, Collingwood argued, thought the reinforcement of American military power would solve the Vietnam's problems. But the war was "as much political as military," and the American military presence "introduced a dangerous element into the political situation." Collingwood concluded by saying that the limit to the number of "round-eyes" South Vietnam could absorb may have been reached. Collingwood had been CBS's man in Asia for many years, and his commentary might be taken as an echo of what at least some television coverage had been like before Vietnam had become a major war and a major story for television. A year and a half later the term *round-eyes* was heard on television again, in a very different context (these were the only two times I encountered it). David Snell of ABC visited a group of GIs relaxing at China Beach. "Is there anything this beach doesn't have?" he asked them. The soldiers yelled, "Round eyes!" And Snell came back, "Aw, you don't really miss *girls*, do you?"[45]

The points of view of these two stories are obviously very different. Collingwood's is political; the ABC story is personal. Collingwood's, though certainly from an American point of view, is about Vietnam; the ABC story is about Americans who happen to be there. Almost all television coverage after mid-1965 was about Americans "in action." This emphasis is hardly surprising. Television people assumed, no doubt correctly, that this was what would most interest the American public. Television, moreover, is a dramatic medium and needs sympathetic characters; it will usually personalize the news whenever possible. This was seen as a journalistic, not a political, choice. But, like many such "choices" (no one thought much about it at the time), it had important political consequences. It meant that the war would be covered from "inside" American policy, from the point of view of those carrying it out, with very little critical distance. And it pushed war coverage strongly toward the Sphere of Consensus. Journalists are as wary as members of Congress of doing anything that might leave them open to the charge of failing to support American troops at war. And the tendency was strong for reporters to identify with young Americans like themselves, whose dangers—and thrills, which are also part of war—they would often share, at least for a brief period. (One consequence of the expansion of American involvement was that after mid-1965 Vietnam was no longer covered by the Collingwoods, foreign correspondents with long experience in Asia, but by young reporters who, like the soldiers, would be rotated out of their dangerous assignments in six months or a year.) In the hundreds of reports that I watched—to return for a moment to the "round-eyes" story—never did I hear a journalist comment on the hostility that many American soldiers felt toward all Vietnamese, whichever side they were on, though one would occasionally hear a soldier use the term *gook* in an interview (this hostility is usually a prominent theme in veterans' recollections of the war). It was sensitive enough to show American troops burning huts, but the issue of racism was apparently too sensitive to touch.

The most striking illustration of this focus on American fighting men—and its political implications—can be found in coverage of the air war. Here are excerpts from a few very typical stories on the air war and related naval action against the North:

ABC, April 28, 1967. Don North reports from the destroyer Shelton. This destroyer will attempt to take out the shore batteries, while our sister destroyers fire on the main target. . . . [T]he pilots [of a spotter plane] radio an assessment of 100 rounds on target, the best shooting we've seen on Operation SEA DRAGON. They won't be using that radar site again for a long time. The *Shelton* turns her fantail toward the sandy coast of North Vietnam and heads to sea.

CBS, September 29, 1967. Don Webster reports from the carrier Intrepid. *Webster begins by talking with a pilot about the strength of North Vietnamese defenses. He then talks with the ship's executive officer, who shows photos of the damage. Turning to politics, Webster then asks:* "What is the effect of knocking down all four of these bridges on shipping into Haiphong? . . . As you know, there's a lot of opposition in the U.S. to

bombing North Vietnam. Is there much debate about it among the pilots?
. . . Of the 75 or so pilots on this carrier . . . how do you think they'd
vote on the question of bombing?"

Finally the reporter gives his summation. "The bad weather . . . is
expected to severely limit the number of Navy air strikes like this. So
these pilots are trying to make every air strike 100 over 100, that is, a
direct hit."

*ABC, March 31, 1972 (air war coverage did not change greatly over the
years).* The carrier *Constellation, reports Ron Miller,* is a conglomerate
of steel, electronic gadgetry, and a community of almost 4500 men. . . .
The pilots, who seem to defy all that is natural and reasonable by taking
off and landing, are considered the best in the world.

Miller and a pilot, whom he introduces as one of the elite, *then describe
the shipboard life of the pilots, who, they say, are set off from the rest of
the crew and honored with special privileges. The pilot talks about the
dangers of flying over the North.*

*Finally, the report moves somewhat obliquely to the question of casualties
from the bombing.* It is ironic, *Miller says,* that the men who control some
of the world's most destructive weapons rarely see the results of their
work. Distance divorces them from ally and enemy.

I honestly don't like the idea of shooting a person, *the pilot says.* I don't
know if I could do that. From good distances up looking down you don't
have a chance to see the good you're doing. We're a tremendously effective destructive force. As far as a deep, true understanding of what
the people feel, yes, you get very divorced from it. To me, that's a
detriment.

Controversy had surrounded the bombing since its onset in 1965.
There were two major political issues.[46] One had to do with whether
the bombing was effective; the other, with civilian casualties and the
moral issues these raised. But television's focus on the pilots as individuals precluded dealing seriously with either. A good deal of air war
coverage simply avoided political issues, focusing exclusively on the
pilots' personal experience, the technology, and so on. "How does this
normally work, when you get a call for a mission?" the correspondent
would ask. "How long does it take you to prepare and get out on target,
get back and so forth? . . . You must get back pretty tired. How is this
move to Thailand going to affect you?"[47]

When political issues were broached, personalization transformed
their meaning in a way that shifted them out of the Sphere of Legitimate
Controversy and into the Sphere of Consensus. The pilots appeared
well briefed on the debate about the effectiveness of bombing and were
prepared with strategic rationalizations of it: that it saved American
lives in the South, that it diverted North Vietnamese manpower, and
so on. But for the most part they interpreted the question of effectiveness as a question of how well they were doing their jobs, how accurately

they were hitting their assigned targets. On this ground there could be no argument. The pilots certainly *were* skillful, and one of the things that made them so appealing as television characters was that they fit one of the great hero-images of modern American culture: they were *professionals* who had mastered technology and could make it perform as they wanted. In fact, the debate about the effectiveness of the bombing had nothing to do with the skill of the pilots. It was a strategic rather than a tactical question and had to do with whether the bombing, accurate as it might be, could affect either the North Vietnamese ability to supply their forces in the South or their willingness to continue the war. If television journalists were aware of these issues, they almost never let them disturb their celebration of, as one report put it, "the hottest jet pilots" around.[48]

As for the issue of civilian casualties—and the unspoken doubt that ran through the Vietnam period about technological warfare—it was usually dealt with as in the ABC report from 1972. The pilot would be asked if it didn't bother him that his bombs might kill innocent civilians, whom he could not even see. And he would say yes, it did bother him, and he did his best not to kill civilians, and meanwhile the bombing was a job that had to be done. The central theme, in other words, was again *professionalism*. The underlying message was that morally as well as technologically we—the news audience—could put our trust in the pilots: they did their jobs well and without vindictiveness, and if civilians were killed, it was not because the pilots wanted to kill them or did not care—it was just "part of the job."

For several reasons the air war was an extreme case. The journalists, in the first place, had no direct access to the battlefield and therefore no way to cover the air war firsthand except by talking to the pilots or by showing film released by the Defense Department (which the networks often did, with commentary like, "The smoking target gives impressive evidence of just how effective these and similar raids have been,"[49] or, "This is the shape of things to come for Communist aggression in Vietnam"[50]). The pilots themselves were an elite volunteer group; their morale was consistently high and they were articulate and well briefed on political issues surrounding their mission. They were also very much like the journalists themselves, upwardly mobile professionals of roughly the same age (many intended to become airline pilots after their service in Vietnam), which may have made it particularly easy for the journalists to identify with them.[51] Journalists had much greater independence covering the ground war; they might, for instance, as Safer did at Cam Ne, rely on their own perceptions if those contradicted what their American sources told them. And on the ground personalization did not always result in coverage that made the war look good: as it dragged on and morale began to break down among U.S. troops, soldiers in the field began to express their frustration to reporters.

But most of the time, especially in the early years, when morale was good, coverage of the ground war from the point of view of the soldiers meant that it too would be treated very sympathetically. The reporting of the war on the ground was far more diverse than air war coverage, and no story can really be called typical. But here are some excerpts, from very different kinds of stories, that give some sense of what this reporting was like:

NBC, February 9, 1966. Dean Brelis reports from An Lao. Brave men need leaders. This is a leader of brave men. His name is Hal Moore. He comes from Bardstown, Kentucky. He is married and the father of five children.

Moore talks about tactics, and then goes on to talk about his men. They are the greatest soldiers in the world. In fact, they're the greatest men in the world. They're well trained, they're well disciplined, their morale is outstanding. Their motivation is tremendous. They came over here to win.

The next day, on CBS, Dan Rather also reported on Moore, whom he introduced as "Lightning" Hal Moore. At 33, one of the youngest full colonels in the army, hero of the Ia Drang Valley in November, and itching for another head-on clash. Colonel, . . . what do you hope to accomplish?

The colonel. We hope to clear out this entire valley, get the VC out of here and let the people come back and live a normal life.

NBC, October 27, 1967, Greg Harris. The army calls this an "insertion" [troops are being dropped by helicopter at a landing zone in "the bush"]. As gunships saturate the landing zone with rockets and machine-gun fire, scout helicopters seek out the VC or spot suspects. Then a squad of the assault, or "blue," platoon is lifted into the location to either engage the enemy or surprise and capture a suspect. In the first twenty-six days of Operation WALLOA, this particular unit killed 270 VC while suffering only three wounded Americans.

We then see the unit move into and search a village. Ammunition is found, and that was enough proof of its being used by the Vietcong. Cong Phu was burned and blasted to death. *We see American medics treating sick and injured civilians, then Harris speaks with the platoon commander. The Vietcong, the lieutenant says, had been moving in, and* the only way to stop it is to eliminate the area. . . . [We are] razing these houses so we'll avoid Charlie coming in and spending his nights.

Harris begins his summation over film first of a body being pulled out of a hole by the hair, then of burning huts. The war in First Corps is changing for the enemy. [Then there is a silence and film of a body.]

Today the Vietcong lost the use of Cong Phu. Tomorrow they will lose
the use of another village, then another.

Each set of reports illustrates an important organizing principle in
coverage of the fighting in the South. The two on Colonel Moore focus
on the soldiers as individuals, the report from Operation WALLOA,
on their job. The Moore stories are of course hero stories, which came
in many forms in the 1965–67 period. Some were about heroes of
combat; some about heroes of technology, the helicopter pilots of the
Air Cavalry, for instance; others were about "moral heroes." Television
loved little vignettes about Americans, often doctors, who helped to
"win hearts and minds" by working with Vietnamese civilians.[52] And
explicit hero stories aside, the competence, humanity, and high morale
of American soldiers was a prominent theme in a great deal of television
coverage.

The WALLOA story was bloodier than the average combat story,
and at the same time more openly upbeat in its ending, in the image
of steady progress Harris painted. But with those qualifications it can
be taken as a good representation of the "typical" report on the most
heavily covered aspect of the war during this period, the "search and
destroy operation." Most such reports simply told the story of how one
unit went about its job on one day of the operation. The tone was
usually "straight": this was the field equivalent of the kind of objective
journalism we examined in Chapter 3. And like their counterparts in
Washington, journalists in the field relied heavily on official sources to
tell the story, usually the commander of the unit the reporter was
traveling with. (ABC occasionally ran stories in which no reporter appeared at all, and the narration was done entirely by a military officer.[53])

The political questions surrounding the search and destroy strategy
being used in the South were closely parallel to those raised about the
air war in the North. On the one hand there was an issue of effectiveness:
there were many, both in Washington and in Vietnam, who believed
a strategy of attrition would lead only to a stalemate on a higher and
higher level; there were also questions about whether a strategy that
involved massive displacement of civilians would be politically coun-
terproductive, overburdening the Saigon government with refugees while
failing to give it roots in the villages. And, on the other hand, there
was a moral issue about whether a strategy—or a war—which required
"scorched-earth" tactics could be justified.

But the average field commander, naturally enough, was not much
concerned about these issues; he was concerned with doing his assigned
job as well as he could. If he brought his men home safely and accu-

mulated some of the prizes of war by which the American command measured performance—enemy killed and captured, supplies destroyed—the operation was a success. And if villages had to be destroyed in the process, to return to the issue raised by Safer's Cam Ne report, that was a necessity of war, a part of the job. Usually, this view was simply implicit in the structure of the narrative, which would treat the burning of a village as a minor event in the course of an operation, with the focus not on the fate of the civilians but on the effort to "clear out" the enemy. At times, however, some reporters would defend this aspect of search and destroy more explicitly: "This is not callousness; this is not wanton destruction," reported NBC's Jack Perkins in one report a few months after the Cam Ne story. "Everything in this area for years was Vietcong."[54] A few days later, reporting from the same operation in an NLF stronghold known as the Iron Triangle, Perkins recounted that the unit he was with went through a "village unabashedly advertising itself with signs and flags as a Vietcong village." The column of Americans was fired on, and air strikes were called in. "There was no discriminating one house from another," Perkins said. "There couldn't be, and there did not need to be. The whole village had turned on the Americans, so the whole village was being destroyed."[55]

The "Big Picture": Ideology and the Role of the Anchor

Most television reports from the field gave a glimpse of one very small part of the war, saying little explicitly about its wider significance. The "big picture" was filled in primarily by the anchor. This was usually done in a kind of "battlefield roundup" which would precede and set the context for any film reports the network might have, and into which other bits of news about the war would be integrated. Here are some of these "roundups."

CBS, August 23, 1965, Walter Cronkite (before a map of Southeast Asia with the words RED CHINA arching over the top.) American Air Force jets gave Communist Vietnamese their heaviest clobbering of the war today, hurling almost half a million pounds of explosives at targets in the North. In one thrust our bombers hit the Long Bon[?] railroad bridge only thirty miles from Red China's border. Other bombs smashed a hydroelectric power station and dam at Banh Thuc, southwest of Hanoi. In that raid, the first at purely economic targets, they dropped one-and-a-half-ton bombs, believed to be the biggest used yet in this war. In the South, Vietcong mortars fired into the big U.S. air base at Bien Hoa, 15 miles from Saigon, and light American casualties were reported. And the International Red Cross in Geneva today got an urgent plea from the Vietcong for medical and surgical supplies, an indication that our bombing raids and infantry sweeps are taking a heavy toll of all kinds of Red equipment.

NBC, January 10, 1966, Chet Huntley. American and allied forces were on the offensive on three fronts today in Vietnam. An assault by units of the First Air Cavalry Division, kept secret for six days, wound up on the east bank of a river separating South Vietnam and Cambodia. The enemy was clearly visible on the other bank, but refused to fire. The sweep has netted virtually no enemy personnel, but three large camps and tons of equipment and supplies have been destroyed. In the Iron Triangle 25 miles north of Saigon the story is about the same. . . . The South Koreans 10 miles north of Qui Nhon have turned in one of the big victories of the war, catching an enemy regiment and killing 185 and capturing 609 suspects. In air operations over South Vietnam four American airplanes were lost yesterday and today.

CBS, October 31, 1967, Walter Cronkite. In the war, U.S. and South Vietnamese troops smashed the second Communist attempt in three days to capture the district capital of Loc Ninh, some 72 miles north of Saigon. The allies killed more than 110 VC, boosting the enemy death toll since Sunday to 365. American losses were reported at 4 dead and 11 wounded.

One thing that is immediately evident about these reports is that there is not much explicit politics in them. The influence of Cold War ideology is certainly strong, as it was throughout Vietnam coverage. In these reports the other side is identified as the Communists or "Reds." In reports from the field one would often hear soldiers—asked by journalists whether they thought that the war was "worth it"—speak about the need to stop the Communists before "we have to fight them in San Francisco." And from time to time journalists would speak of the "battle for democracy" or the fight against "Communist aggression"; one of the more colorful battlefield roundups, which preceded a report on the GI's views of the 1966 election, went like this:

Today, after meeting three days of desperate, almost suicidal resistance by the Vietcong, our troops find the enemy gone into sullen hiding, our firepower too powerful to face. For in the three weeks of what has been named Operation ATTLEBORO, the infantry has killed more than four hundred, captured scores, overrun strong point after strong point. As the fighting rages once again to preserve democracy, the GIs themselves have an eye on the elections back home.

But there was little discussion on television about the "global stakes" in Vietnam, as there was in the *Times* in earlier years; and the little phrases that gave television coverage such a heavy Cold War flavor in 1965 moved further into the background as time went on. CBS and NBC, for example, had dropped the term *Reds* by the beginning of 1966; ABC did so somewhat later.

Television reporting of Vietnam was structured primarily by a different, much less conscious level of ideology: it was structured by a set of assumptions about the value of war—not so much as a political instrument, but as an arena of human action, of individual and national self-expression—and by images and a language for talking about it. This understanding of war was formed primarily in World War II, and later, no doubt, etched into the national consciousness by the popular culture about war that developed simultaneously with the political ideology of the East-West conflict: the films of John Wayne and Audie Murphy, for example, and the culture of sport, particularly football. World War II reporting, by the way, also contained little explicit politics. Once the war was under way, its political purposes were taken for granted and public attention focused on the effort to win it.[56] That was how it was with Vietnam as well in this early period. This understanding of war, as it was manifested in most early Vietnam coverage, can be summarized with a set of unspoken propositions.

War is a national endeavor. From the beginning there were some who refused or were at least reluctant to accept Vietnam as "our" war. Even many mainstream politicians sometimes spoke of "Johnson's war," though this was done cautiously; in the Nixon years it would become more open. And radical critics questioned more directly the line the administration had drawn between "us" and "them"; "No Vietnamese ever called me 'nigger' " was a slogan of black opposition. But television respected that line, and anchors, especially, frequently spoke of the war effort in the first person.

War is an American tradition. Sometimes television reports would explicitly evoke the memory of World War II, placing Vietnam in a continuous tradition descending from it. NBC's Dean Brelis, for instance, closed one report (aired on the Fourth of July, 1966) by signing off from "the First Infantry Division, the Big Red 1 of North Africa, Omaha Beach, Normandy, Germany, and now the Cambodian border." The effect of this—making Omaha Beach and the Cambodian border equivalent—was to take Vietnam out of historical context, making it instead a part of a timeless American tradition of war, understood in terms of its most powerful and positive symbol. At times, this tradition would be pushed even farther back, as correspondents used the language of the frontier. Americans in Vietnam, for instance, referred to Vietcong-controlled territory as "Indian country," a phrase which reporters sometimes adopted.

One example of the use of the frontier metaphor is such an interesting illustration of the way ideology can structure the political meaning of the news without the journalist's awareness that it is worth a brief digression. It came later in the war, in a 1971 documentary on CBS entitled *The Changing War in Indochina*. Charles Collingwood was reporting on the progress of the pacification program in Kien Hoa province in the Mekong Delta, once an NLF stronghold. To illustrate the progress pacification had made in that particular district (the documentary had a kind of good news/bad news message, and this was part of the good news) he took a boat trip down a canal with the U.S. district advisor. The advisor painted a picture of gradual progress, illustrating his narration by pointing to the scenery along the banks, where peasants were building new houses farther and farther out. At one point, the scenery changed abruptly: the smiling faces of the children disappeared and the land was suddenly scarred and the trees broken. Near the place where the scenery changed was a fortified outpost. As the boat approached it, Collingwood asked the advisor, "Does this mean we are getting into what you call 'Indian Country'?" And the advisor replied, "This is almost like St. Louis on the move into the frontier."

This was good television. The simple theme of gradual progress in pacification meshed perfectly with the visual aspects of the story, and changing scenery, and the movement of the boat. The sudden change along the banks and the danger it implied gave the story an element of drama. And the analogy with the frontier not only made the news entertaining, but made the situation in the Mekong Delta, which was very remote from the experience of the audience, seem familiar. And this is no doubt why the metaphor was used: it made a good story. But it also has important political implications—and in important ways distorted the image the audience was given of the war in the Mekong. The Mekong Delta was not a wilderness: it was the most heavily populated region of Vietnam, the center of rice production, with an old and complex culture and social structure. The reason it looked like a wilderness in 1971—something Collingwood mentioned, but without emphasis, since it was outside the organizing frame of the story—is that it was devastated by B-52 strikes in the late 1960s. And what was going on there was not a move into the uncivilized wilderness of frontier mythology, but a political conflict in which the balance of power had been changed, for the time being, by that American firepower. Much of the use of metaphors in news reporting is of this character: journalists use them to make unfamiliar events entertaining and comprehensible, without being aware of the political baggage they carry.

War is manly. A society's political ideology is closely tied to its conceptions of sexual identity. The understanding of war that dominated American thinking in the 1950s and 1960s went along with certain ideas about what it is "to be a man." We have already caught a glimpse of this conception of masculinity in the "hero" stories examined above. Two elements are especially important: toughness and professionalism. War was seen as manly, first of all, because it was thought to give a man, and a nation, the opportunity to prove they could "take it," that they could face danger and pain without flinching. "They are marines," said NBC's Garrick Utley, narrating a report about an early amphibious landing in Vietnam. "They are good, and they know it. But every battle, every landing, is a new test of what a man and a unit can do.[57] And Dean Brelis, in the Fourth of July, 1966, report which he signed off by invoking the memory of Omaha Beach, reported, "But they were bloody, and that's what they wanted. They had chased the hills and the mountains looking for the enemy and after many frustrations they had found him, and the price is blood and tears." This was one of few really bloody film reports from Vietnam, and illustrates why it should not be assumed that the capacity of television to represent the suffering of war makes it an inherently pacifist technology. Suffering and death are part of the mystique of war. By seeking them out, Brelis's infantrymen proved they had, as a football coach would say, "motivation" and "desire"; and these were an important part of the masculine ideal of the time.[58]

War also gave men a chance to prove mastery and control, to show that they were not only tough but were "pros"—men who could "do the job." We have already seen a number of examples, particularly in stories about the air war. On occasion, the connection with sexual imagery would be expressed directly. On December 12, 1967, for instance, NBC ran a report on a new helicopter, the Cobra (reports on new technologies of war were common during Vietnam, and were usually very upbeat). "Mr. Davis," the correspondent asked, "what do you like best about piloting the Cobra?" The pilot replied, "it's kind of like a hard woman: it's something you can't like very well, but you can love it."

Winning is what counts. This theme is closely related to the conception of masculinity discussed above. It is interesting to contrast that conception with another image of masculinity that competes with it in American culture. If we turn from the 1950s and 1960s back to the 1930s, and from John Wayne to Jimmy Stewart, we see a very different kind of masculine ideal. The hero of Frank Capra's *Mr. Smith Goes to Washington*, for instance, is an awkward and sensitive country boy, who stands in contrast to tough and professional Washington, and in the end wins both the "girl" and the respect of the younger generation because he, unlike Washington's "pros," sticks to his convictions. He is masculine because he is independent and firm in his moral beliefs. The male hero of Vietnam coverage is masculine for very nearly the opposite reason: he renounces individuality and dedicated himself single-mindedly to the pursuit of ends he does not question—winning, doing the job.

A great deal of the language of television reporting of Vietnam put the war on this sort of footing. While some television reports would put it "above" moral or political judgment by reference to the Cold War, what was far more common was language that essentially put the war *below* such judgment by treating it as a sporting event or a day's work. Bruce Morton of CBS, for instance, closed one report based on Defense Department bombing footage, with this narration:

> This next run is a pilot's dream, the bomb landing squarely on a railroad bridge. . . . The Communists will have to detour now, and the flow of supplies will be slowed. Barges make a handy target for pilots with some spare rockets as they head for home, perhaps planning a ward-room party after hitting that bridge.[59]

Notice the similarity of this report to the typical beer commercial that shows workers coming home after a long day to enjoy the rewards of a job well done.

Here are some other characteristics of the language of Vietnam reporting that seem to have the same effect of "purging" the war of political and moral implications.

> Use of words that portray war as a technical process, for example, "clear" an area, "work them over," "take out" a target, "mop up."

> Action words that give violence a slightly trivialized, cartoon-like character:

> "American marines with heavy air and artillery support *smashed* a Vietcong unit near Saigon."[60]

> "Above the DMZ . . . U.S. naval power is *pounding* communist targets."[61]

> The language of sport:

> "[O]ur airplanes should have even better shooting in the days ahead."[62]

> "American and Australian forces had somewhat better hunting today."[63]

> "Operation MASHER has begun paying off."[64]

> "[T]he total score now stands at 695 enemy bodies counted and several hundred more captured."[65]

> "American soldiers today captured the biggest prize so far in the biggest offensive of the Vietnam War."[66]

> "The VC are here somewhere. They have to be found and destroyed. Second Lieutenant James Palmer of Franklin, North Carolina, heads this squad, and he's found his quarry. . . . Four VC were spotted running,

tiny dots in the tropical glare, so every gun on the APCs opened up while they gave chase."[67]

War is rational. Eventually, one of the things that may have soured the American public on the war in Vietnam is the fact that it was a war of attrition, without fronts or fixed objectives, and therefore appeared irrational: it was never clear whether any given battle or operation should be considered a victory or defeat, or how it contributed to the achievement of more general strategic objectives. But this was not how the war appeared on television for the first two years. Here the role of the anchor is particularly important. The anchor's battlefield round-ups—the four quoted at the beginning of this section are all good examples—gave Vietnam the appearance of structure Americans had come to expect from their wars, complete with "fronts" and "big victories" and a sense of driving, goal-directed energy. These roundups were based on the daily press briefing in Saigon (known to reporters as the 'Five O'Clock Follies"), and the claims of victory presented there were taken most of the time at face value.[68] So this reporting, combined with reporting from Washington on optimistic statements by the administration and a fair number of upbeat reports from the field, meant that militarily the war appeared to be going very well for most of 1965, 1966, and 1967. Of all those battles or operations in the sample for the pre-Tet period for which journalists offered an assessment of success or failure, 62% were presented as "victories" for the United States and South Vietnamese, 28% as successes for the other side, and only 2% as inconclusive. The United States and its allies were also generally reported as holding the military initiative; this was the case in 58% of television reports on military engagements.[69] The "enemy" was described as holding the initiative in 30%, and 11% were described as cases of mutual advance or attack. (By some estimates the reality was very much the other way: the Office of Systems Analysis in the Defense Department estimated in 1967 that "the VC/NVA started the shooting in over 90% of the company-sized fire fights."[70]) This impression of American initiative was reinforced by the fact that most film reports, at least until the fall of 1967, showed U.S. troops "on the move," usually in large-scale sweeps, and by a heavy emphasis on the potency of American firepower and the technology that delivered it. Finally, 79% of the assessments of the overall military situation—assessments, that is, not of the outcome of particular engagements, but of progress in the overall "war effort"—presented on television described the situation as favorable to the United States, 7% as favorable to the other side, and 7% as "stalemated."[71] It must have been very hard in this early period for the average television viewer to imagine the possibility that American arms might not ultimately be successful in Vietnam.

The "Bad Guys": Coverage of the North Vietnamese and "Viet Cong"

I felt that many of the commentators and Congressmen who professed outrage about My Lai were not really as interested in the moral questions raised by the Calley case as they were interested in using it to make political attacks against the Vietnam war. For one thing, they had been noticeably uncritical of North Vietnamese atrocites. In fact, the calculated and continual role that terror, murder and massacre played in the Vietcong strategy was one of the most underreported aspects of the entire Vietnam war.   RICHARD NIXON[72]

The tragedy was . . . that night after night . . . all you would see was the Americans and the South Vietnamese as the instigators of violence, suffering and so forth. . . . But you never saw what the VC did day after day. . . . Can you imagine if we had been able . . . to travel with the VC the same way we traveled with the American and South Vietnamese troops?   A network official and former Vietnam correspondent,
interviewed in 1981

In certain ways, because Vietnam was an undeclared war without censorship, coverage of the enemy was different than in previous wars. If journalists could get access to the North Vietnamese or the Vietcong, they were in theory free to report the war from both sides. (*Vietcong* was originally a derogatory slang expression, used by the South Vietnamese government and its supporters to refer to the organization that called itself the National Liberation Front; American journalists rarely used this latter term.)[73] In December 1966, the first American correspondent was admitted to North Vietnam, Harrison Salisbury of the *New York Times*. He sent back a series of "straight" dispatches: reports which treated the North Vietnamese as though they belonged to the Sphere of Legitimate Controversy, summarizing their views as a Washington reporter might summarize those of American officials. "The aims, aspirations and operations of the National Liberation Front are viewed by its leadership in terms sharply different from the picture held by many Americans," began one dispatch. "This contrast in view was the highlight of an interview given by a member of the Central Committee."[74] The press was deeply divided by this crossing of the normal boundary of political debate, and Salisbury was heavily criticized by many of his colleagues.[75] Still, all three networks ran long interviews on the evening news after his return.

But Salisbury's reports were not typical of reporting on "the enemy,"

Table 2   Statements Presented on Television That Are Favorable
and Unfavorable to Various Actors of the
Vietnam War, August 1965–January, 1968

Object of Statement	Statements Presented on Film		Journalists' Editorial Comments	
	Favorable	Unfavorable	Favorable	Unfavorable
U.S.	65	31	11	3
GVN[a]	3	1	2	2
DRV, NLF[b]	2	8	0	20
Domestic opposition	0	6	0	2

Notes: [a] Includes Cambodian and Laotian government forces.
[b] Includes Cambodian and Laotian Communist forces.

most of which was not so different from that of previous wars. Television
painted an almost perfectly one-dimensional image of the North Vietnamese and Vietcong as cruel, ruthless, and fanatical—clearly beyond
the bounds of Legitimate Controversy. Just as television journalists
often waived the strictures of objectivity to celebrate what was seen at
the beginning of the war as a national consensus behind it, they also,
much more consistently, waived them to denounce the enemies of that
consensus—the inhabitants of the Sphere of Deviance—both in Vietnam and, as we shall see, at home as well.

We can begin with some statistics that give a sense of the different
journalistic standards applied to different actors in television's Vietnam
coverage. Table 2 gives two sets of figures. The first is a summary of
statements presented on television—usually in film clips of press conferences, speeches, and interviews—supporting or criticizing the actions
and policies of various parties to the war. The second gives a count of
journalist's "editorial comments." A word of explanation about the
second set of figures is needed. It is very difficult to measure objectively
the "slant" of a journalist's presentation of the news. This measure,
therefore, is scored very conservatively: it only includes the most explicit instances of editorializing or of interpretation of the news that is
clearly favorable or unfavorable to one or another major actor in the
war. This is why the figures are small. Even though many stories in this
period appear very "biased," relatively few—only about 6% if commentaries are excluded—contained any statements that qualified under
the standards of this measure as *explicit* editorializing. Despite the
conservative scoring, there remains a good deal of subjectivity in the
coding of this sort of thing, and the exact numbers should be taken

Table 3 Frequency of Editorial Comments in Television Coverage of Major Actors of the Vietnam War, 1965–73

	Number of Editorial Comments	Comments per Hour of Coverage
Coverage of U.S. policy, activity	99	4.0
Coverage of domestic opposition	27	5.0
Coverage of South Vietnamese government	63	10.2
Coverage of North Vietnam, NLF	65	19.7

with a grain of salt. The difference we are interested in here, however, is not subtle: both sets of figures clearly show a dramatic contrast between the favorable balance of coverage given the Johnson administration and the extremely negative balance of coverage for its adversaries in Vietnam and, though here the numbers in the sample are very small, also at home.[76] Table 3 gives another perspective on varying journalistic standards.[77] It shows how common editorializing was in coverage of those actors relative to the amount of television time devoted to each. Journalists were much more likely to depart from objectivity in coverage of the enemy than in coverage of other actors, and least likely to do so in coverage of administration policy. Unlike most other aspects of television coverage, coverage of the North Vietnamese and NLF did not change greatly over the course of the war. In the period after the Tet offensive, April 1968 through January 1973, for instance, negative statements about the NLF and North Vietnamese outnumbered positive ones by 45 to 6. Negative comments by journalists outnumbered positive ones by 29 to 10. Of 12 positive comments by journalists throughout the war, 10 concerned the effectiveness of enemy forces: this was the only element of television's image of the enemy that changed substantially. In 1965 and 1966, in the general atmosphere of enthusiasm about U.S. firepower, the North Vietnamese and NLF were often portrayed as being "on the ropes." "Last week when Hanoi and Haiphong were bombed for the first time the Communists claimed they had shot down seven American airplanes and said it was a significant victory," Chet Huntley reported in July 1966. "In fact only one airplane was lost in the raid. The same night, Wednesday, they tried hard to shore up morale in Hanoi by parading a captured American pilot through the streets of the capital."[78] By the middle of 1967, as we shall see in the following chapter, television was beginning to treat

American's adversaries in Vietnam as formidable ones.[79] What did not change was the dark picture of evil painted by the coverage we are about to examine. For this reason, we shall abstract from differences over time here, and look at coverage of the North Vietnamese and NLF during the entire period of this study, 1965–73.

Following are two stories which give a good sense of the content of television's image of the enemy, and of the implicit political message carried in contrasting journalistic standards. Both happen to be from the later period of the war.

On September 15, 1968, NBC's Howard Tuckner reported on the burning of a Vietnamese village by American troops. As in so many stories we have seen, he explained that troops often burned villages because they provided cover and support to the Vietcong, and he showed signs around the village that showed that it was, indeed, a base for the NLF. Then he interviewed the lieutenant who commanded the unit, who explained that he had ordered the village burned because he had taken fire from it. In the end, however, Tuckner was not convinced. He had heard no shots fired, he said, and he concluded that the lieutenant would "have to live with his decision."

In October 1970, a North Vietnamese artillery shell slammed into the city of An Hoa, hitting an orphanage. An ABC camera crew was there to record the aftermath. Correspondent George Watson narrated, "No one was prepared for the massacre, the irrational murder that the North Vietnamese inflicted on An Hoa."[80]

Clearly we are dealing here with two entirely different kinds of journalism. Consider Tuckner's phrase, "the lieutenant will have to live with his decision." It conveys two messages. On the one hand it is clearly critical; this was one of the relatively few reports scored for negative interpretation of U.S. activities. On the other hand it conveys a respect for the lieutenant's moral judgment: it implies that the lieutenant, the reporter, and the audience all belong to the same moral community, sharing common values by which they judge one another's actions. This same message is also carried in the overall structure of Tuckner's report, particularly in the fact that the journalist's interpretation is *separated* from the description of the event. This implies that the interpretation is open to question, that the journalist might be wrong and the lieutenant right, or, in other words, that this disagreement belongs to the Sphere of Legitimate Controversy (remember that we are dealing here with a story from a later period than most we have encountered in this chapter, a period when the early consensus was much weaker).

The underlying message of Watson's An Hoa story is precisely the opposite. By collapsing description and interpretation into the single phrase "irrational murder," Watson implies that he and the audience do *not* share common values with the North Vietnamese and that there is no need, therefore, either to understand their motives (about which nothing is said in his story) or to entertain the possibility that the morality of their action is open to question. Watson thus draws a hard line between the moral community he represents and the North Vietnamese, whom he places outside that community. This story was scored under a subcategory of the "editorializing" variable, intended to measure "loaded" word choice—the use of words and phrases with an openly emotional or evaluative content. Only very strong terms were coded— for example *savage, brutal, murderous*—or, on the positive side, *heroic*.[81] Not surprisingly, this form of editorializing—a particularly extreme departure from objectivity because of the collapsing of commentary and description—occurred almost exclusively in reports on the enemy. Of twenty-four instances of loaded word choice that occurred in the sample, sixteen (all negative) were in reference to the North Vietnamese and NLF (an additional five were in reference to the antiwar movement at home).

Here again we have run into the issue of civilian casualties, and it seems a good idea to pause for a moment to consider the background to it. Civilian casualties in Indochina had a number of different causes. Much of the devastation and suffering, first of all, was the by-product of day-to-day military operations, which involved extremely heavy firepower.[82] It was of course the Americans who relied most heavily on massive firepower, but operations by the North Vietnamese and their allies could also cause great destruction, particularly in the later part of the war, as continued escalation and attrition changed the conflict from a small-unit, politically focused guerrilla war to a conventional conflict fought primarily by North Vietnamese regulars. William Shawcross reports that one Khmer Rouge bombardment of Phnom Penh in February 1974 destroyed 10,000 homes.[83]

Some civilian suffering was also caused by atrocities in the narrowest sense of the word: deliberate attacks on civilians carried out for their own sake, without any strategic or tactical purpose. Atrocities of this sort are hardly unique to the Vietnam War, but there was much about that war to encourage them—the fear and frustration felt by American soldiers fighting in a place where the whole population often seemed to be their enemy; the hatreds aroused by twenty years of civil war; and the bitter ethnic antagonisms between Khmer and Vietnamese that exploded into genocidal fury when the war came to Cambodia. Large-scale massacres like My Lai (coverage of which is discussed in Chapter

5), however, were not a normal part of the war. Small-scale My Lais seem to have been more common—pot-shots taken at peasants from helicopters or individual rapes and murders committed in the field.[84]

Finally, the least understood cause of civilian casualties was the fusion of political and military struggle that characterized the war in Vietnam. Many civilian casualties resulted not from the actions of individual soldiers, as at My Lai, or from the unintended (though certainly not unforeseen) effects of the use of massive firepower, but also from systematic policies followed by the two sides. Neither side regarded civilians as mere bystanders. Winning the allegiance or establishing control over the population was central to the objectives of both sides. This meant, for one thing, that each side made a vigorous effort to eliminate the other's political cadres. The NLF was very effective at assassinating and intimidating political representatives sent out by the Saigon government—village chiefs, school-teachers, and so on—and those who cooperated with them. (The "Hué massacre," in which the NLF executed hundreds of government officials and supporters during their Tet occupation of Hué, was in part a "crash program" of such assassinations.) The Americans and South Vietnamese also had programs for eliminating the other sides's political cadres; this was known in the jargon of the war as "rooting out the infrastructure."[85]

For the Americans and South Vietnamese, eliminating individual political cadres was a tactic of limited usefulness. The NLF was too deeply entrenched in the villages and could too easily reestablish its "infrastructure." U.S. strategy, therefore, came to rely heavily on "clearing out" villages and whole areas regarded as sympathetic to the enemy. This, most likely, is what was happening at Cam Ne, as in many of the television stories we have examined. Officials were fond of quoting the Maoist dictum that the guerrilla lives among the people like a fish in the water, and reasoned that if the fish could not be caught any other way, they could least be caught by draining the water: by depriving them of the civilian population that provided them with supplies, recruits, and intelligence. Guenter Lewy has described this policy as follows:

> Plans for the relocation of non-combatants had been developed by MACV [Military Assistance Command, Vietnam] since the summer of 1966, and in the course of the year 1967 what amounted to the encouragement and creation of refugees became accepted policy. In view of the great difficulties experienced in bringing security to the people it was considered easier to bring the people to security, and until late 1968 the prevalent but uncodified policy was that of compulsory relocations and displacement by military pressure through combat operations, crop destruction and the

Table 4 Attribution of Responsibility for Civilian Casualties
and Abuse of Prisoners in Television Coverage of Vietnam, 1965–73[a]

	Attributed to Action or Policy of:			
	U.S., Allies	DRV, etc.	Neither or Both[b]	Total
Civilian casualties, general	30	58	23	110
	27.4%	52.4	20.2	100.0
Kidnapping, murder of civilians	3	21	0	24
	13.1	86.9	0.0	100.0
Massacre[c]	13	7	0	21
	65.3	34.7	0.0	100.0
Refugees and orphans	9	5	23	37
	24.8	14.0	61.2	100.0
Destruction of homes, etc.	15	11	12	38
	39.4	29.5	31.1	100.0
Total civilian casualties	71	102	56	230
	30.9	44.4	24.7	100.0
Abuse or torture of prisoners	10	5	1	15
	62.4	31.8	5.8	100.0

Note: [a] Figures may not add to totals because of fractional weighting and rounding.

[b] Includes, among others, casualties described as acccidental or attributed to "war" in general.

[c] Scored only when killing of civilians is explicitly described as a massacre.

creation of specified strike zones [also known as "free fire" zones, in which anything that moved was considered hostile]. During 1967 the total number of refugees almost doubled. It reached close to one million by the end of 1967.[86]

It was also American policy, at certain times, that villages could be bombed immediately and without warning if U.S. troops took fire from them.[87]

The North Vietnamese and NLF, for their part, would also sometimes punish villages considered hostile, burning them or executing or kidnaping inhabitants. They also made their presence known to South Vietnam's urban population, especially after Tet, by firing rockets and artillery into government-controlled cities. The purpose of these attacks was political: they were intended to demonstrate to the population in the cities that the South Vietnamese government did not have the war under control. This presumably was what was going on in Watson's An Hoa report. (It seems unlikely, however, that the North Vietnamese actually intended to hit an orphanage, as Watson implies. Not only would this have been an "irrational" target, as he puts it, but it would

Table 5 Attribution of Responsibility for Civilian Casualties
Shown on Film in Television Coverage of Vietnam, 1965–73[a]

| | Attributed to Action or Policy of: | | | |
	U.S., Allies	DRV, etc.	Neither or Both[b]	Total
Civilian wounded	10	18	4	32
and dead	30.4%	57.6	12.0	100.0
Refugees	8	2	21	31
	24.5	7.2	68.3	100.0
Destruction of	11	10	12	33
homes, etc.	34.4	29.1	36.4	100.0
Total	28	30	37	95
	29.9	31.4	38.7	100.0

Note: [a] Figures may not add to totals because of fractional weighting and rounding.
[b] Includes, among others, casualties described as accidental or attributed to "war" in
general.

have been exceptional marksmanship to pick out a single building and
hit it.)

Tables 4 and 5 show how television assigned responsibility for civilian
casualties it reported. Reporting on mistreatment of prisoners is also
included. Table 4 includes all references to casualties in television coverage, both verbal and visual, including those made in stories on domestic debate. So, for example, a charge made by an opponent of the
war at home, reported on television, would show up in these figures.
Table 5 includes only civilian casualties shown on film. The two tables
show that although certain types of civilian casualties were more often
attributed to the Americans and South Vietnamese, overall more attention was given to civilian casualties caused by the North Vietnamese
and NLF. The fact that journalists traveled only with American and
South Vietnamese troops did not at all mean they could cover the
harshness only of their own side. To some degree, in fact, it was the
other way around. When the North Vietnamese or NLF moved into a
village to assassinate South Vietnamese government officials or fired
rockets or artillery into a town, it was easy enough for American journalists to be notified and provided transportation to the scene. When
American bombs or artillery fell on a village in the South or a factory
in the North, journalists much of time had no way even to know about
it much less to cover it firsthand. At the time of Salisbury's visit to
North Vietnam, administration officials had complained that attention
to casualties of American bombing of the North "obscured . . . the
acts of terrorism . . . directed against civilians in South Vietnam by the
Communists."[88] But only 6.5% of all references to civilian casualties

Table 6 Distribution of Television Time
in Coverage of North Vietnamese and NLF, 1965–73

Subject	Minutes of Coverage
Military activities, forces[a]	94.3
Terrorism	28.7
POWs in South Vietnam	25.0
DRV policy	17.7
Diplomatic activity[a]	14.5
Civilian casualties in North	11.8
Other	6.2

Note: [a] Estimates of total television time in sample broadcasts; see note 77 in the text.

on television were to those in the North. One time trend is worth noting, especially since it runs counter to the pattern of increasingly "negative" coverage that we will see most often as we begin to explore later television coverage. In the pre-Tet period, a majority of the civilian victims shown on film were victims of American and South Vietnamese activity; in the later period a majority were victims of North Vietnamese and NLF activity. This is probably best explained by the fact that the Americans were engaging in fewer and the North Vietnamese in more large-unit operations in the later period;[89] much of the bloodiest coverage appeared during the North Vietnamese spring offensive of 1972, when American ground troops were for the most part out of the fighting.

The theme of terrorism directed against civilians was central to television's image of the enemy. The sample contained thirty-six "atrocity stories"—reports like Watson's from An Hoa of deliberate attacks on civilians by the North Vietnamese and NLF (as well as the Khmer Rouge in Cambodia)—eight of them film reports. This does not amount to a particularly large proportion of television's total coverage of the war (there were, for example, 124 film reports on ground combat in the sample), but it loomed large indeed in relation to television's total coverage of the enemy, who remained faceless in most reporting. Table 6 shows the amount of television time devoted to various subjects in television coverage of the North Vietnamese and NLF. "Atrocity" stories were the second most common type of coverage, followed by stories on enemy prisoners in South Vietnam, which were also often concerned with terrorism. There were no stories in the sample—and in fact I never encountered a television story—that dealt primarily, or at any sub-

stantial length, with the political tactics, history, or program of the
North Vietnamese or the NLF. Journalists were not unaware that politics might have had something to do with the strength of the Vietcong,
and late in the war some stories would have a phrase like, "Out of fear
or perhaps genuine disbelief in the government, well over half the
people in Ku Chi are still influenced by the Communists."[90] But, like
the early *New York Times* coverage examined in Chapter 3, television
coverage of the North Vietnamese and NLF focused on terror to the
almost total exclusion of politics.

Television reports dealing with civilian casualties caused by American
action usually were very specific. In keeping with the usual conventions
of "objective" reporting, they described a single incident and were not
concerned with larger policies or patterns. No television report I encountered ever suggested that the United States might have any sort
of general policy of targeting civilians. Attacks on civilians by the enemy, on the other hand, were routinely assumed to result from a calculated *policy* of terror. They were also—in some ways television's
stereotype of the enemy was contradictory, as outgroup stereotypes
often are—treated as manifestations of a savage and irrational nature.

Let's consider one more of television's atrocity stories. On November
1, 1967, CBS covered a Vietcong attack on a village in the Central
Highlands, where the Special Forces had been struggling to recruit the
non-Vietnamese tribespeople, called *Montagnards* by the French, who
inhabited that sparsely populated region. (Contrary to the image presented in Francis Ford Coppola's *Apocalypse Now*—of the awe-struck
savage worshiping the white man as a god—the *Montagnards* were
fiercely independent and shifted allegiance as their own interests seemed
to dictate. The Americans were often able to take advantage of their
hatred of all Vietnamese, North and South.) The story began with the
camera panning across a scene of destruction, then focusing on correspondent John Laurence. "This is how South Vietnamese independence is marked by the Vietcong," Laurence began (November 1 was
the anniversary of the overthrow of Diem), "by burning hamlets, by
kidnapping civilian officials, and by terrorizing people. Three hundred
fifty *Montagnard* villagers were burned out of their homes, their pigs
and chickens slaughtered, the assistant village chief kidnaped, and five
others taken hostage when a dozen Vietcong slipped in at night for a
few hours of terrorism. It seems the Americans from a nearby Special
Forces camp were trying to build Tra Trung into a model village for
the rest of the countryside—a new schoolhouse, a deeper well, and a
lumber mill were in progress. But that was coming too close to pacification for the VC." Laurence then interviewed a Green Beret advisor,

who described American efforts to help the people of Tra Trung. "With the help of the American Special Forces and the local government," he concluded, "the villagers will survive to rebuild their homes. And maybe by Independence [Day] next year they'll have something to celebrate."

Both elements of television's stereotype of the enemy are here. The attribution of a systematic *policy* of terror, first of all, is implicit in Laurence's use of the present tense and plural (again description and comment are merged): though he is reporting only a single incident, he says, "This is how South Vietnamese independence *is marked* by the Vietcong: by burning *hamlets*. . . ." In other reports, the attribution of a policy of terror was more explicit. Walter Cronkite, for instance, began a report about a bus full of refugees which hit a land mine, presumably planted by the Vietcong, by saying, "The Johnson administration and Saigon have long insisted that the Communist domination of South Vietnam's countryside was based primarily on terrorism. Well, today the war provided a bloody example of that terrorism."[91] Cronkite's report is a particularly good illustration of the power of stereotypes to structure reporting. Although the Tra Trung attack reported by Laurence presumably was a deliberate effort to terrorize *Montagnards* who had cooperated with Americans, Cronkite had no way of knowing—so far as one can tell from the story as reported—whether the Vietcong land mine was intended for a bus of refugees or a military convoy (nor is it immediately clear how blowing up buses of refugees would provide control over the civilian population). If the refugees had been killed, say, by American fire in a "specified strike" zone, the theme would have been the "tragedy of war," not "terrorism." The image of the Vietcong as savage terrorists was so strong in the early years that a wide range of events was bent to fit it, including in a few instances routine military encounters. ABC's Peter Jennings once reported what he called "another of those small but [and here he paused a moment for dramatic effect] harrowing VC butcheries."[92] The incident turned out to be a Vietcong ambush of an American patrol, a routine contact between two military units.

The terrorism theme went along with another closely related cluster of images of the enemy, also illustrated in part by Laurence's Tra Trung story. While Laurence implies that the attack was deliberate and reflected a normal practice on the part of the enemy, he makes little attempt to describe the reasoning behind it, to say what the North Vietnamese hoped to gain. And with the phrase "a dozen Vietcong slipped in at night for a *few hours of terrorism*" he makes it sound as if they were merely amusing themselves, merely passing the time. Like the movie *The Deer Hunter*, in which enemy soldiers, for no apparent reason, force American prisoners to play Russian roulette, Laurence's story implies that their actions were motivated by a love of cruelty for its own sake.

The theme of terrorism as an element of North Vietnamese and NLF policy had the important effect of putting them outside the political realm, making them appear more as criminals than as a political movement or rival government. The language of law and order was common in television coverage: while a South Vietnamese government official taken by the Vietcong was "kidnaped," an NLF political cadre—or any Vietcong, since television made no distinction between the political and military sides of the NLF—taken by the government was always a "Vietcong suspect."[93] And with the imagery of gratuitous savagery television went a step further. Like most twentieth-century war propaganda, television coverage of Vietnam dehumanized the enemy, drained him of all recognizable emotions and motives and thus banished him not only from the political sphere, but from human society itself. The North Vietnamese and Vietcong were "fanatical," "suicidal," "savage," "halfcrazed."[94] They were lower than mere criminals (there is usually some "human interest" angle in crime reporting): they were vermin. Television reports routinely referred to areas controlled by the NLF as "Communist infested" or "Vietcong infested."[95]

Despite some ambiguities that came through in this situation of extraordinary freedom for the war correspondent, the dramatic structure of the uncensored "living-room war" of 1965–67 was simple and traditional: the forces of good were locked in battle once again with the forces of evil. What began to change in 1967, as we shall see in the following chapter, was the conviction that the forces of good would inevitably prevail.

5

"We Are on Our Way Out," 1968–1973

You would kill ten of my men and I would kill one of yours. But even at that rate you would be unable to hold on, and in the end I would carry the day.   HO CHI MINH, 1946[1]

In the spring of 1967 the war over Vietnam escalated on two very different "fronts." The North Vietnamese began concentrating large numbers of troops in Quang Tri and Thua Thien provinces, just south of the Demilitarized Zone (DMZ). This significantly changed the pattern of fighting. Before, most attention had been focused on mobile search and destroy operations, in which American troops would "sweep" through territory controlled by the NLF and North Vietnamese. But in April 1967 attention turned to a series of battles in which American outposts were besieged by large numbers of North Vietnamese regulars, setting up bloody fights from fixed positions. The battle for hills 861 and 881 in April was followed by Con Thien in September, Dak To in November, and finally the seventy-seven-day siege of Khe Sanh, which began January 21, 1968.

The other escalation took place in the halls of the Pentagon. This battle had begun to heat up in the summer and fall of 1966. Until then, civilians in the Defense Department, despite some doubts, had accepted the strategy formulated by military commanders.[2] But when the Joint Chiefs of Staff (JCS) submitted their recommendations for 1967, proposing a continued buildup in U.S. force levels and expanded bombing of North Vietnam, McNamara balked. He concluded that he could see "no reasonable way to bring the war to an end soon," argued that further escalation would cause serious political problems both in the United States and South Vietnam (in part due to its effect on the South Vietnamese economy), and proposed a stabilization of the U.S. commitment—"A military posture that we could credibly maintain indefinitely."[3] A basic disagreement had thus emerged over U.S. strategy. Westmoreland and the Joint Chiefs believed increased military pressure would raise North Vietnamese and NLF losses to the point that they could no longer go on with the war. Their civilian opponents, concentrated primarily in the Office of Systems Analysis, argued that the North Vietnamese could sustain indefinitely the losses they would suffer even with substantial increases in U.S. military activity. Against the strategy of attrition, therefore, they proposed increased emphasis on pacification and strengthening South Vietnamese forces, and an effort to limit the cost of the war to the United States and thus the potential for a collapse of domestic support.

Johnson, for the moment, accepted McNamara's recommendations, which called for gradual escalation during the first few months of 1967. The military did not vigorously oppose this decision at first, although the developing Pentagon factions continued to skirmish, primarily over bombing policy. But on March 18, 1967, General Westmoreland submitted a request for 200,000 additional troops, beyond the ceiling of 470,000 previously planned for 1967. Westmoreland estimated that the war would last two more years if his request was fulfilled, three years with a "minimum" increase of 100,000 troops. The systems analysts and other civilian officials opposed the escalation, and the battle raged unabated through the remainder of 1967. It broke partly into the open in August, when McNamara and the military clashed before a Senate committee over the bombing, which the military wanted to intensify and McNamara, convinced it was ineffective, to cut back. Johnson approved only part of Westmoreland's troop request, an increase to 525,000. But he allowed substantial escalation of the bombing, and finally broke with McNamara, who resigned and moved to the World Bank.

For all the concern with the possibility of a collapse of domestic support, the Johnson administration had not yet lost its ability to keep internal debates out of the press: relatively little of the spring policy debate leaked to the public. But the prospect of another round of escalation, combined with the increased fighting near the DMZ, did have an effect on the tone of television coverage. On April 12, for instance, Mike Wallace reported for CBS on the building of a new U.S. military headquarters in Saigon:

> The new MACV will be a sprawling structure, built to last. Because, without exception, the feeling here is that we are in for a long war. One high-ranking official who reflects the feeling in top circles in Saigon says he sees no possibility of a negotiated settlement until after the U.S. presidential election, not before January 1969 at the earliest. The official said he thought the enemy was willing to take a million casualties, which at

the current ratio would mean 200,000 U.S. casualties, with at least 25,000 killed [in the end it was 57,000], and that figure may be conservative.

"Will the American people accept those losses?" I wondered.

"Do they have any choice?" was his rejoinder.

"Then the real war out here is just beginning?" I asked.

The official nodded his head in assent.

The next day Cronkite reported:

The war in South Vietnam's northern province has apparently reached a crisis, and our diplomatic correspondent, Marvin Kalb, has learned in Washington that the U.S. commander in Vietnam, General William Westmoreland, has asked President Johnson to dispatch at least one more American division to the war to counter a massive Communist buildup in and around the Demilitarized Zone [Westmoreland's minimum request was actually 2⅓ divisions] . . . in addition to the 438,000 U.S. troops now committed to the war.

[The broadcast then cut to an unusual shot of Cronkite standing by a map of Vietnam, showing with a pointer the progress of the fighting.] So far in Quang Tri [he concluded], thinly stretched marine and government forces have been unable to halt the Communist buildup, now estimated at 35,000 men. And there's talk in Saigon of having to evacuate Quang Tri's quarter of a million population.

The optimism of the previous years was by no means gone. On May 3, for instance, Chet Huntley gave a reassuring view of the increased fighting and, perhaps without knowing it, of the strategy of attrition:

From Hill 881 to the Mekong Delta . . . the enemy has chosen to stand and fight conventionally in relatively large numbers. And it has been his undoing. The U.S. has immeasurably greater firepower and mobility. . . . The principal campaigns so far bear this out. In the Mekong Delta the 25th Infantry Division killed 195 members of a VC battalion. The South Vietnamese operating west of Hué killed 150 . . . the 4th Infantry Division killed 136.

Hills 881 and 861 were eventually taken, the media reported another American victory, and the crisis in Quang Tri was for the moment forgotten.

Nevertheless, the first signs of a major shift in television's image of the war had appeared. The change would continue gradually through the rest of the year, as political divisions and the pace of fighting increased, and accelerate with the Tet offensive and the dramatic political events of 1968. Two sets of statistics illustrate its magnitude. Before Tet, editorial comments by television journalists ran nearly four to one in favor of administration policy; after Tet, two to one against. Before Tet, of the battles journalists ventured to describe as victories or defeats, 62% were described as victories for the United States, 28% as defeats, 2% as inconclusive or as stalemates. After Tet, the figures were 44% victories, 32% defeats, and 24% inconclusive.

From 1961 to 1967, for all the tension between the media and government, and for all the mythology about the press as an adversary or watchdog of the state, the independence of the American news media— at least those parts of it we are considering here—was very limited. Even on an issue as explosive as Vietnam, an undeclared war in a distant and often hostile land, without censorship or extensive restrictions on access, the media were remarkably docile. State secrets of enormous political sensitivity were effectively contained; official perspectives dominated the headlines; much of the coverage was not only restrained in criticizing American policy, but positively enthusiastic about the "land war in Asia" officials had so feared to acknowledge.

But what are we to make of the later years of the Vietnam War? The mood of the media clearly turned more skeptical in those years, the nation was locked in conflict over the war, and Nixon, despite an intense desire not to be the first American leader to lose a war, felt he had no choice but to withdraw American forces, until he could get from the North Vietnamese no more than a "decent interval" before their final offensive. Did a fundamental change take place in the tight relation between media and state described in the preceding chapters? I shall argue that it did not. What happened is expressed well by Max Frankel, who told Todd Gitlin:

> As protest moved from the left groups, the anti-war groups, into the pulpits, into the Senate—with Fulbright, Gruening and others—as it became a majority opinion, it naturally picked up coverage. And then naturally the tone of the coverage changed. Because we're an establishment institution, and whenever your natural constituency changes, then naturally you will too.[4]

Television was as much an establishment institution in the post-Tet period as it was in the early years of the war. But by 1968, the establishment itself—and the nation as a whole—was so divided over the war that the media naturally took a far more skeptical stance toward administration policy than in the early years: Vietnam, in other words, entered the Sphere of Legitimate Controversy, and the administration could no longer expect to benefit consistently from consensus journalism. It is impossible to say exactly what elements of the general collapse of consensus most affected the media (it is interesting that Frankel shifts in mid-sentence from talking about establishment opinion to majority opinion—on the assumption, perhaps, that these ultimately coincide and there is no contradiction between the establishment status of the news media and their other identity as a representative of the public). But three elements seem most important in the case of television: growing divisions in Washington, declining morale among American troops in the field, and the spread of the antiwar movement into parts of the political mainstream. We shall see how each of these factors affected television coverage.

This is not to say that television's role in the collapse of consensus was purely passive. Though there is no way to measure the impact of television's changing images of the war, they must surely have affected public opinion, both directly and through their impact on opinion leaders; during Tet, especially, images from television were frequently invoked in political debate over the war. But for the most part television was a follower rather than a leader: it was not until the collapse of consensus was well under way that television's coverage began to turn around; and when it did turn, it only turned so far. The later years of Vietnam are a remarkable testimony to the restraining power of the routines and ideology of objective journalism. At a time when much of the nation's intelligentsia was in a militant and passionate mood, when members of Congress, employees of the U.S. embassy in Saigon, and business executives could be seen demonstrating in the streets against the nation's foreign policy, most television coverage was dispassionate; "advocacy journalism" made no real inroads into network television. The administration retained considerable power to manage the news: it should not be forgotten that Richard Nixon was able to keep public support for his handling of the war through four years and more than a hundred thousand American casualties. And many potentially explosive issues never penetrated television's relatively narrow agenda. We shall return to this argument, about the limits of television's turn toward a skeptical stance, but first we must explore in more detail the change itself.

"An Important Point Where the End Begins to Come Into View"

From April through the end of 1967, television's image of the war became increasingly contradictory. Much of the time, the "gung ho" enthusiasm described in the previous chapter prevailed; at other times a much more conflicted image emerged. Two periods will be considered here which illustrate this more ambivalent mood.

July 1967. McNamara traveled to Vietnam to assess the situation. He professed optimism about the war—probably more optimism than he actually felt—though he acknowledged that pacification was going badly, producing a spate of television reports about lack of progress in that area. But intense fighting was taking place again near the DMZ, and reports on this fighting were often juxtaposed with McNamara's professions of optimism. On July 7, ABC reported:

> Even as the Defense secretary said that the U.S. is winning, the marines were, and still are, being heavily pounded by North Vietnamese artillery near the DMZ. Our reporter Bill Branigan in Saigon cables today that as the intense shelling near the zone enters its sixth day, it marks the seventh day since military authorities in the South Vietnamese capital were saying how weak were the enemy supplies and how much his troops were hurting.

News of the dispute over Westmoreland's troop request, meanwhile, was beginning to leak.[5] In Washington, when the secretary returned, the president tried to put forward the appearance of unanimity he had maintained in previous years, delivering a classic performance at a July 13 press conference:[6]

> *Alvin A. Spivak (United Press International).* Will this increase, Mr. President, in whatever form it takes [as usual no details were released] fully meet the request that General Westmoreland has made?
> *The President.* The General can answer that as well as I can. But we have answered it before. The answer is: Yes, we have reached a meeting of minds. The troops that General Westmoreland needs and requests, as we feel it necessary, will be supplied. General Westmoreland feels it is acceptable, General Wheeler thinks that it is acceptable, and Secretary McNamara thinks that is acceptable. It is acceptable to me and we hope that it is acceptable to you. Is that not true, General Westmoreland?
> *General Westmoreland.* I agree, Mr. President.
> *The President.* General Wheeler?
> *General Wheeler [Chairman of the JCS].* That is correct, Mr. President.
> *Secretary McNamara.* Yes, sir.
> *The President.* Mr. Spivak?
> *Mr. Spivak.* Yes, sir.

By this time there was enough controversy over Vietnam that television reports were no longer simply recitations of official press conferences. But television seemed uncertain how to handle the growing official disunity. In the post-Watergate era, the correspondent would likely have treated the public press conference as a performance and, contrasting it with the "real story," reported on the basis of unnamed official sources. But in 1967 television still treated public proceedings as the "real story" most of the time, mixing them, however, with reporting on what officials were saying in private—with the result that the reports were often extremely ambiguous. The "schizophrenia" that characterized *New York Times* reporting in 1964–65 now was beginning to appear in television as well. On the day of Johnson's press conference, ABC's Frank Reynolds reported:

> The president does not like to read or hear speculation about disunity in the administration family. In the last few days there have been reports that Westmoreland might not receive all the troops he has requested. . . .
> [At the press conference] they were a friendly group, and there wasn't the slightest sign of a disagreement. Mr. Johnson put to rest reports that he had lost confidence in Westmoreland. . . . Westmoreland, who reportedly wants another 100,000 men, denied that he had requested any specific number of troops. . . . As the president beamed at him, he said, "I am being provided the forces I have recommended." The general also described reports of a military stalemate as a complete fiction . . . .
> Nevertheless, he admitted [the North Vietnamese] are continuing to send troops and supplies to South Vietnam, and there was no prediction today of an early end to the war. . . .
> Mr. McNamara is just back from Vietnam and he and the president apparently agree: "The children are growing, slowly, to be sure, but steadily."

Howard K. Smith then reported in a commentary that sources in Washington were saying the United States was losing the military initiative to the North Vietnamese. "American military officials," he concluded, "believe that with more troops they can wreck this Communist strategy as they have past ones. However, they have no good answer to the fact that North Vietnam can escalate too."

September–November. In the fall, with a presidential election year approaching, the Johnson administration launched a "progress offensive" to convince the public that the war was being won. Politicians of both parties were flown to Vietnam for progress reports and then brought before the press at home to say things were going well. And finally General Westmoreland was brought back to give the same assurance. Westmoreland never uttered the famous line about seeing the "light at the end of the tunnel" (that came from the poetic Frenchman Henri Navarre). But, in his own bureaucratic idiom, he said something similar. "We are now in a position from which the picture of ultimate military success may be viewed with increasing clarity," he said in September.[7] And, in November: "We have reached an important point where the end begins to come into view."[8] Television reports on the optimistic official statements of this period were generally "straight," neither playing them up nor expressing much skepticism about them. The last entry in an Associated Press Close-to-the-News Book on Vietnam, put out at the end of 1967, reads, "Nov. 16—Gen. Westmoreland asserts situation in Vietnam is 'very, very encouraging.' "[9]

The North Vietnamese, meanwhile, launched an offensive of their own, stepping up their attacks near the DMZ and the Laotian border. The progress offensive therefore shared the news with reports on two of the bloodiest battles of the war, at Con Thien and Dak To, which provoked a significant change in television's image of war. The "guts and glory" reporting of 1965–66 had persisted through the summer of 1967. And, indeed, it continued through the fall to dominate coverage of the air war and of the search and destroy operations still going on farther from the DMZ. "South Vietnamese troops and their American Special Forces advisors," reported Bert Quint in an October 31 story on CBS, "surrounded for a while in their own camp at Loc Ninh, broke the noose and mauled the enemy, sending him scurrying back to his haven in Cambodia. . . . Now Dog-Face Battalion, 1st of the 18th of the 1st Infantry Division, the Big Red 1, is tracking them."

The enthusiasm of the early years could be seen in the reporting of Con Thien and Dak To as well, but it coexisted with reporting of a much graver and less confident tone. Given that the reporting from other fronts changed so little, and the eagerness with which journalists greeted any good news coming out of Con Thien and Dak To, it does not seem likely that any major change in their political attitudes had taken place. To a large extent, the change in coverage probably reflected strained morale among the troops themselves; in this period, for the first time, soldiers interviewed on the news can be heard expressing less than enthusiasm for the war. To the American command, battles like Dak To and Con Thien seemed a valuable opportunity to bring American firepower to bear on large concentrations of North Vietnamese troops. But the troops who were the "bait" in this war of attrition found themselves on the defensive for long periods, an unusual situation for American troops in Vietnam, and often taking high casualties for pieces of ground which were of little significance in themselves. So television's focus on the individual soldier, which had been a political asset for U.S. policy until this point, began to have different implications.

Statistically, there was no decline in the fall of 1967 in the percent of battles described as American victories; that would come later. But there was a decline, from 68% before Con Thien to 49% between Con Thien and the Tet offensive, in the number of engagements in which the United States was described as having the initiative. Following are a number of excerpts from the reporting of Dak To and Con Thien.

September 28, CBS. A platoon commander tells John Laurence. I think we're just occupying ground, and we're losing too many men. If we were to stay here two months longer, we wouldn't have much left of this platoon.

Laurence. Isn't that all a part of war, as the generals say?

Lieutenant. Sure it is, but for seven months up here one battalion ain't going to have much left. If that's a part of war, they ought to rotate a little more.

September 29, NBC, Dean Brelis. Major Cook, are you hurting the enemy by being here?

Major. Oh, I think we are. . . .

Brelis. In other words, you feel that it's worth keeping this ground.

Major. Definitely.

Brelis. Do you think the North Vietnamese could ever take this post from the marines . . .?

Major. That's kind of a leading question there. I'll say, I don't think so. We'll give it a bloody go, and I don't think they'll take it away from us.

Brelis. The Vietnamese call this area the Plain of Angels. The marines just call it Hell. [Here is the traditional attitude: "War is Hell but it makes you a man." Notice the contrast with the tone of the Brelis story below.— DH]

CBS, November 17, Cronkite. American troops today won a dramatic victory in the battle for Dak To. . . . As darkness approached, one company commander radioed battalion headquarters, "We are low on people. . . ." Back came the answer from headquarters, "I don't want you to back off the hill unless you're kicked off." The response was a final drive which brought the men to the top of the hill, and the message to headquarters, "We're here to stay."

NBC, November 22, Brelis. One thing was certain. In the process of destroying an obstinate enemy with an apparently endless supply of all kinds of ammunition, the 173rd Airborne was destroying a good part of itself.

CBS, November 22, Cronkite. The battle for Dak To has now become the bloodiest of the war for American and North Vietnamese troops. . . . U.S. pilots said they could not see how the North Vietnamese survived the constant bombardment, and a senior field officer commented, "I have to give the enemy his due. Obviously he has outstanding morale and discipline."

Murray Fromson. The question every GI asks and cannot answer is, "Was it all worth it?" No one really knows.

Tet

In December, 1967 Westmoreland warned that the enemy in Vietnam could be expected to make a "maximum effort" in the near future. He expected that effort to take place around Khe Sanh, which the North Vietnamese indeed besieged late in January. But on January 30 and 31, the North Vietnamese and NLF launched simultaneous attacks on more than a hundred cities and towns from one end of South Vietnam to the other, achieving almost complete surprise. The fighting that followed was the heaviest of the war to that point, causing great destruction in urban areas, which until then had seen little fighting. The standard view of the Tet offensive today is that it was a significant military setback for the North Vietnamese and NLF, despite the initial surprise, and very likely a setback in the political conflict against the Saigon government as well.[10] Having decided to abandon the jungle and expose themselves to American firepower in conventional combat, the North Vietnamese and NLF suffered enormous casualties. Those casualties were particularly high, moreover, among those most difficult to replace, NLF cadres deeply rooted in South Vietnam. The South Vietnamese government and army did not collapse. And the failure of the offensive may have significantly damaged the prestige of the NLF: the peasant may have been a much less willing recruit to the revolution after such a slaughter, the citydweller less inclined to see an NLF victory as inevitable.[11]

But Tet is also remembered as the event that shattered American morale at home; and it is Tet that is most often pointed to as the event that demonstrates the immense power of the media. "It was the first time in history a war had been declared over by an anchorman," wrote David Halberstam.[12] As we shall see, Tet appeared in the news as a dramatic and disastrous turn of events. But its impact on public opinion and on policy is more complex and less dramatic—though certainly not insignificant—than generally supposed. Tet was less a turning point than a crossover point, a moment when trends that had been in motion for some time reached balance and began to tip the other way. "A battle, no matter how important it may be," as North Vietnam's Gen. Vo Nguyen Giap put it, "can only represent the high point of a developing situation."[13]

Late in 1965, when American troops were first committed to Vietnam in large numbers, the public had rallied to the cause, and there had been an initial surge of support for the war. But the initial rally was short-lived, and early in 1966 a steady erosion in public support began— at a time, it is important to note, when television was still strongly committed to the war. Well before Tet, in October 1967, a plurality of the public believed the United States had made a "mistake" going into Vietnam.[14] Considerably earlier, at least by the beginning of 1967, a plurality were saying they disapproved of Johnson's handling of the war.

The initial public response to Tet itself was to rally to the war effort: the number of people calling themselves hawks, for example, jumped from 56% to 61% in the immediate aftermath of the Tet attacks. Tet did, however, produce an increasing perception that the war was going badly: from November 1967 to the end of February 1968, the percent believing the U.S. was making progress dropped from 51 to 32. By the end of March, shortly before his withdrawal from the campaign, Johnson's approval rating on the war had dropped 13 points, to 26 percent, and the percent believing the United States had made a mistake in entering the war, which had stabilized immediately after Tet, was once more on the rise.[15]

The decline in Johnson's rating on the war may have been as much a response to what people were not hearing from Washington as to what they were hearing from Vietnam. If Johnson had been able to take some action—or to create the appearance of taking action—he might well have profited from the "rally round the flag effect" that typically boosts presidential popularity in the immediate aftermath of a foreign policy crisis.[16] But the administration was embroiled in an extended policy debate and remained mostly silent on the war for two months after Tet. At the same time, moreover, the administration faced a second embarrassing international incident to which it was also unable to respond: the seizure by the North Koreans of the intelligence ship *Pueblo*. The administration's silence probably accounts in part for the reaction of the media as well as that of the public: the Tet period seems to confirm the pattern we discovered in 1964–65, that the media are most active when the administration fails to maintain the initiative on a major public issue.

Tet certainly was a period of exceptional journalistic activity. The percent of television stories in which journalists editorialized or made commentaries on the news jumped from a pre-Tet average of 5.9% to 20% during the two months following the Tet attacks, and then fell back to 9.8% after Tet. Walter Cronkite made an extraordinary personal statement on the war. Many newspapers ran front page editorials. And one piece of "investigative reporting" caused a major stir in Washington: a story in the Sunday *New York Times* on March 10 revealing the "stirring debate" under way in the administration over a request from the Joint Chiefs for an additional 206,000 troops. Neil Sheehan and Hedrick Smith pieced the story together mainly from congressional sources; and, as Walt Rostow later lamented, it "churned up the whole eastern establishment."[17] If the administration had been clear enough on its direction to maintain an active public stance, Cronkite might never have ended his famous broadcast (quoted below) with a policy statement of his own, and the Sheehans and Smiths might have been kept busy reporting the official line. But, like in the aftermath of Pleiku in 1965, there was no official line in February and March of 1968.

The silence was broken by Johnson's surprise announcement at the end of March that he would decline to run for reelection and would curb the bombing of North Vietnam. That announcement had a dramatic effect on public opinion, perhaps more significant than the effect of Tet itself. Johnson's approval rating jumped sharply upward, as did support for a bombing halt. And the percent of the public calling themselves doves jumped to the point that hawks and doves were nearly evenly balanced for the first time.[18] Once the president acted, the public seemed to follow his lead, as it usually does in foreign policy.[19]

And what of the impact of the media's reporting of Tet on policy itself? Halberstam's comment that the Vietnam War was declared over by a television anchorman referred to Cronkite's report on the war, a CBS special shown after Cronkite had traveled to Vietnam to report personally on Tet. Cronkite had concluded:

> To say that we are closer to victory today is to believe, in the face of the evidence, the optimists who have been wrong in the past. To suggest we are on the edge of defeat is to yield to unreasonable pessimism. To say that we are mired in stalemate seems the only realistic, yet unsatisfactory conclusion.[20]

Johnson is said to have watched the broadcast and concluded, as Bill Moyers put it, that "Cronkite was it."[21] A number of officials have recalled being "fed up with the 'light at the end of the tunnel' stuff" in official reports from Saigon, and becoming "more persuaded by what I saw on the tube and in the papers."[22] It seems likely that Tet coverage emboldened political opponents of the administration to speak out; and it is clear that there was great concern among policymakers about the impact of Tet on public opinion.

At the same time, however, the decision to stop escalating the war can hardly be reduced to Johnson's or other officials' reactions to what they saw on the "tube." By the time of Tet one secretary of defense had already concluded that an end of escalation was essential. Clark Clifford, brought in to replace McNamara, was delegated to study a new proposal for a troop increase put forward by the Joint Chiefs after Tet. And Clifford too concluded that escalation did not promise a military victory in the foreseeable future. "I couldn't get hold of a plan to win the war," Clifford recalled. "When I asked how many more men it would take, would 206,000 more men do the job, no one could be certain. . . . It was a dead end."[23] After Clifford submitted his report, Johnson convened a sort of council of the foreign policy establishment, the so-called Wise Men, including past secretaries of state, chairmen of the Joint Chiefs, and similar notables, and they too recommended a change in the country's course in Vietnam. Public opinion was certainly a factor in their deliberations, but they did not rely, any more than Clifford did, on Walter Cronkite to brief them on the military situation in Vietnam.[24]

Ironically, to the extent that official Washington was affected by "alarmist" reports of a military crisis in Vietnam, the military itself may have been as important a source as the media. When military commanders prepared the proposal for an increase of 206,000 men—which, as Clifford discovered, they could not promise would be the last—they thought of it not as an emergency augmentation to meet the Tet crisis, but as a force which would permit an expanded strategy in the future and reduce the strain of American strength in other parts of the world. But when he presented the proposal in Washington, Wheeler, fearing that the administration would be unresponsive to an appeal for more troops based on an expanded military strategy, packaged the request instead in the context of a somber picture of the military situation in South Vietnam. His report apparently caused considerable alarm.[25]

Journalists generally accepted the official claim that Tet was a military defeat for the North Vietnamese and NLF. "First and simplest," Cronkite reported, "the Vietcong suffered a military defeat."[26] But they often rejected official optimism about the overall course of the war, suggesting that in one way or another the victory was Pyrrhic. They stressed its costs both for American and South Vietnamese troops and for civilians. There was heavy emphasis on the destruction the fighting caused in South Vietnam's cities, a theme which came to be symbolized by the words of an American major at Ben Tre, who told the AP's Peter Arnett, "It became necessary to destroy the town in order to save it."[27] A faithful television viewer, watching the evening news five nights a week, would have seen film of civilian casualties and urban destruction in South Vietnam an average of 3.9 times a week during the Tet period (January 31 to March 31), more than four times the overall average of 0.85 times a week. Film of military casualties jumped from 2.4 to 6.8 times a week. Tet was the first sustained period during which it could be said that the war appeared on television as a really brutal affair; even later, only the period of the North Vietnamese spring offensive in 1972 would resemble it for sheer volume of blood and destruction. And along with the emphasis on the costs of war went a heavy skepticism about whether any military advantage the United States might have reaped wouldn't be offset by damage to pacification, the prestige of the Saigon government, and morale back in the United States. Here are some examples.

Three days into the offensive, on February 2, the South Vietnamese attacked the An Quang pagoda—a center of non-Communist opposition to the government since the days of Diem. CBS had three reports on Tet that day, and one dealt with the fighting at An Quang. The film showed heavy, seemingly chaotic fighting in the streets of Saigon, wounded civilians, and finally South Vietnamese troops taking away prisoners they said were Vietcong. The narrative was terse, letting the pictures dominate the report, something which was common during Tet; this shift to heavily visual coverage was one of many breaks in the routine of television news which added to the atmosphere of crisis. (The most important such break was probably Walter Cronkite's presence in the field, away from the controlled setting of the studio, wearing a steel helmet.) Don Webster wrapped up, as the prisoners were being taken away:

> These pathetic-looking people may be Buddhists rather than Vietcong, and there's little record of the Buddhists and the Vietcong working very closely together. About the only thing certain is the government hasn't won any friends here today. If the purpose of this war is to win the hearts and minds of the people, the capture of An Quang pagoda can be considered a defeat.

That same day those who watched NBC, after they saw the fighting at An Quang, saw the most famous television footage of the war—of South Vietnam's General Loan carrying out a summary execution in the streets of Saigon. The narration, by Howard Tuckner, was again terse:

> Government troops had captured the commander of the Vietcong commando unit. He was roughed up badly but refused to talk. A South Vietnamese officer held the pistol taken from the enemy officer. The Chief of South Vietnam's National Police Force, Brigadier General Nguyen Ngoc Loan, was waiting for him.[28]

Then the film.

On February 20, NBC's David Burrington reported from Hué:

> American marines are so bogged down in Hué that nobody will even predict when the battle will end. . . . More than 500 marines have been wounded and 100 killed since the fighting in Hué began. . . .
>
> The price has been high and it's gained the marines about 50 yards a day or less in a heavily populated part of the citadel. Still, nothing is really secure. . . .
>
> Most of the city is now in rubble. This is a middle-class section. Some of South Vietnam's best-known intellectuals live here. Now the war has finally come to them.

The palace, considered South Vietnam's spiritual capital, is expected to be destroyed, and many Vietnamese say the fight isn't really worth it now that their city is dead.[29]

For the most part, journalists seem to have interpreted Tet, without consciously making the distinction, for what it *said* rather than what it *did*—as proof, regardless of who won or lost it, that the war was not under control. This was a perspective they shared with much of the U.S. mission in Saigon, which was divided over the significance of Tet, and with many in Washington, both in Congress and in the administration itself.[30] This attitude developed so rapidly that it is perhaps best to see it, initially at least, as a coincidence of views rather than as a product of mutual influence. It may be one of the many ironies of Tet coverage that it gave the public a more accurate view of the overall course of the war through the *inaccurate* view it gave of the outcome of the particular battle. Before Tet, 48% of the public thought the war would last two years or less, 32% that it would continue more than two years, with the rest unsure. After Tet the respective percentages were 35 and 30, with fully 35% unsure—a much more realistic assessment.[31]

Many of the journalists also considered the impact of Tet on American politics to be of overriding importance. One reporter, asked to comment on the charge made by his colleague Peter Braestrup that the media had turned a North Vietnamese defeat into a victory, replied, "Braestrup was basically a war correspondent. I was a political reporter." Tet is an interesting illustration of the "uncertainty principle" at work: the journalists were inescapably a part of the political process they were reporting. If they said Tet was a political defeat for the administration, they were helping to make it so; if they resisted the journalistic instinct to put Tet in that context, they were helping the administration out. Most of them followed that journalistic instinct.[32]

Simultaneous with Tet was the seventy-seven-day siege of Khe Sanh, another battle of attrition which received heavy coverage and was generally treated on television both as a symbol of the frustration of the Vietnam War and as a potential disaster in the mold of Dien Bien Phu—a ghost evoked in eleven of thirty-one film reports on Khe Sanh.[33] A typical wrap-up:

CBS, March 29, Jeff Gralnick. So there is no end in sight. The North Vietnamese out there beyond the fog show no inclination to pull back or attack. U.S. commanders show no inclination just yet to drive them back. So for the marines and the Seabees and the rest here, there is nothing to do but sit and take it, just to wait, and hope they'll rotate out, leave before they join the roster of the wounded and dead here.

As it turned out, the North Vietnamese melted into the jungle just a week after this report, after taking tens of thousands of casualties. The media have since been criticized for making so much of the siege of Khe Sanh and the possibility it would be taken (which was in fact unlikely), seizing on it as an ongoing story that made better drama than the usual sweeps and partols that seemed to end so ambiguously.[34] No doubt it did make a difference that Khe Sanh, where a definite objective seemed at stake, had a better dramatic structure than other battles. But the media were also responding to heavy official concern with Khe Sanh. Westmoreland had at first interpreted the Tet offensive as a diversion and said the real battle would come near Khe Sanh; and Johnson, himself fearing a Dien Bien Phu, had a model of Khe Sanh built in the White House and took the extraordinary step of ordering the Joint Chiefs to sign a formal declaration of their confidence that the outpost could be held.[35]

"Business as Usual at the Country Store": The New Image of War

The Tet–Khe Sanh period was unique. By April Cronkite was back in his studio, General Loan was off the screen, and the news had settled back into its normal routine. But television's image of war had been permanently changed: the "guts and glory" image of the pre-Tet period was gone forever.

This is not to say that television had become *anti*war. It was still unusual for journalists to take an openly critical stance; most reporting was "straight" and dispassionate (fewer than 10% of news stories, labeled commentaries excluded, contained editorializing according to the measure described in Chapter 4) And most of the time, the war was reported from inside American policy: a story had a "happy ending," in other words, when American policy succeeded, a "sad ending" when it did not. The Americans and to a lesser extent the South Vietnamese were still the "good guys," though they were now more fallible, less macho than the good guys of pre-Tet mythology. "The idea," said one correspondent, reporting on pacification on an island off the coast of South Vietnam in 1970, "is to take an area that was formerly controlled by the Communists, an area where the natives were driven out, and give it back to them, help them to relocate and make sure they're safe."[36] How were the "natives" driven out of their homes? Presumably, since it was a Communist-controlled area, by American military action. But journalists still deeply believed that American motives were good, and there remained a strong tendency to emphasize the positive in reporting American actions. Identification with "our side" was still strong enough that journalists would sometimes slide back into consensus journalism, occasionally, for example, participating vicariously in the war effort. "We have the target marked here," said NBC's Robert Rogers, flying with the Laotian air force in 1972, "and we're going to go in and clobber it."[37] Some elements of the old hero image of American troops—the image of the pilot as a hero of technology, for instance—persisted, as did television's old image of the "bad guys" on the other side.

But the change was nevertheless dramatic. Let us go through, one by one, the characteristics of television's pre-Tet image of war noted in the preceding chapter.

War Is a National Endeavor. Before Tet, Vietnam was "our" war; after Tet, most of the time, it was simply "the" war: as it entered the Sphere of Legitimate Controversy, journalists began to distance themselves from it and use of the first-person plural dropped off.

War Is an American Tradition—Invocation of the Memory of World War II. Never, after Tet, did I encounter a television story that mentioned World War II; Vietnam was now cut off from that legitimizing connection with tradition.

War Is Manly. The change here can be seen in the handling of casualties. Never after Tet does one hear a phrase like, "They were bloody, but that was what they wanted." There was increasing focus on the costs of the war to American troops, and less inclination either to bury them in statistics or to treat them as proof of the masculinity of war. Every Thursday the Public Affairs Office in Saigon released the weekly casualty figures, or "body count." And for years the networks put them up, every Thursday, usually next to little American, South Vietnamese, and NLF or North Vietnamese flags. In the later years of the war, however, they began apologizing in various ways for the coldness of the numbers. At times they would use still photographs of wounded soldiers instead of the flags. And at times they would introduce them with a comment, like this one by David Brinkley, on June 26, 1969:

> Today in Saigon they announced the casualty figures for the week, and though they came out in the form of numbers, each one of them was a man, most of them quite young, each with hopes he will never realize, each with family and friends who will never see him again. Anyway, here are the numbers.

In reporting from the field, too, there was an effort to humanize the costs of the war. One thing that made the pre-Tet "living-room war" seem so pale in comparison to other accounts was the fact that the people killed almost never had names—or families, friends, childhoods, etc., which go along with having names. In part, this was because television took care not to identify specific American casualties to insure that relatives not yet officially notified would not learn the fate of their loved ones from the evening news. But later, as the political consciousness changed, reporters began to think of ways around this problem. One report closed with film of a number of soldiers looking down at the bodies of three friends killed that day, remembering them.[38] The bodies were never shown and the people were not named, but the story was much more powerful than many more graphic ones.

It is important to add here that it was the costs of the war to Americans that was stressed more heavily in the later years, more than its costs to the Vietnamese. There was a considerable increase in the sheer volume of reporting on ARVN casualties as Vietnamization put the South Vietnamese army in the news (the trend is shown in Figure 2). But the special effort to humanize the casualties of war applied primarily to Americans. Coverage of North Vietnamese and NLF casualties remained mostly statistical. Coverage of civilian casualties was an important feature of the news; it was not uncommon for a reporter to wrap up with a comment about the villagers being the "biggest losers" when the fighting was over. But the total amount of coverage of civilian casualties did not increase—it dropped considerably after Tet, in fact, rebounding only with the 1972 spring offensive (again, see Figure 2). And the tone, if anything, became more matter-of-fact. Rarely does one find after Tet either the shock expressed by Safer when he first saw a village being burned or the defensiveness other reporters had expressed about similar events.

War Is Rational. The image of the efficient American war machine moving inexorably toward victory was supplanted to a large extent by an image of war as eternal recurrence, progressing nowhere. The typical story on ground combat in the post-Tet period would be a matter-of-fact report on the day's activities, without any direct statement one way or the other about their larger significance, but with a closing line something like, "The Special Forces and the enemy fought this battle to a standstill. And there was nothing left but to tend to the wounded, and fight again another day."[39]

In other reports, the theme of endless repetition was expressed more directly:

CBS, May 5, 1969, Tony Sargent. This flimsy little North Vietnamese cooking hut sort of symbolizes the reason that U.S. troops may be in South Vietnam for quite a while, because you come through and tear it down one day; three days later you come back, and there it is again.

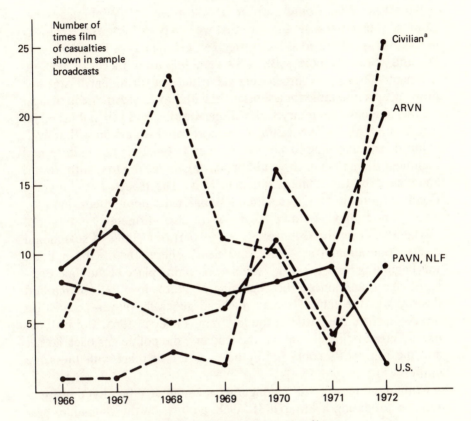

aIncludes film of refugees and of destruction of homes.

Figure 2 Film representation of casualties in television coverage, 1966–1972

NBC, June 16, 1969, Jack Russell. This hill was taken, as hills usually are in this war. But, as often happens, it was difficult to assess the value of this captured objective.

CBS, June 18, 1969, Don Webster. These tanks and armored personnel carriers are assaulting an area called the "Country Store" [because so much enemy equipment had been captured there over the years]. It illustrates one of the frustrations of fighting here. The troops have held so many assaults here they've long ago lost count of the number. . . .

There are dozens of areas in Vietnam like this one. We enter, either fight the enemy or find they've just left, we leave, and the Communists return. The soldiers on these vehicles will serve their full twelve-month tour of duty here and then return home. Most will believe they've accomplished something. But in all probability it will still be business as usual at the Country Store.

Winning Is What Counts. I have saved for last the "Winning is What Counts" theme because it is here that we can get a better sense of why news coverage changed as it did after Tet. On the day of Don Webster's "Country Store" report, CBS had several important pieces of news on Vietnam. Unnamed sources were reporting that President Nixon was drawing up a timetable for a substantial withdrawal of American troops. Former Defense Secretary Clifford, meanwhile, had just published an article in *Foreign Affairs* calling for a more rapid American withdrawal; Clifford was interviewed on the broadcast. Finally, the military had identified the units which would be leaving under the first withdrawal, announced by the administration in May. The troops assaulting the Country Store, in fact, had suffered a major disappointment that day, when rumors they would be leaving were disconfirmed.

The assault on the Country Store was part of a series of search and destroy operations (or "search and clear" operations, as the military was beginning to call them)[40] which were taking place at the time President Nixon announced the beginning of Vietnamization. Search and destroy was the same strategy that had generally played so well on television since the battle of the Ia Drang Valley in 1965. But in 1969, in a different political context, the soldiers, the politicians back home, and the journalists could hardly be expected to react with the same enthusiasm.

Winning, after all, was no longer what counted. When Lyndon Johnson was preparing his March 31, 1968, address on the war, aides persuaded him to change the opening line from "I want to talk to you of the war in Vietnam" to "I want to talk to you of *peace* in Vietnam."[41] And from that point forward, the message Americans heard was—to quote a 1968 cable sent by NBC News to its correspondents in the field—"We are in our way out of Vietnam."[42] Richard Nixon entered office promising that he would end the war, and though he also promised "peace with honor," he never publicly talked about military victory. For all the polarization that followed Tet, a new national consensus of sorts had been formed: everyone agreed the country wanted out of Vietnam. One interesting statistic bears this out. When statements reported on television in the post-Tet period—most of them from administration officials or members of Congress—were coded according to the criteria used in evaluating Vietnam policy, about 42% of the classifiable statements were argued on the basis of whether administration policy would help end the war. An additional 23% referred to related themes, including the costs of the war to the United States and the need to protect American troops and get back prisoners of war. Fewer than 6% referred to the familiar themes of the pre-Tet period, halting "Communist aggression," preserving democracy, and so on.[43]

In theory, American military strategy had switched at the beginning of 1969 from an emphasis on attrition of enemy forces to an emphasis on maintaining control of population centers. But, in fact, the large-unit operations of this period were often indistinguishable from those of previous years.[44] Some involved little contact with the enemy; but when contact was made, intense battles would often follow for pieces of ground far from any population center. The objective would be taken and quickly abandoned, but the real purpose of the operation was to run up a large number of enemy dead. This was usually achieved. Along the way, however, the unit would run up a fair number of casualties of its own, something which few questioned when the country was assumed to be seeking a military victory, but which was hard to justify given the new consensus.

A series of assaults in May on a ridge the soldiers dubbed "Hamburger Hill," because of the number of men ground up on its slopes, produced particular resentment among the troops.[45] Back in the United States Hamburger Hill and the general policy of search and destroy became a major political issue. This period produced an unusual burst of explicit questioning of military tactics in television reports from the field. Richard Threlkeld, reporting on the battle for "Million Dollar Mountain," a precurser to Hamburger Hill, summed up:

> The elite Special Forces have fought well and bravely as usual, but for a military objective of doubtful value. . . . After you've been here a while and seen all the casualties . . . you come away with the distinct impression that the principal reason that these Special Forces have been ordered to take Million Dollar Mountain is simply because it's there.[46]

After the controversy over Hamburger Hill, orders went out from the White House to limit American casualties,[47] and major battles of attrition involving American troops became rare—as did commentaries from television correspondents in the field like those of 1969. But men continued to die, by ones and twos rather than fifty at a time, and the collapse of morale among American troops continued as soldiers began to worry about being the last casualty in the lame-duck war. "Fraggings," for instance—assaults with fragmentation grenades usually directed at officers considered too willing to risk their men's lives—increased from 126 incidents in 1969 to 333 in 1971, a fivefold increase, correcting for the declining number of American troops in the war.[48] Drug use, racial conflict, and refusals to obey orders were also on the

Table 7   Positive and Negative References to Morale of U.S. Troops

	Positive References	Negative References
Before Tet offensive	4.0	0.0
After Tet offensive	2.5	14.5

rise. Table 7 gives a count of the number of stories dealing primarily with the morale of U.S. troops, showing the large increase in negative stories after Tet. Stories in which American morale is mentioned but is not the major subject of the story are also scored, but weighted one-half. The small numbers for the pre-Tet period reflect the fact that the morale of American troops was largely taken for granted then, and therefore not discussed explicitly.

Reporting of My Lai and other war crimes cases, which was extensive in the last few years of the war, should also be mentioned in this connection. Stories of these incidents of course focused attention on civilian victims of the war, and no doubt contributed to some weakening of the moral dichotomy television had set up between Americans and the enemy—though some television commentary made a point of reinforcing that dichotomy on the occasion of My Lai. ("My Lai was for Americans an exceptional horror," said ABC's Howard K. Smith. "My Lais for the other side are a daily way of life."[49]) But My Lai coverage was usually cautious and dispassionate, a great deal of it focused on legal issues in the trial of Lieutenant Calley, rather than on the massacre itself, which of course became an "alleged massacre" once charges were filed. So it may be that for much of the viewing public, My Lai was less an atrocity, comparable to those they had heard about on the other side, than confirmation that American morale was on the decline. Many Americans, incidentally, did not believe the news of the My Lai massacre.[50]

This is not to say that the average story on American troops was about fragging, drug abuse, or war crimes. The portrayal of American soldiers remained highly sympathetic through the end of the war, but the image of the soldier eager for a fight gave way to that of the reluctant warrior whose battle was mainly to survive. One reporter, wrapping up a story that included footage of an officer persuading reluctant troops to go out on a mission by assuring them it was not an offensive operation, but necessary to protect other troops, concluded, "[O]ne thing does seem for sure: the average American soldier no longer wants any part of this war—even in a defensive posture."[51]

The Home Front: Vietnamization and
the Silent Majority

The new consensus to end the war confronted the Nixon administration
with a difficult political problem. For Nixon was not willing lose the
war; he wanted "peace with honor," which meant in effect the full
achievement of the original American objective of an independent,
anti-Communist South Vietnam.[52] Vietnam policy during the Nixon
years was contradictory and erratic in the extreme: the administration
was trying simultaneously to withdraw from the war and to force its
adversaries to back down; at one moment it would be deescalating,
pulling American troops out of the South, at the next, escalating the
air war to new levels of intensity or expanding the American commitment into Laos and Cambodia.

It is tempting to attribute the erratic character of Nixon's Vietnam
policy to his own character—his "sense of beleaguered isolation"[53]—
and to that of the policy's other architect, Henry Kissinger. The decision-making process *was* exceptionally personal during the Nixon years,
and no doubt it reflected Nixon's and Kissinger's characters to a degree.
But it also had deeper roots. Nixon was not the only one who remained
committed to achieving "peace with honor"; that sentiment was widely
shared in Congress and the media and presumably among the general
public.[54] Yet it is not clear there was a rational policy to be found, as
long as the nation held to the contradictory objectives of getting out
of the war and at the same time not "losing" South Vietnam to the
Communists. In a sense American policy in Vietnam had always proceeded according to what H. R. Haldeman called the "Madman Theory."
Haldeman quotes Nixon as saying:

> "I call it the Madman Theory, Bob. I want the North Vietnamese to
> believe I've reached the point where I might do *anything* to stop the war.
> We'll just slip the word to them that, 'for God's sake you know Nixon is
> obsessed about Communists. We can't restrain him when he's angry—
> and he has his finger on the nuclear button—and Ho Chi Minh himself
> will be in Paris in two days begging for peace.' "[55]

But it was American policy all along to convince North Vietnam that
the United States would do whatever it had to to win in Vietnam, even
if that seemed an irrational attitude toward a distant conflict in which
American costs could clearly be very high in relation to any real American interest. What had changed was that it was even more difficult to
sustain the credibility of the threat once the decision had been made
to deescalate.

The political environment during the Nixon years was exactly the kind of environment in which a president is likely to have trouble managing the news and, presumably, public opinion. The administration, like its predecessors, but much more blatantly, was sending out contradictory signals about its policy. Political elites were openly divided about the war. Relations between the president and Congress proceeded toward ever greater levels of tension. The antiwar movement was making major inroads into the political mainstream. The administration itself was rent by division, and the effect of this was magnified by a centralization of power in the White House that left even senior policymakers often unsure of the administration's direction and unable to participate in the policy-making process except through the press.

Yet the Nixon administration did not do badly at keeping the support of what it called the "Great Silent Majority." Nixon's approval rating averaged 57% over his first term, a very respectable showing;[56] he won reelection against George McGovern, whose major issue was Vietnam, by a landslide.

The most basic reason for this success with the mass public was no doubt the policy of Vietnamization itself. By turning over the burden of ground combat to the South Vietnamese, the administration lowered American casualties from more than 14,000 killed in 1968 to 300 in 1972.[57] The war continued with great intensity, and this infuriated those who were actively opposed to it. But mass dissatisfaction with the war had different sources from the active opposition of the antiwar movement. For the antiwar movement, as Howard Schuman put it in a study contrasting student and public attitudes toward the war, the issue was "what we are doing to the Vietnamese"; for the mass public it was "what the Vietnamese are doing to us."[58] In a sense it was the very fact that the Nixon administration's Vietnam policy was so contradictory that made it an effective political strategy. Nixon promised what the public wanted: to end the war and win the peace.[59] He lowered the cost of the war while at the same time presenting himself, in contrast to his domestic opponents, as the one who would stand firm against the Communists and achieve peace with honor.

Table 8 shows from one angle how Vietnamization worked on television. The announcement of that policy in May 1969 was accompanied by a major public relations effort intended to focus attention on the transfer of responsibility for ground combat to the South Vietnamese. In Washington there was a heavy volume of statements lauding the progress of the South Vietnamese; in South Vietnam there was a series of ceremonies transferring one base or another to South Vietnam, always accompanied by more official statements lauding South Viet-

Table 8 Positive and Negative References to Performance of
South Vietnamese Armed Forces, Before and After
Announcement of Vietnamization

	Positive References	Negative References
Before Vietnamization	8.5	3.0
After Vietnamization	43.5	14.5

Note: The beginning of Vietnamization is dated May 9, 1969.

namese progress. These "pseudo-events," as Daniel Boorstin has called them,[60] were automatically "hard news" according to the conventions of newsworthiness discussed in Chapter 3, and the journalists had to report them, even if they were personally skeptical—and, as we shall see, journalists were generally skeptical about the South Vietnamese government. As the figures show, however, the administration not only succeeded in putting Vietnamization on the news agenda, but was able to produce a favorable balance of coverage of the South Vietnamese army.

Figure 2 (see page 177) gives another angle on the impact of Vietnamization. It shows how often the sample included film of casualties in each full year for which data are available, from 1966 through 1972. Television's greater sensitivity to the costs of the war kept the representation of American casualties relatively stable until 1972 (the drop-off actually began earlier, after the Laotian invasion in February 1971). The figures are boosted, for instance, by the still photographs sometimes shown with the weekly body count in the latter part of the war. But *relative* particularly to South Vietnamese casualties, the representation of American casualties declined substantially.

In Washington coverage the Nixon administration never enjoyed the kind of patriotic reporting Johnson did near the beginning of the war. The war no longer belonged to the Sphere of Consensus. But if Nixon did not get the active collaboration of television, he nevertheless retained a good deal of the power his predecessors had to manage the news. The pattern of television's response to Nixon's Vietnam policy is very close to the pattern we observed in the *Times*'s coverage during the Kennedy and Johnson years. When the administration maintained the initiative, it was usually able to dominate the news. Television coverage in such a period would generally take the form of "straight" objective reporting: official statements would be presented with little interpretation and few "balancing" statements from the opposition. When the administration was confused or divided about its policy, and therefore unable to present a united front, others would become active (or would be regarded as more newsworthy, or both), and it would partially lose control. It would have to share the news with political opponents, and the journalists would become more active interpreters of the news.

The twists and turns of the Nixon administration's political strategy and the media's response to them are far too numerous to trace from beginning to end. But let us consider three important episodes that illustrate both the administration's problems and its power: the beginning of Vietnamization in May–June 1969; the opening of the first major cracks in the administration's unity in September 1969; and the peace initiative that preceeded the congressional midterm elections of 1970.

The Beginning of Vietnamization. Vietnamization was introduced with the kind of public relations blitz that typically accompanies a policy expected to be politically popular. For several weeks a flood of official leaks, background briefings, and press conferences kept the new policy at the top of the news agenda. There was opposition, and it got some coverage (the CBS interview with Clark Clifford following publication of his *Foreign Affairs* article has already been mentioned). And the journalists were sometimes bolder than in previous years. "Reporters kept coming back to a key question," said Robert Pierpoint, reporting on a press conference by Henry Cabot Lodge, the U.S. representative to the peace talks: "Why should the Communists negotiate if the U.S. is preparing to withdraw anyway?" Lodge's reply was that he didn't think one could "assume a helter-skelter withdrawal." "But," Pierpoint concluded, "Ambassador Lodge did not explain what the president's plan to start soon an *orderly* withdrawal of U.S. troops might do to the Paris talks."[61] This was the exception, however; in May and June the administration dominated most Washington reporting.

Patrick Buchanan, the presidential speech-writer who wrote the attacks on the media which Vice President Agnew would deliver in November 1969, later told a reporter he felt the president should have the "right of untrammeled communication with the American people."[62] And in order to assert that "right," the Nixon administration would more and more try to have the media without the journalists. Nixon held fewer press conferences as time went on, for instance, and gave more prime-time speeches. But a good deal of the time "the right of untrammeled communication" was exactly what the president and other officials got on the evening news. Often the role of the Washington correspondent, though it was beginning to increase (recall that early in 1966 correspondents did not appear in most Washington coverage), was still limited to paraphrasing or introducing official statements. On May 9, for instance, the day news of Vietnamization was first leaked, ABC's Bill Gill reported:

> The president is acutely aware of congressional criticism of his Vietnam policies [nothing about what the critics say]. He is acting with controlled haste to deescalate the Vietnam War. Mr. Nixon is spending a good part of his time here and at Key Biscayne with a full study of the Vietcong ten-point peace proposal from Paris. . . . The stage is set for the beginning of Mr. Nixon's Vietnam War deescalation.

On May 15, after a Nixon address, NBC's Brinkley reported:

> The president has now made clear what he would like to see done in Paris and how. The main points of what he said are these. The withdrawal of American and North Vietnamese troops in a year, an international body of some kind to supervise the withdrawal and arrange a cease-fire, and free elections. And that is the base from which this country will negotiate from now on.

A long clip—a minute and twenty seconds—followed, of a statement by Ambassador Henry Cabot Lodge, about to return to the Paris peace talks.

On June 10, when Nixon returned to Washington from a conference with President Thieu at Midway, the CBS report on his return lasted a little under two minutes thirty seconds. Dan Rather, the White House correspondent, spoke just under thirty seconds, only long enough to set the scene. The rest of the report showed unedited the last two minutes of the president's statement. It was followed by a brief report on a statement by Averill Harriman, who had been Johnson's ambassador to the Paris talks; this was the only time in these three reports that critics of the administration were covered.

The image of authority these reports project is probably as important as anything they say about policy (they do not, in fact, say much about policy). The president appears in control of events ("acutely aware," "controlled haste," "full study," "the president has made clear"); and although the reporters no longer refer to administration policy as "our" policy, the reporting is full of cues that the president is to be seen as speaking for the nation as a whole: the fact that Brinkley puts the president's remarks in the context of "this country's" position at Paris, for instance, rather than in the context of the political debate at home. To the extent that the journalists mediate between officials and the public here, their primary role is to establish the legitimacy of presidential authority, not to interpret events on their own.

"Is There a Firm Vietnam Policy?" To the extent that there was a coherent strategy for achieving "peace with honor" in the Nixon administration, it was Vietnamization: the idea was to strengthen the South Vietnamese army and government to the point that, with limited American assistance—limited enough that it could be sustained indefinitely—the South Vietnamese could fight well enough that the North Vietnamese would be convinced they could not win. It may have been wishful thinking, but it was a plausible, consistent strategy. This had been the policy Clark Clifford had urged during the Johnson administration; its primary champion in the Nixon administration was the new Secretary of Defense, Melvin Laird.

But the White House did not fully embrace Vietnamization; for Nixon and Kissinger, as Haldeman put it, "the threat was the key," the threat of what Kissinger called "savage, punishing blows" if North Vietnam did not come to terms.[63] Soon after the beginning of Vietnamization, Nixon leaked word to the press that he was considering such a move.[64] But Hanoi did not bend, delivering in August a "cold rebuff" of the peace terms that accompanied the threat of escalation. Another round of troop withdrawals was supposed to be announced in August, but was not, and the administration said little in public about the change of policy. In September Ho Chi Minh died, and following a three-day truce called by the North Vietnamese, the administration suspended B-52 raids against North Vietnamese and NLF forces in South Vietnam for thirty-six hours, and then abruptly started them again. The apparent indecision, and above all the apparent shift away from Vietnamization, caused alarm both in Congress and in the administration itself. In the administration, moreover, the centralization of power in the White House was beginning to become clear. Officials reacted by going to the press, and Washington was soon awash in leaks about the growing internal divisions of the Nixon administration.[65]

And as usually happens when the administration fails to provide a clear direction, the media began to become more active. The response of television to the growing sense of crisis is best illustrated by an unusual report on the *CBS Evening News* on September 12. Cronkite brought into the studio the three correspondents covering the basic foreign policy beats, Dan Rather from the White House, Marvin Kalb from the State Department, and Steve Rowan from the Pentagon. "Gentlemen," Cronkite began, "there seems to be . . . a considerable confusion about American policy in Vietnam. The *New York Times* has ticked off the indications this morning [in an editorial]. . . . Dan Rather, is there in fact a firm Vietnam policy at this time?" Here are excerpts of the conversation, more than eight minutes long, that followed.

Rather. Walter I believe there is . . . I think the president's long-range policy is still in the process of being formulated. That is what the big meeting today at the White House has to do with. . . . [But] yes, I think we're in the midst of President Nixon formulating and perfecting a long-range policy for Vietnam which will include at the minimum a withdrawal of 200,000 U.S. troops by the end of next year.

Kalb. What we find now all over the administration—this is not just stuff that comes from the State Department—you have the feeling that indecision, indecisiveness, and kind of vacillation . . . and a clear feeling that the president has not really faced up to the key question, which is, "What price for peace in Vietnam?" If the Communists are putting a price that it must be the elimination of the Thieu government, the president indicates that he's going to ride with the Thieu government, so that you're really at the same kind of loggerheads that President Johnson was.

Rowan. I think people in the Pentagon are worried . . . about the fact that we [thought] we had a policy, back in May and June when the president went to Midway, but that policy seems to have changed vastly in the past few weeks.

Rather. I think that's overstated . . . and the reason for it being overstated up and down government, in the Defense Department, in the State Department, is because the Nixon policy . . is very tightly kept between President Nixon and his principal foreign policy advisor, Dr. Kissinger. . . .

Cronkite [looking concerned]. Gentlemen, does this indicate . . . that the State Department and the Pentagon are not privy to the plans in the White House?

Rather. I believe that to be the case. . . .

Rowan. I get the impression that Secretary Laird may *not* be privy to all the president's thinking. Certainly Laird's people are very concerned about the direction that things have been taking for the past few weeks, and they seem to feel that President Nixon has decided to use as his principal advisors on Vietnam Ambassador Bunker and General Abrams, and to bypass the counsels of the Joint Chiefs of Staff and . . . others in the Pentagon.

This is "establishment journalism" in a period of political crisis. The focus is firmly on official views of American policy; even Congress did not receive much coverage during the September crisis. But with officials divided and communication channels within the administration inoperative, the media became a forum for airing political differences rather than a tool of policy. The journalists also moved in the direction

of more active news analysis, since it fell to them to make sense out
of the confusion over U.S. policy.

The postscript to the story of the September crisis is that Nixon
regained the initiative relatively quickly. On September 16 he gave a
speech announcing the withdrawal expected in August—and getting
over two minutes of uninterrupted time on the evening news.[66] On the
eighteenth he spoke at the United Nations, and again got long blocks
of air time. On the twenty-fifth, Senator Charles Goodell put foward
a plan for a timed withdrawal of American troops, and CBS ran a story
on "growing restlessness" in Congress. That story took a backseat to
a Laird press conference, however (Goodell spoke for twenty seconds,
Laird for a minute ten; two other interviews boosted Congress' time
to an unusually high fifty seconds). The next day Nixon responded to
Goodell, getting two minutes twenty seconds.[67]

The Mid-Term Election Peace Offensive. Nixon's popularity sagged
during the confusion of September–October, from a July peak of 65%
approval of his performance as president to 56% in mid-October. About
that time, on October 15, the antiwar movement held its most
impressive, and most favorably covered, protest to that point, the Moratorium, which penetrated into the hinterlands of America as no previous protest had done. Some have credited the Moratorium with
scuttling the administration's plans for massive escalation against the
North.[68] Then, on November 3, Nixon delivered his most famous speech
on Vietnam, calling for the "Great Silent Majority" to stand behind
him. The administration was furious about the "instant analysis" following the broadcast, in which some commentators observed that the
speech contained "no new initiatives" and was unlikely to satisfy the
opposition; this was the occasion for Agnew's attacks on the media,
and the background to Buchanan's remark about "the right of untrammeled communication." But, all in all, the speech got a good reception
in the news. ABC's report the next day was organized using the president's categories, contrasting the "Silent Majority" of Nixon supporters with the "Vocal Minority"—blacks and demonstrators opposed to
the war. The terms appeared in a graphic shown at the beginning of
each segment of the broadcast. Nixon's popularity jumped twelve points
following the address.[69]

On April 30, 1970, Nixon sent American troops into Cambodia. The
move provoked a dramatic upsurge in antiwar activity and congressional
opposition. The Gulf of Tonkin resolution was repealed in June and
the most serious attempts yet to limit the president's war-making power
were introduced, though they did not yet have majority support. Cambodia also provoked a large volume of criticism from journalists (though

this came mostly in formal commentaries, which are listened to less than anything else on the news;[70] regular news reports were "straight" as usual, but unusually full of dramatic conflict on the home front). The public reaction was different: the invasion was followed by another jump in support for the president.[71] But the stage was set for what was expected to be a bruising battle over Vietnam in the 1970 congressional elections.

Nixon took the offensive with a peace proposal delivered in a speech on October 7, 1970. At first glance, the proposal was new. The American negotiating position to that point had hinged on the concept of mutual withdrawal: the United States would withdraw its troops from South Vietnam if the North Vietnamese would do the same. This was an appealing proposal from the point of view of domestic politics, since it appeared evenhanded. But it offered no prospect of serious negotiations. It required the North Vietnamese and NLF to renounce entirely their political goals in the South, since attrition and Vietnamization had been successful enough that the NLF by itself was no longer a match for the Saigon regime. And, in any case, the North Vietnamese had no incentive to accept it, as the United States was withdrawing unilaterally. In his October speech Nixon stayed away from the mutual withdrawal formula, calling instead for a standstill cease-fire. But in fact American policy had not changed. The president indicated that American withdrawal would be based on "principles" he had "previously outlined," that is, mutual withdrawal, and reiterated to reporters the next day that American withdrawal was contingent on North Vietnamese reciprocation.[72] The North Vietnamese of course denounced the proposal. But the speech had other purposes; it was intended, as Kissinger put it, "at a minimum [to] give us some temporary relief from public pressures."[73] And that it did. Congressional doves—many of whom had called for a cease-fire proposal—praised the president's initiative. On television American "reasonableness" was contrasted with North Vietnamese "intransigence." On October 8, Brinkley reported:

> President Nixon's new peace plan for Vietnam was formally offered at the Paris peace talks today, and the Communists reacted with sneers, wisecracks, and sarcasm. But actually that's about what was expected of them; no one thought that was their final reaction, and the American ambassador said he was not discouraged. . . . [I]t's taken for granted they will talk seriously some time later. In this country the president's plan has won wide support and approval in both parties.

Here we come to one of the most important reasons for Nixon's success with the news. Ever since the Senate Foreign Relations Committee hearings of February 1966, journalists had been uncertain whether to treat the war as a political issue or as a matter of national security—uncertain whether it belonged to the Sphere of Legitimate Controversy or the Sphere of Consensus. No doubt politicians and the public at large were just as uncertain. After 1968 the consensus was increasingly that it was to be considered a political issue. But the uncertainty never entirely went away, and the president could usually knock the issue at least partly back into the Sphere of Consensus with a peace proposal which would focus attention on the confrontation between "this country" (no longer just "the Nixon administration," once things were moved to the plane of Cold War politics) and the Communists. No journalist—at least not on the visible medium of television—was about to say anything that might seem to place him or her on the wrong side of that line. Whenever relations with North Vietnam came up, television journalists reverted either to consensus journalism not unlike that of 1965–66, or to the most deferential "objectivity." The result was a consistent image of American flexibility contrasted with North Vietnamese unreason.

"All that came out of the meeting," Chet Huntley reported in 1969, "was a hint that more Americans might be withdrawn if the enemy shows any inclination to be reasonable, to be willing to give and take."[74] And in 1971 Robert Pierpoint reported from the Western White House:

> In Paris, for the first time according to a high official here, the Communists are showing apparent flexibility. President Nixon wants to find out whether this flexibility is *only* apparent, simply an attempt to exploit domestic pressures, or whether Hanoi now feels for its own reasons that it is now finally time seriously to negotiate.[75]

In each story the onus for lack of progress toward peace is removed entirely from the Nixon administration and put onto the North Vietnamese.

The Republicans lost twelve seats in the House in 1970, but gained two in the Senate, a good showing for the president's party in an off-year election.

The Nixon period is remembered as one of exceptional tension between the administration and the media. Following a *New York Times* story in May 1969, revealing the secret bombing of Cambodia, wiretaps had been ordered to monitor contacts between reporters and officials (television, incidentally, did not report the secret bombing story). The vice president publicly attacked the media—the first time in modern American history an administration had publicly criticized not merely particular news organizations but the institution of journalism itself. The president relied increasingly on prime-time addresses which enabled him to bypass the journalists. And the administration, considering the journalists active opponents of its policies, carried on an unprecedented campaign to use the power of the state to pressure the media, the most potent tactic probably being an effort to organize owners of affiliate television stations, most of whom were Republicans, against the networks.[76] For their part, many journalists were becoming quite hostile in their personal feelings about the administration and its policies. "[O]ne day some CBS journalists were so angry," Herbert Gans observed, "that they rewrote a lead story to read, 'The President of the United States today cheapened the United States' highest military decoration for bravery by using a medal of honor award ceremony for a spite-ridden attack on Americans who dare to disagree with him.' "[77] They did not, of course, use that lead. When one looks at daily news coverage, the relation between the media and the administration does not appear dramatically different in the Nixon period. The reporters set aside their passionate leads and wrote "objective" ones. The administration dominated the news most of the time, and it did so not because of its often clumsy attempts at intimidation, but because the familiar routines of journalism gave it advantages only marginally diminished from those of its predecessors.

The Home Front: Dissent

There was a strong consensus in support of the war in the early years; but there was never unanimity. As Kennedy and Johnson both had feared, dissent was quick to surface as the war escalated. It was expressed somewhat fitfully, since liberal Democrats were reluctant to hurt the leader of their own party, Republicans wary of putting themselves in a position where they could be charged with having sabotaged the war effort, and both groups worried about charges they were failing to back American boys at war. But both did speak out from time to time; they were covered about equally on television.[78] In the military there was unhappiness about the administration's unwillingness to escalate the war faster and more widely. Active military officers did not challenge the president publicly; like McNamara and other civilians in the administration who had doubts on the other side, the policy of gradualism gave them enough of what they wanted and enough hope that policy would go their way eventually that they continued to play the quiet bureaucratic game.[79] Their views did come out through their allies in Congress, however. "Hawkish" views were also expressed at times by lower-level military personnel unhappy about restrictions the administration had place on the use of American forces. It is probably

inevitable that many of those who fight in a limited war—who have an unlimited commitment to a cause the nation considers only one priority among many—should feel betrayed. And given the rhetoric of an ultimate global struggle that served to justify the war, it is natural enough that this feeling of betrayal would be translated into a desire to go "all out." "You either go into a war to win or you stay out," said the father of a nineteen-year-old marine killed at Con Thien, interviewed on CBS in August 1967.[80] "They just keep feeding more and more men into the death trap." The marine's parents had returned a letter of sympathy from President Johnson, complaining that restrictions on the bombing of the north endangered the troops. Finally, from outside the established arena of political debate, the war was challenged by the diverse antiwar movement, which brought together, among others, religious pacifists, the "Old Left," the largely student-based "New Left," and parts of the civil rights movement.

Beginning with the live coverage of the parts of the Fulbright Committee hearings in February 1966, dissent became a regular feature of television coverage. From 1966 on about 20% of all Vietnam coverage—at least on CBS, for which the data are available—concerned the various forms of domestic controversy. No doubt this is one of the reasons for the public war-weariness that began to grow just about this time, early in 1966. The Fulbright hearings pushed the war at least partly into the Sphere of Legitimate Controversy, and coverage of more traditional forms of dissent was respectful, even in the years when television coverage was generally very favorable to the administration. But the reporting of the antiwar movement was another matter.

Among the many arguments made about the political impact of television is the view that it provided a new avenue to power in the United States, a means by which previously powerless groups could break into the political process.[81] And, in fact, the antiwar movement did play to the television cameras, often successfully grabbing the media spotlight, perhaps more rapidly than it would have done without television. On October 16, 1967, for instance, when antidraft demonstrations were held around the country, CBS led its broadcasts with a series of four film reports from different regions of the country. The story ran on page 3 of the *New York Times* the next day. But television was hardly a passive tool to be used by the new movement, and the costs of this route to influence were high. When the established boundaries of the Sphere of Legitimate Controversy were challenged from the outside, the journalists rose to defend them, employing a host of symbolic "weapons" or (better) "markers" which served to neturalize the ideological threat by placing it in a recognized location in the Sphere of Deviance. Coverage of the antiwar movement became more "objective" only as it began to penetrate established centers of power, and even then the ability of the movement to break into the process of political debate in a substantial way was limited.

It is worth looking closely at a number of television stories on the antiwar movement from the pre-Tet period, for they provide a look at a face of journalism we have not yet seen: journalism as an agency of social control.

On October 27, 1965, ABC's Peter Jennings introduced a report on an antiwar group called the May Second Movement by saying, "While Americans fight and die in Vietnam, there are those in this country who sympathize with the Vietcong." Jennings went on to say that an ABC reporter had "exposed" the activities of the May Second Movement. This brief introduction is a good example of the heavy load of ideological meaning that can be packed into a word or two. Parts of the antiwar movement in the United States did in fact support the NLF and North Vietnamese, and the May Second Movement was one of them—we learn in the story that it was planning to send blood to the NLF—but this does not mean that the ABC report can be taken simply as factual reporting. This can be seen if we simply reconstruct Jennings's introduction a little bit: "While Americans fight and die in Vietnam, there are those in this country who question whether the enemy there is really a foreign aggressor as President Johnson has claimed." To "sympathize" with the enemy is to be a traitor; to "question" whether the enemy should in fact be an enemy is to have a political opinion. Most of the time television spoke of the antiwar movement as a threat to "internal security," not as a participant in political debate.

The aid-and-comfort-to-the-enemy theme was standard. In one NBC report, following a story on demonstrations in Britain, Chet Huntley remarked, "Meanwhile, Hanoi was having paroxysms of joy over the demonstrations in this country over the war in Vietnam."[82] Also common was the contrast drawn in Jennings's report between the troops in Vietnam and the antiwar movement, a contrast which again has the effect of taking antiwar activity out of the context of policy debate. On October 14, 1965, the day before the first nationally coordinated demonstrations against the war, CBS gathered a group of GIs in Vietnam and showed them a film of a lecture on draft resistance produced by an antiwar organization in the United States. Morley Safer then solicited the soldiers' reactions: "You're getting shot at," Safer said to one GI. "Five of your buddies were killed down the road the other day. How did you feel watching that film?" The story closed with an emotional soldier saying he wished the fellows in the film, not his buddies, had been going down that road.

The antiwar movement also appeared on television as a threat to "law and order" at home. "Antiwar demonstrators in New York provoked a series of clashes today with counter-demonstrators and police," said Walter Cronkite, introducing one report.[83] All we learn about how demonstrators had "provoked" these confrontations is the following: one of the marchers was carrying an NLF flag, and "the sight of the flag was too much for some of the onlookers . . . the angry crowd along the roadway jumped in to do away with the Vietcong symbol."

If this series of reports suggests there was a heavy emphasis on the most radical factions and most militant tactics of the antiwar movement, that is correct. "The journalistic premium on clash and theatrics," as Todd Gitlin puts it, "was wrestling with the [journalists'] political interest in moderation. Trapped in [their self-contradictory] conventions [the media] encouraged the same extremists [they] deplored."[84] Not being recognized as a part of the normal political process, the antiwar movement could rarely become news except by playing the deviant role, usually by "provoking" violence or charges of aiding the enemy.[85] So the factions that played this role the best were the ones that grew most rapidly, and the movement increasingly defined *itself* according to the deviant role in which it was cast by the media. This is no doubt a major reason the antiwar movement was hated by most of the public even when the public had turned against the war.[86] It may also be a further reason Nixon was able to hold political support: besides the October peace offensive, the administration's other tactic in the 1970 congressional elections was to run against the "anarchy" of the antiwar protests.[87]

One final example from the early period illustrates the parallel that often exists between coverage of political dissent and of deviance in general. To set up this parallel it will be useful to look for just a moment at coverage of homosexuality in the British press in the 1950s and 1960s. That coverage, according to a study by Frank Pearce, portrayed society as though it were composed of three kinds of people: "normal" people, who belonged to the mainstream of society; the weak and vulnerable who lived on the edges of the mainstream; and the "hard-core" deviants, who stood essentially outside of society.[88] Deviance was explained as corruption of the weak and vulnerable by the hard-core. This imagery is reassuring because it places the origin of deviance outside the mainstream of society. It can be applied to political as well as to any other sort of deviance; it is familiar in politics as the "outside agitator" theory of political conflict.

A story by ABC's John Rolfson on the subject of American war resisters in France, shown during the Tet offensive on March 5, 1968, fits this model closely. The story began with a report on French policy, and then moved to a set of interviews that served to introduce the Americans. Most seemed to have tried to emphasize their political opposition to the war, but the interviews, as edited, focused primarily on their personal histories. Each would appear only for a few seconds, long enough to say, for instance, "I read some antiwar literature, then heard that many people were going to France." Having introduced the war resisters, Rolfson then turned to the question of why they had defied the conventions of their society. "The deserters," he said, "are recruited or helped by various groups. Our contact with them is only a voice on the telephone, a man called Mr. Cook. He was in the apartment with some of his associates, behind the big sheet, running the show. We tried to learn something about the mysterious Mr. Cook. . . ." Mr. Cook did not want to be photographed, so he was separated from Rolfson and the camera crew by a sheet. He did not have much to say about who he was.

Rolfson then turned from the causes to the consequences of deviance: "So the opposition to the Vietnam War gives these deserters a more or less reasonable excuse. Propaganda work with other deserters gives some of them a purpose in life temporarily. But life is not easy for these young misfits in a strange land." In a second set of interviews Rolfson asked the "deserters" (one said he considered himself a refugee, not a deserter, but Rolfson pointedly continued to call him a deserter) about their life in France. His final question emphasized the norms the men were violating: "What do you think of the idea of the obligations of citizenship in the United States? Do these ideals mean anything to you?" And then he concluded by saying, "Obviously [the deserters are] being used against the United States."

Several things are notable about this report. It explains "desertion" or "resistance," first of all, in terms of the groups or individuals who "recruit or help" the war resisters, not in terms of politics. The "mysterious Mr. Cook" receives far more attention than the war in Vietnam. The aura of mystery Rolfson builds further softens any threat to consensus that might be posed by the reporting of political deviance. Rolfson could have explained that Mr. Cook seemed mysterious because he was concerned about his security. Instead, he used Mr. Cook's mystery to establish an atmosphere that made the story seem as though it were being reported from the distant nether reaches of the social world. In general, television places high value on its ability to bring the audience "close" to events, something which it usually accomplishes by bringing the people of the story to life so the audience can empathize with them and feel a "part" of the story. This was what was done in most reporting on the war itself. But here the opposite is done: the phenomenon of war resistance is made to seem distant, sinister, and foreign to the lives of the audience. Finally, Rolfson's report stresses the cost of deviance: "life is not easy for these young misfits." This was common in television reports about war resisters; reporters often pressed them about whether they were aware of the penalties they could incur, an emphasis which reinforced both the definition of their act as criminal rather than political, and the impression that they belong to Pearce's category of the "weak and vulnerable," unaware of the full implications of what they were doing.

To understand how and why the reporting of the antiwar movement changed after the Tet offensive and the Johnson "abdication," it will be useful to take a look at a more recent television story, a CBS report on the nuclear "freeze" movement in California in 1982. Here is a brief excerpt from the narration:

> Parts of the movement have evolved from predictable sources: people against nuclear power now turning their energies to nuclear weapons [video: "hippie" types dancing to rock music]. . . . traditional liberal groups used to marching for causes [video: "traditional march"]. . . . Yet polls show that more than any issue in recent memory this one cuts across age, income, and political party lines. . . . Statewide support is two to one, much of it from people not previously known for political activism.[89]

Later in the report, most of which was very positive in tone, pollster Mervin Field predicted that the movement would become a major factor in upcoming elections.

In general, the media place a low value on political involvement by ordinary citizens; this is perhaps a general characteristic of contemporary political culture in the United States.[90] Political protest usually receives favorable coverage under two circumstances. First, it is favorably covered when it can be interpreted as an expression of individual conscience by people who do not "make a habit" of political involvement. One of the few favorable stories about war protesters in the early Vietnam period was a CBS report on a school-teacher in Indiana who was being fired for attending a demonstration against the war. The closing line was, "In a small town, it's difficult to be different."[91] It was essentially a human-interest, not a political, story. Second, protest is favorably covered when it becomes an acknowledged force in the established—legislative and electoral—political arena.

The event that did the most to change the media's portrayal of the antiwar movement was the 1968 New Hampshire primary. Eugene McCarthy, as a peace candidate backed by legions of young activists, ran nearly dead even with the incumbent president's write-in campaign, an exceptional feat in a day when incumbents were nearly always renominated. Those who voted for McCarthy in New Hampshire were by no means all doves on the war—many voted for George Wallace in November[92]—but the antiwar movement had broken into the Sphere of Legitimate Controversy. And the part of it that had done so was now both sanctioned by the media and held up as confirmation of the legitimacy of established political boundaries. *Time* magazine's comments on the New Hampshire primary express this particularly well:

> In an era when many young Americans are turning away from involvement in the democratic [i.e., electoral] process by dropping out either to psychadelia or to the nihilism of the New Left, the cool, crisply-executed crusade of Eugene McCarthy's 'ballot children' provides heartening evidence that the generation gap is bridgeable—politically, at least.[93]

Television reports in subsequent years would frequently plug opponents of the war who chose to "work within the system." In May 1970, for instance, after the wave of protests that followed the invasion of Cambodia, Walter Cronkite did a sympathetic report on the "earnest, clean-shaven college students, full of facts, not rhetoric, carrying well-written resolutions and legal briefs in their hands" who had remained behind to lobby in Congress. "These emissaries," he said, "are just about as weary of high-flown oratory as their elders."[94]

Still, the boundaries marking the limits of acceptable political activity were not unaffected by the dramatic political events of 1968 and subsequent years. Dissent in general, inside or outside the "system," had become a political issue by the Nixon period, and the standards of objective journalism were therefore increasingly applied to all forms of protest. The openly condemnatory tone of early television coverage of the antiwar movement vanished rapidly after 1968—after New Hampshire and the Democratic Convention. Journalists for the most part dropped the loyalty issue; one can see stories in the post-Tet period in which antiwar activists are shown in offices with NLF flags on the wall, and the journalist never mentions their presence.[95] At times the movement even benefited from the "objective" practice, standard in stories on officially sponsored events, of framing an event in the terms provided by its sponsors. "The Moratorium demonstration was historic in its scope," said Walter Cronkite of the October 15 protests. "Never before had so many demonstrated their hope for peace. . . . With scattered exceptions the Moratorium was a 'dignified, responsible protest,' in its sponsor's words, that 'appealed to the conscience of the American people.' " The Moratorium, which did much to move forward the legitimization of the antiwar movement, fit the media's two criteria for a "good" protest: it involved large parts of the political establishment and also brought in normally "nonpolitical" people from the "nonpolitical" hinterlands of America.

The extension of "objective" reporting to the antiwar movement did not, however, mean that the movement had gained an extensive ability to project its message to the American public. Within the Sphere of Legitimate Controversy, not all are equally legitimate. The notion of balance notwithstanding—let alone the notion of the media as an adversary of government—the choices journalists make about who will be heard follow closely the hierarchy of formal political authority. Even congressional critics had limited access to the news compared with the administration: not only were they granted much less time to speak when they appeared on the evening news, as we saw above, but they had nothing comparable to the day-to-day ability of the administration, through its position as the primary provider of authoritative information about world events, to affect news coverage—nothing like the power of the "high administration official" of the Pierpoint story quoted above. The antiwar movement stood at the bottom of the media's hierarchy of legitimate political actors, and its access to the news and influence over it were still more limited. Superficially there was almost perfect "balance" in the representation of the administration and its critics in post-Tet television coverage: administration representatives and supporters appeared 249 times in the sample, domestic critics, 258 times. But this did not translate into a balance of real power to communicate.

The ability of the administration to influence the framing of news can be contrasted with the antiwar movement's consistent inability to control the way its actions were presented. In 1965, when the Students for a Democratic Society, the leading organization of the New Left, was faced for the first time with the opportunity and the danger of national publicity, an internal memorandum prepared by the organization expressed prophetically the problem the movement would have communicating through the media.

Table 9 Focus of Statements on Antiwar Movement
Presented on Television

	All Statements Before N.H.	Journalists Statements After N.H.	Other Statements After N.H.	All Statements After N.H.
Violence, disruption, legality, restoration of order by authorities	1 7.7%	21 27.5	35 31.6	56 29.9
Political views	1 7.7	11 14.7	9 8.4	21 11.0
Efectiveness of demonstrations	0 0.0	9 11.3	12 10.8	20 11.0
Public support, participation	0 0.0	9 11.8	7 6.7	16 8.8
Organizing techniques	1 7.7	7 9.3	7 6.1	14 7.4
Loyalty, effect on enemy, U.S. morale	4 38.5	3 4.4	8 7.4	12 6.2
Appearance, style (long hair, etc.)	0 0.0	7 9.8	2 1.7	9 5.0
Demography (students/"middle class")	0 0.0	6 7.4	2 2.0	8 4.2
Other	4 38.5	3 3.9	28 25.3	31 16.6
Total	9 100.0	76 100.0	111 100.0	187 100.0

Notes: "Other" includes, among other things, simple statements of like or dislike, statements questioning manhood or courage of people refusing to fight, and statements about right to dissent in wartime.

Figures may not add to totals because of fractional weighting and rounding.

The important thing is never to let our critics get us debating about communists in the movement, the reactions of Hanoi to marches, the wisdom or legality of draft-card burning. The issue is the war, and we must not let anyone forget it.[96]

In fact, coverage of the antiwar movement did focus primarily on the movement itself as an issue, not on what it had to say about the war. And this was nearly as true after 1968, when the tone of coverage had become more neutral, as before. Some evidence on the issues or "angles" stressed in antiwar movement coverage appears in Table 9.

For the period after the 1968 New Hampshire primary, the table gives
two sets of figures. The first is a summary of the focus of statements
about the antiwar movement—by officials, soldiers, antiwar demonstrators themselves, and many others—presented on television. The
second is a count of journalists' news angles. Like the "editorializing"
measure introduced in Chapter 4, this is a difficult variable to code
reliably, and the figures should be assumed to be rough. For the most
part, what they measure are the themes stressed in the leads and wrap-
ups of stories, where the most evident "framing" of a story takes place.
For the pre-1968 period, because so few stories on the antiwar movement were included in the Defense Department Kinescopes, the two
sets of figures are combined.

The figures suggest that the political views of the antiwar movement
were for the most part overshadowed by other themes: the "aid-and-
comfort-to-the-enemy" theme before 1968, and afterwards the tactics
of the movement (there was a good deal of discussion, mostly negative,
about whether protests had any effect on policy) and, above all, its
conflicts with authority. The issue of violence and disruption was particularly important. Journalists often made a point in later years to
promote moderation. But ironically this meant that the theme of violence often dominated reports of protests in which there was none:
"Today's protest was *different*," began one report on the Moratorium,
"peaceful, within the law, and not confined to a radical minority."[97]
And violence still drew coverage. Cronkite began one report on college
antiwar protests by saying, "The Cambodia development set off a new
round of antiwar demonstrations on U.S. campuses, and not all of them
were peaceful."[98] The film report, not surprisingly, was about one of
the ones that was *not* peaceful, and dealt mainly with the professionalism shown by the authorities who restored order.

This report, on the unpeaceful demonstration following Cambodia,
contained not a word about the Vietnam War, and in this it was typical:
64% of film reports on the antiwar movement contained no substantial
discussion of the war.[99] Only 16% of film reports on antiwar marches
and rallies had film of speeches with natural sound. When they were
shown, representatives of the antiwar movement often appeared only
for a few seconds. Their fate was frequently like that of a demonstrator
at a campaign rally for Democratic vice presidential candidate Edmund
Muskie in 1968. Muskie had offered the demonstrators a deal: if they
would stop heckling, he would let them select a representative to address the crowd for a few minutes. Their representative appeared on
television for perhaps five seconds, long enough to say, "We're here
to make our voices heard."[100] Then the story cut away and returned

to its major theme, Muskie's skill at handling demonstrators. The openness of the political process was symbolically confirmed, but little power to communicate was given away.

A few more statistics will round out the discussion of antiwar movement coverage. Negative statements about the antiwar movement outweighed positive ones in television coverage by about two to one after the New Hamsphire primary. Journalists' editorial comments also ran about two to one against critics of the war (here the figure is for all critics, including congressmen and other elites). (Interviews with journalists during this period have generally found strong hostility to the "Vietniks," as the protesters were often called, despite the journalists' unhappiness with administration policy.)[101] Finally, 49% of all domestic criticism of administration policy reported on television came from public officials and former public officials. Sixteen percent came from reporters in commentaries and interpretive comments, and 35% from all other sources, including antiwar protesters, soldiers, and other citizens. As a forum for political debate, television remained open primarily to official Washington, despite the rise in political protest.

With Friends Like These . . .

It is appropriate that our discussion of the coverage of those for whose benefit the Vietnam War was ostensibly fought—the South Vietnamese—should come so late in this book, and as brief as it will be. Coverage of the South Vietnamese government, politics, and economy took up something under 10% of television coverage of the war (not counting the coverage of the South Vietnamese army that accompanied Vietnamization). But this figure exaggerates the attention television paid to the South Vietnamese: most of this coverage was in its own way very American centered. Just as the *New York Times* in the early 1960s spoke of "weak regimes on China's fringes" which "hampered" efforts to "stem Communist aggression," so television throughout the 1965–73 period spoke of the South Vietnamese primarily as a problem for U.S. policy. Most coverage focused on the South Vietnamese government and its urban political opposition; the peasant figured in the news mainly as a victim and prize of the conflict.

Not all coverage of the South Vietnamese government was negative. Journalists often came to identify with and "root" for South Vietnamese troops they accompanied or programs they covered, just as they did with American programs. There were many sympathetic stories about the South Vietnamese, and indeed many stories that exuded a naive and somewhat paternalistic enthusiasm for the progress of "political development" in South Vietnam. An ABC reporter, closing a report on the South Vietnamese military academy, made the following analogy:

> In the early nineteenth century the young United States was faced with problems of war, pacification, the extension of government control, and the development of natural resources. Graduates of the Military Academy at West Point played key roles in solving these problems. Hopefully history will repeat itself in South Vietnam.[102]

There was, however, a heavy emphasis on corruption in the South Vietnamese government, on political conflict, and later on worsening relations with the Americans, and it seems most likely that the main effect of this coverage was to feed American war-weariness, the sense that American lives were being wasted. Beyond that, Americans did not learn much from television about South Vietnamese of any political coloring, Anti-Communist, Communist, or otherwise.

Americans went into Vietnam assuming the conflict there had two sides, "our" side and the Communists'. But South Vietnam was divided along many lines. There were, for one thing, many personal rivalries which periodically led to political trouble. And there was also a good deal of antiwar sentiment, often favoring negotiation with the NLF (which was itself not an altogether monolithic organization), of anti-American sentiment, and of political opposition to the authoritarian Thieu/Ky government which the United States backed, in one form or another, from late 1965 through the end of the war. The sharpest poliltical conflict occurred in the spring of 1966, when dissident troops took over the cities of Hué and Danang and the Buddhist Struggle Movement launched protests across South Vietnam, directed both at the Ky government and at its American backers. There was another wave of self-immolations and a brief civil war within a civil war before Ky regained control.

Only fragments of television coverage of South Vietnamese politics prior to 1968 are available, but these suggest two things. First, television was hostile to the political opposition in South Vietnam, portraying it, like the antiwar movement at home, as a threat to law and order ("once again the forces of anarchy in Vietnam are on the march"[103]) and treating the whole political conflict as a distraction from the fight against the Communists. (Administration officials were spreading the word— falsely—that the protests were instigated by Communist agents, and had some success with the media.[104]) Second, the South Vietnamese government was apparently successful in legitimating itself through elections, at least to judge from the available CBS coverage of the Constituent Assembly elections in September 1966.[105] Virtually nothing is said in the few stories available for analysis about the content of the opposition's grievances against the government.[106] Here are two examples of television coverage from 1966.

CBS, May 15, 1966, Marvin Kalb. Among high administration officials tonight there is the deepest fear that South Vietnam may be on the verge of a new kind of civil war, in which anti-Communist forces will be fighting against one another. Almost invariably, this will help the Communists.

CBS, August 15, 1966, Richard C. Hottelet. Right now the Communists and dissidents of various kinds are trying to persuade people to boycott the election. . . . Cases of threat and terror are reported in increasing number. If the people turn out in a large vote in spite of this, it will be a vote against the Vietcong and for the constitution.

The CBS rundown sheet for the eve of the election (a full transcript is not available) bills the story as, "Vietnamese vote for the first time democratically while Vietcong terrorist [*sic*] continue anti-election activities and many were wounded in Saigon." A more important election was held in 1967 (pro-Communist and "neutralist" candidates were barred from running and restrictions on the ability of opposition candidates to campaign were many, but the election was clean enough that the Thieu/Ky ticket managed only a plurality of 35%). Transcripts of the reporting of that election are not available, however.

Coverage after 1968 was no more substantial in its representation of the political lines of division in South Vietnam. But it is clear that the South Vietnamese government had relatively bad press in that period. Three themes contributed to the negative image of the South Vietnamese government. First, there were reports on incompetence and, most important, corruption in the government. A typical bit of narration sounded like this, "Theft and corruption are so common in South Vietnam they've become a cliché. But surely stealing from hungry refugees reaches a low point in heartlessness."[107] Second, there were reports on dissent, repression, and political conflict (Thieu had cracked down on the opposition after his poor showing in the 1967 election). And, third, there were reports on increasing tensions between the Thieu government and the Americans, as the United States moved toward what amounted to a separate peace with North Vietnam. South Vietnamese reluctance to go along with that peace prompted Frank Reynolds to say of Vice President Ky in a 1969 commentary, "With friends like him, who needs enemies?"[108] This is perhaps as good an illustration as any of how little Americans had learned about the Vietnamese in more than a decade of fighting with and against them: just as reporters reacted

Table 10   Positive and Negative
References to Democracy in South Vietnam,
Performance of South Vietnamese Government,
U.S./South Vietnamese Relations, After Tet Offensive

	Positive References	Negative References
Democracy in South Vietnam	3.5	37.0
Performance of GVN	7.5	10.5
U.S./Vietnamese relations	7.5	33.5

with indignation when the North Vietnamese and NLF refused to be "reasonable" and surrender the aims of forty years of war so that the United States could have "peace with honor," they often reacted similarly when their former allies stood in the way of American extrication from the war.

Table 10 shows the balance of positive and negative references (defined as in Table 7, above) in coverage falling within these three themes. The last set of figures, for U.S./Vietnamese relations, includes stories not only on relations between the two governments, but also, for instance, on demonstrations against the U.S. presence and on tensions between U.S. troops and South Vietnamese troops or civilians.

Again, The Great Debate that Wasn't: A Last Look at Objective Journalism

In December 1968 the *CBS Evening News* included an unusual two-part special report on the pacification program.[109] CBS had chosen its topic well. "Pacification" involved the struggle for political support or hegemony in the villages of South Vietnam, and this was what the war was ultimately about—or at least had been when it started. So here was an opportunity, at an important point of transition between two administrations, to pause and take another look at the roots and implications of the war. The report was unusually long for television, a total of thirteen minutes, and it included a long interview with a critic of administration policy (Senator John Tunney of California), a sign that perhaps the old tendency simply to report how official policy was being carried out might be giving way at last to a real discussion of what American policy should be.

How did CBS pose the issues raised by pacification? Here are Walter

Cronkite's introduction to the report and correspondent Murray Fromson's wrap-ups to the two segments:

> *Cronkite.* American officials in Saigon came up with their most optimistic pacification report of the war today. They said that almost three-fourths of South Vietnam's seventeen million people now live in relatively secure areas controlled by the Saigon government. . . . Tonight we look at one of [the] contested areas.
>
> *Fromson (concluding Part I).* So pacification does not stand still. It moves forward, it moves back. But what is the balance? What is the trend . . . ? An effort is being made to measure this, and we'll look at the measurements in our next report.
>
> *Fromson (concluding Part II).* Another offensive by the Communists would undermine the program. . . . But the momentum seems to be in the other direction. Since the November 1 bombing halt government and U.S. troops have taken over nearly 800 hamlets. . . . The goal is to occupy another 300 of these hamlets by the anniversary of the Tet offensive.

There was no great debate here, nor any reexamination of the roots of the war. The story was structured from beginning to end around the question of the *effectiveness* of existing policy. Reporting on the deaths of two civilians, killed when an American tank fired into the village, Fromson said, "What may be regarded as a military necessity also creates problems for the pacification team." The whole of Part II was devoted to the computerized Hamlet Evaluation System (HES), which produced the official figures on the progress of pacification. That was where Senator Tunney came in: he was not there to debate the wisdom of the justice of American policy in Vietnam, but simply to offer an opposing view on the accuracy of the figures produced by HES. At one point Fromson broached the important question of *why* the peasants of the village chose sides as they did—and not always as Americans assumed they should. "Out of fear or perhaps genuine disbelief in the government," he said, "well over half the people in Ku Chi are still influenced by the Communists." But he quickly dropped the issue, and canceled the doubts potentially raised by the phrase "genuine disbelief in the government": "The hope of winning them over depends on security," he continued, and went on to discuss the effectiveness of the local militias being organized by the government to help "break the grip" of the Vietcong.

Why this purely "technical" approach to a story that could so easily have served as a vehicle to explore more fundamental issues? Surely one reason is simply that it is easier. It is undeniably difficult for a reporter to go into a culture very different from his or her own, in a situation of political conflict vastly different from the American experience, and say anything very substantial about the causes of the conflict or its meaning to the people involved. Add to this the fact that— Vietnam being a limited war for Americans—reporters, like soldiers, served limited tours (television correspondents often served only six months, rarely much more than a year),[110] and that almost none spoke Vietnamese (though at least one member of a three-man television crew almost always would), and it is not surprising that journalists fell back on simpler issues.

But the tendency to analyze events in terms of strategy and tactics, success and failure, "momentum" and lack of momentum is not confined to situations where the reporters are relatively ignorant outsiders. It is a general characteristic of news analysis in American journalism, most evident, in fact, in the reporting of the story reporters know best, that of the presidential election.[111] The focus on tactics and effectiveness in coverage of the antiwar movement is another example. It is related to objectivity, and brings us around to a last look at the political consequences of the conventions of objective journalism.

Here is one final way of posing the dilemma of objectivity: on the one hand the journalist is supposed to adopt, as Lippmann put it, an attitude of "disinterested realism"; on the other hand the journalist is expected to explain the news at least to some degree, to provide background and context, and this expectation is strongest in a period like the post-Tet period of the Vietnam War, when political elites are at odds and the world seems out of joint. So the journalist has to provide interpretation and analysis without appearing to depart from objectivity. And the easiest way to accomplish this is to focus on "technical" questions that do not embroil the journalist in the conflicts of interest, perspective, and value that are the dangerous stuff of political life. It is much easier to discuss with an attitude of "disinterested realism" the accuracy of the HES than, for example, the question of whether American intervention in Vietnam was ultimately good or bad for the Vietnamese peasant.

Journalists do not, of course, only report and analyze events. They also report what people of various kinds *say* about events. But the debate over the war, as it appeared on television, was also very narrow in focus. No doubt this was due both to the quality of the debate itself and to the journalists' standards of newsworthiness. It was, as we have seen, the debate in Washington that dominated news coverage, at least as far as substantial discussion of the war is concerned. There were periods when this debate burst the normal bounds of political discussion; at the 1968 Democratic Convention there was a debate over the origins of the war and the question of whether the United States should have gotten into it to begin with. Later on there were periods when the relative power of Congress and the presidency in foreign policy were debated. But the day-to-day discussion of the war that dominated most television coverage was narrowly focused on immediate policy issues: would the invasion of Cambodia get the country into another "quagmire"? Would the Laotian operation destroy Vietnamization? Did that operation violate congressional limitations on the use of U.S. troops? Should the president announce a timetable for withdrawal?

The routines of what I have called objective journalism had particularly contradictory consequences in the later period on the war. On the one hand they continued often to be a source of power to an adminstration which knew how to use them to manage the news. On the other, when the morale of the troops was collapsing or Washington officials were at odds, the journalist began to look much more like the independent "watchdog" his critics and champions so often fancy him to be. The journalist clearly responded to the shifting of political boundaries, extending to a wider range of political views the right to a hearing; at the same time journalistic conventions also set bounds on the range of issues that would be seriously discussed. Many aspects of objective journalism contributed to this narrowing of the bounds of discourse. Two have been mentioned: the tendency to anlayze events in technical terms and the emphasis on official Washington as the locus of political discussion. To these might be added the focus of most news on specific, day-to-day events (discussed in Chapter 3): the issue was, "How is the war going today?" not, "What is this war about?" "How did it happen?" "What can we learn from it?"

This limiting of the focus of the news had two interrelated consequences. First, it meant that the dominant political ideology of American society was to a large extent protected from the threat Vietnam could potentially have posed; here is one more important sense in which the modern American press must be seen as an integral part, not an adversary of the state. For certain parts of the American public, mostly among the college-educated young, Vietnam led not only to dissatisfaction with certain policies or incumbent politicians, but to a questioning of basic assumptions about the character of the American political system and the American role in world politics. There was, for one thing, a questioning of the legitimacy of the foreign policy decision-making process, which resulted in large part from the revelations of the official "management" of opinion we have explored in previous chapters. And there was a questioning of the benevolence of American power: many came to see Vietnam not merely as a "tragic miscalculation," but as an aggressive war motivated by power, com-

parable to the Soviet intervention in Czechoslovakia, which happened
to coincide with the deepening of American divisions over Vietnam.
Some of these issues are now beginning to be debated, and this is no
doubt a delayed effect of Vietnam, resulting in part from the fact that
the generation socialized to politics during the war is now coming into
positions of power. In the reporting of Central America, for instance,
there has sometimes been open discussion of the appropriateness of
the Cold War perspective that has dominated U.S. foreign policy in
the postwar period; there has even been discussion of whether the
American role in the region has been a benevolent or an imperialistic
one.[112]

But during the Vietnam War issues of this sort were simply not on
the news agenda. Never, for example, did I hear an American utter
the word *imperialism* on television. On those rare occasions (rare, that
is, after Tet) when the underlying reasons for American intervention
were discussed explicitly, what journalists did was to defend the hon-
orableness of American motives.[113]

As for the legitimacy of the foreign policy decision-making process,
we have already seen that television continued to accord the administration most of the trappings and privileges of authority that previous
administrations had enjoyed. There was, of course, considerable discussion of the "credibility gap" as well as debate over the power of the
presidency. But the limits of discussion in this area can be seen in the
fact that only seven stories in the sample contained any references—
and this includes reporting of statements by domestic critics—to deliberate government deception of the public.[114] The most substantial of
these was a brief story on the Pentagon Papers, mentioning what the
documents revealed about Johnson's 1964 statement that he would not
send American boys to Asia. Very little of the substance of the *Pentagon
Papers*, however, got into television coverage.[115] The controversy over
the leaking and publication of the Papers, on the other hand, being
"hard news" rather than "mere history," was covered very extensively.

Vietnam fits a pattern that has often been observed in situations of
political crisis: the media in such periods typically distance themselves
from incumbent officials and their policies, moving in the direction of
an "adversary" conception of their role. But they do not make the
"system"—or its core beliefs—an issue, and if these are questioned,
usually rise to their defense; this happened with Watergate as well.[116]

More broadly, the narrow immediacy of television meant that none
of the larger questions posed by the war was raised in any substantial
way in the news. There was no discussion of the origins of revolution
("Guerrilla war, like hives, can break out any time, any place," one

correspondent explained[117]). There was no second look at the doctrine of containment or its application to a conflict like Vietnam: should such a conflict be treated as one "front" in a global struggle? There was no discussion of why this war eventually seemed to contradict so drastically the image of war and the image of themselves Americans held when they went into it: Why the violence that came to be symbolized by My Lai? Why the collapse of morale? Why the hostility of so many of those we thought we were saving, even the ones fighting with us?

The reply television people usually give to this sort of criticism is that lack of time makes it impossible for television to do more than deal with daily headlines, and that that function is performed by other elements of the news media: by documentaries, news magazines, "op-ed" articles, and the like. To this I would make several responses. First, a large part of the public learns of world affairs only from daily journalism; the typical television documentary is shown in a low-rating slot, seen by only a small fraction of the audience for the evening news. The levels of American journalism that are supposed to provide deeper reporting, moreover, including the television documentary, share many of the characteristics that limit the ability of daily news to deal with wider issues, including the focus on Washington's agenda and the technical angle in news analysis.[118]

Finally, though it is certainly true that the time constraints imposed on television journalism by the commercial nature of the medium limit what it can do, the limits that result from ideology, culture, and journalistic routines seem much more fundamental. Television covered Vietnam nearly every day for more than seven years, producing hours of reporting on the war. Some of that reporting concerned events of great immediate significance. But the majority did not: it was taken up with routine battle coverage (several days old because most film was shipped by air); reports on technology; human-interest vignettes about the troops; occasional "light" stories about such trivia as what it is like to parachute out of an airplane;[119] and many speeches and press conferences, relatively few of which were of real historical significance. When one looks at it all in a concentrated period of time, it is clear that a great deal of television's coverage had no significant value as information about the war. The problem with Vietnam coverage was quality, not quantity.

The media probably bear a good deal of the responsibility for the political troubles they have had in the post-Vietnam era. Americans went into Vietnam believing it was a replay on a smaller scale of World War II: a struggle to defend democracy against aggression, which we would surely win, not only because we were more powerful but because the right was clearly on our side. Television held this view strongly, perhaps more strongly than the public itself. It didn't work out that way, and eventually television brought the bad news. But it never explained *why*: it never reexamined the assumptions about the nature of the war it had helped to propagate in the early years. So to the public, the bad news must have seemed nearly as incomprehensible as an earlier "American defeat" in Asia: the "loss" of China. The Chinese revolution triumphed just when the Cold War consensus was becoming solidified, and only a few unhappy souls were so foolish as to suggest some historical development might be taking place in China that could not be reduced to the global struggle between democracy and totalitarianism. Add to this the fact that the United States had clear military superiority at the time, and it is hardly suprising that a great deal of the public should have accepted the notion that treason was the only reasonable explanation for defeat. In the same way, it is hardly surprising that Americans should gravitate toward the view that "loss of Vietnam" resulted simply from a lack of American will, which leads easily to the conclusion that the media were to blame: no more sophisticated explanations were put before them.

6

Conclusion

It is a miracle, in a way, that our people have stayed with the war as long
as they have.   McGEORGE BUNDY, 1968[1]

Did the media "lose Vietnam"? I shall argue that this is not the most
important question to ask about the media's role in that war. But it is
worth taking up initially, in more precise and less sensational formu-
lation. Could American power have been used more effectively in Vietnam if officials had had more control over the media? Perhaps. But the
case is by no means as strong as often supposed.

As we learned in Chapter 4, voluntary guidelines for the protection
of military information worked well. There were only a handful of
violations of those guidelines by the press, and there is no evidence
that the military considered the press a source of significant damage to
military operations. As a strictly military problem press coverage was
entirely trivial compared with, say, interservice rivalries, which resulted—to name only one of many inefficiencies—in predictable American air traffic over North Vietnam.[2]

Officials sometimes complained of diplomatic damage done by press
coverage. But again there is little evidence that this was extensive. The
bombing of Cambodia in 1969, for example, was kept secret, as officials
have later told the story, not only to prevent opposition in the United
States, but because it was believed that Sihanouk and the North Vietnamese would be more likely to protest if the bombing were officially
acknowledged.[3] They were therefore furious when the *New York Times*,
using official sources, disclosed it; aside from the *Pentagon Papers* case,
in which the courts concluded the government had been unable to show
evidence of harm to national security, this is the episode most often
cited as evidence press leaks were harming American diplomacy. But
it is not obvious that it would have been of enormous significance if
these protests had occurred, unless perhaps protests from Sihanouk
made the bombing an issue in the United States (the bombing of Cambodia did not become a political issue until years later).[4] And, in any

211

case, it turned out that neither Sihanouk nor the North Vietnamese did protest. The most significant diplomatic secret of the war was Kissinger's meetings in Paris with Le Duc Tho—and this secret was kept.

So the case would seem to come down to the impact of the press on the "home front." This case can be made in a number of different ways. At times, for example, officials believed that if only the United States could send a clear enough "signal" of its resolve to the North Vietnamese, the latter could be expected to back down. And the ability to project an image of unity at home was seen as crucial to the communication of this signal. But the notion that "signaling" by itself would have induced the North Vietnamese and NLF to give up a goal they had been pursuing for decades seems very dubious—an illusion born of the assumption that the Vietnamese revolutionaries were merely proxies for the Soviet Union and China, and that Vietnam was a limited war for them just as it was for us.

The military generally believed that the war could have been won if the United States had escalated more rapidly and with fewer political limits. And it is certainly true that considerations of public opinion were in part responsible for some of the limitations placed on the use of U.S. military power. Bombing targets were limited, for instance, in part because extensive civilian casualties were seen as politically damaging. And yet it seems very likely that if Johnson had chosen to go "all out" in Southeast Asia, he could have sold that policy to the public, perhaps more easily, in fact, than the policy of limited war. Limitations on the bombing, after all, were at least as controversial a political issue as civilian casualties in the North. The *New York Times* would not have liked it if Johnson had given the military free reign, nor would the *St. Louis Post-Dispatch* or Walter Lippmann. But the *Daily News* (which was calling in 1964–65 for an invasion of China) and the *Chicago Tribune* would have been ecstatic; and my own guess is that the media in general would have been swept uneasily but powerfully into war fever. Indeed, it was in part the fear that the public would respond too vigorously to an unrestrained call to arms, pushing the country into precisely the kind of confrontation favored by the *Daily News*, that motivated the decision to keep the war limited. The Johnson administration chose to fight a limited war not so much because it felt political opposition gave it no choice, but because it was unwilling to sacrifice other political priorities to an all-out war effort, because it feared the war could grow out of control, and because many officials—an increasing number as time went on—were not convinced the expanded measures advocated by the military would bring victory at reasonable cost.

Eventually public opinion did become a powerful constraint on U.S.

policy. After Tet (or, perhaps correctly, after the Johnson administration declined to take the final opportunity Tet provided to mobilize the country for all-out war) political divisions made it impossible for the United States to persist even in a limited war. So in the end one could say that public opinion was indeed decisive, as Ho Chi Minh and many others had predicted it would be.

But it is not clear that it would have been much different if the news had been censored, or television excluded, or the journalists more inclined to defer to presidential authority. It should not be forgotten that public support for the shorter and less costly limited war in Korea also dropped as its costs rose, despite the fact that television was in its infancy, censorship was tight, and the World War II ethic of the journalist serving the war effort remained strong.[5]

A comment Dean Rusk made to reporters on the subject of censorship is revealing. "Unless we are in a formal state of war," he said, "with censorship here [in Washington], there is no point in having censorship [in Vietnam]. . . . Here is where most of the leaks come."[6] Republicans in Washington were questioning the president's credibility on the war long before most television correspondents were. At least a year before Cronkite called the war a "bloody stalemate" and urged negotiation, the secretary of defense had reached essentially the same conclusion. The collapse of America's "will" to fight in Vietnam resulted from a political process of which the media were only one part. And that process was deeply rooted in the nature and course of the war—the fact that it was a limited war, not only in its tactics but in its relevance to vital American interests; and also the fact that it was an unsuccessful limited war, which expanded well beyond the level of commitment most policymakers would have considered rational at the outset.

The behavior of the media, as we have seen, is intimately related to the unity and clarity of the government itself, as well as to the degree of consensus in the society at large. This is not to say that the role of the press is purely reactive. Surely it made a difference, for instance, that many journalists were shocked both by the brutality of the war and by the gap between what they were told by top officials and what they saw and heard in the field, and were free to report all this. But it is also clear that the administration's problems with the "fourth branch of government" resulted in large part from political divisions at home, including those within the administration itself, which had dynamics of their own. In a sense, what is really remarkable, as Bundy observed, is that the press and the public went as far with American policy in Vietnam as they did. And it is hard to see how, short of a real turn to authoritarian government, political doubt and controversy could have been contained much longer. Perhaps even a shift to authoritarian government would not have changed the outcome. It remains to be seen whether the Soviet Union will have the "will" to persist to a clear-cut victory in Afghanistan, even though Afghanistan is more comparable to Mexico than Vietnam in its relevance to Soviet security. Maybe the lesson of Vietnam is not that it is difficult for an open society to fight a limited war, but that it is difficult to fight a limited war against an enemy for whom it is not a limited war.

I have put the word *will* in quotation marks because its use implicitly begs another, more basic question: Should the United States have wanted to persist in Indochina, or to intervene there to begin with? The answer to that question of course depends on a number of others. Could the United States have won at any reasonable cost? How substantial a national interest did the United States have in the outcome of the various political struggles of Indochina? What possibilities of political compromise existed? And, finally (a question which did not in fact affect policy, but should have), what outcome was best for the people of Indochina? My own view is that the United States could not have defeated the Vietnamese revolution at any reasonable cost, to itself or to the Indochinese, and had little real national interest there, the hostility of the Vietnamese Communists to the United States being no more inevitable in the long run than that of the Chinese. I also suspect that while an early Communist government in South Vietnam might have been harsh, as revolutionary regimes usually are for some period, it would eventually, like the Chinese, have moderated and set out on a course of serious modernization within a socialist framework, probably more rapidly if it had come to power while it still had political roots and alliances in the South—before the NLF was destroyed—and through political rather than military means.

These issues carry us well beyond the scope of this book. What can be said here, however, is that they were never seriously discussed in news coverage of the war, not, at any rate, in *New York Times* coverage during the years when the decision was made to intervene, or in television coverage in subsequent years. They were not discussed because the constraints of ideology and of journalistic routines tying news coverage to Washington perspectives excluded them from the news agenda. From this angle the implications of government control over the media looks very different.

There is no doubt that control of images and information is central to the exercise of political power. Once a set of goals is decided upon, there are often, for example, important tactical advantages in secrecy;

this is obvious to anyone who has engaged in negotiations. (There are also important advantages in publicity and credibility; this is one of the dilemmas of modern politics.) But if we learned from Machiavelli that deception is honorable in the conduct of war, we learned from Thucudides that it is prudent for a world power to consider the justice and larger political wisdom of its actions. Politics is not a football game: winning is not the only thing that counts. The wise use of power is as central to the art of politics as its effective use.

I would not be so foolish to as to suggest that an open political process will always produce wise political results. Perhaps if political systems were to move in the direction of more sustained active discussion of political affairs, and a major process of political education were to take place, that would be true, at least when conflicts of interest were not sharp. But that kind of democracy is a long way off. Still, in the case of Vietnam, it seems likely that greater openness would have produced a better decision. Those who imagine that political elites would govern better without the press and the public looking over their shoulders should look back to the decision-making process of the early 1960s that led to American intervention in Vietnam; the foreign policy decision-making of that period is probably as close as the United States can come in peacetime to the ideal expressed by much of the political science of the 1950s, and, now again, by conservatives of the 1970s and 1980s, that after elections "the ordinary citizen must turn over power to elites and let them rule."[7] It is true enough, as conservatives have argued, that every society must maintain a balance between democracy and authority. But in the case of Vietnam excessive authority looks more like the source of imbalance than excessive democracy.

Notes

Introduction

1. Richard Nixon, *The Memoirs* (New York: Grosset & Dunlap, 1978), p. 350.
2. James Reston, "The End of the Tunnel," *New York Times* (*NYT* hereafter), April 30, 1975, p. 41.
3. Robert Harris, *Gotcha! The Media, the Government and the Falklands Crisis* (London: Faber and Faber, 1983), pp. 61–65.
4. "Ban on Press in Grenada Linked to Vietnam Role" (UPI), *Los Angeles Times*, Nov. 19, 1983.
5. David J. Garrow, *Protest at Selma: Martin Luther King Jr. and the Voting Rights Act of 1965* (New Haven: Yale University Press, 1978).
6. Seymour Martin Lipset and William Schneider, *The Confidence Gap: Business, Labor and Government in the Public Mind* (New York: Free Press, 1983); Norman H. Nie, Sidney Verba, and John R. Petrocik, *The Changing American Voter* (Cambridge: Harvard University Press, 1979).
7. Michel J. Crozier, Samuel P. Huntington, and Joji Watanuki, *The Crisis of Democracy* (New York: New York University Press, 1975).
8. Samuel P. Huntington, *American Politics: The Promise of Disharmony* (Cambridge: Harvard University Press, 1981).
9. Much of this literature is listed in Daniel C. Hallin, "The Media, the War in Vietnam, and Political Support: A Critique of the Thesis of an Oppositional Media," *Journal of Politics* 46 (Feb. 1984).
10. Quoted in Edward Jay Epstein, *News from Nowhere* (New York: Vintage, 1973), p. 10.
11. Telephone interview, Sept. 13, 1984. The term *watchdog* was introduced by me: I asked if Reston agreed that the media increasingly came to play a watchdog role during the Vietnam years, and he said no, that they always had. It was the younger reporters—the Wickers and Frankels and Halberstams—who believed the change had taken place.
12. David Halberstam, *The Powers That Be* (New York: Knopf, 1979), pp. 450–51.
13. Jeffrey C. Alexander, "The Mass Media in Systemic, Historical and Comparative Perspective," in Elihu Katz and Tamas Szeskö, eds., *Mass Media and Social Change* (Beverly Hills: Sage, 1981), p. 33.
14. Herbert J. Gans, *Deciding What's News* (New York: Pantheon, 1979), chs. 2, 6.
15. Halberstam, op. cit., p. 578.
16. The phrase is from Douglass Cater, *The Fourth Branch of Government* (New York: Vintage, 1958).
17. Francis Donald Faulkner, *Bao Chi: The American News Media in Vietnam, 1960–1975*, Ph.D. dissertation, University of Massachusetts, 1981, pp. 128–29.

217

18. *Daily News*, Feb. 26, 1968. Here are a few other *Daily News* heads: "GI Who Hungered for a Fight Gets Wish to Go to Vietnam" (Nov. 18, 1965); "Battered Battalion Itching for a Fight" (Nov. 20, 1965); "Cops at Greatest Strength for Vietnik March Today" (April 15, 1967); "Old Glory Flies Over a Hue Fortress" (Feb. 7, 1968).

Escalation and News Management

1. *Public Papers of the Presidents of the United States: 1961* (Washington, D.C.: U.S. Government Printing Office, 1962), pp. 336–37.
2. The account of the Gulf of Tonkin incident which follows is based primarily on Joseph C. Goulden, *Truth Is the First Casualty: The Gulf of Tonkin Affair—Illusion and Reality* (New York: Rand McNally, 1969), and Eugene V. Windchy, *Tonkin Gulf* (Garden City, N.Y.: Doubleday, 1971). See also Wallace J. Thies, *When Governments Collide: Coercion and Diplomacy in the Vietnam Conflict, 1964–1968* (Berkeley: University of California Press, 1980), pp. 41–52.
3. Arnold H. Lubasch, "Red PT Boats Fire at U.S. Destroyer on Vietnam Duty," *NYT*, Aug. 3, 1964, p. 1.
4. Thies, op. cit., p. 43.
5. Goulden, op. cit., p. 152.
6. Ibid., p. 156. Herrick recently told the *Los Angeles Times* he thought probably no torpedo was fired. Robert Scheer, "Tonkin—Dubious Premise for a War," *Los Angeles Times*, April 28, 1985, p. 1.
7. *Pentagon Papers*, Senator Gravel, ed. (Boston: Beacon Press, 1971), Vol. III, pp. 106–251; Thies, op. cit., pp. 21–41.
8. *Pentagon Papers*, III, p. 150.
9. Thies, op. cit., p. 30.
10. *Pentagon Papers*, III, p. 109.
11. On the concept of "frame," see Todd Gitlin, *The Whole World Is Watching: Mass Media in the Making and Unmaking of the New Left* (Berkeley: University of California Press, 1980), pp. 6–7.
12. Richard E. Neustadt, *Presidential Power: The Politics of Leadership with Reflections on Johnson and Nixon* (New York: Wiley, 1976).
13. Samuel Kernell, *Going Public* (Washington: Congressional Quarterly Press, 1985).
14. "Raid from Laos Alleged by Hanoi" (AP), *NYT*, Aug. 2, 1964, p. 1.
15. Peter Grose, "Sabotage Raids on North Confirmed by Saigon Aide," *NYT*, July 23, 1964, p. 1. And see Georges Chaffard, "Des commandos sud-vietnamiennes entraînées par les Americains opèrent depuis longtemps au Tonkin," *Le Monde*, Aug. 7, 1964, p. 1.
16. Jean Planchais, "Les circonstances du second combat naval demeurent imprécises," *Le Monde*, Aug. 8, 1964, p. 2. See also I. F. Stone, "What Few Know about the Tonkin Bay Incidents," *In a Time of Torment* (New York: Random House, 1967).
17. Thies, op. cit., pp. 40, 42.
18. William E. Porter, *Assault on the Media: The Nixon Years* (Ann Arbor: University of Michigan Press, 1976). These were only two elements of a multifaceted campaign against the media.
19. "[S]ome of the higher agents of these media are themselves either among the elites or very important among their servants." C. Wright Mills, *The Power Elite* (New York: Oxford University Press, 1956), p. 315.
20. The story of press coverage of the Bay of Pigs, and of the *Times* decision specifically, has been told many times: Harrison Salisbury, *Without Fear or Favor: An Uncom-*

promising Look at The New York Times and Its Times (New York: Ballantine, 1980); Tom Wicker, *On Press* (New York: Viking, 1978); Neal D. Houghton, "The Cuban Invasion of 1961 and the U.S. Press in Retrospect," *Journalism Quarterly* 42:3 (Summer 1965); Victor Bernstein and Jesse Gordon, "The Press and the Bay of Pigs," *Columbia University Forum*, Fall 1967; Gay Talese, *The Kingdom and the Power* (New York: World Publishing, 1969), pp. 4–5.

21. David Halberstam, *The Powers That Be* (New York: Knopf, 1979), pp. 651–61.
22. Salisbury, op. cit., pp. 153–54.
23. Ibid., pp. 155–56.
24. Ibid., p. 154.
25. See Steven Lukes, *Power: A Radical View* (London: Macmillan, 1974); John Gaventa, *Power and Powerlessness: Quiescence and Rebellion in an Appalachian Valley* (Urbana, Ill.: University of Illinois Press, 1980); Murray Edelman, *The Symbolic Uses of Politics* (Urbana, Ill.: University of Illinois Press, 1967); and the large literature employing Gramsci's concept of hegemony: Antonio Gramsci, *Selections from the Prison Notebooks*, ed. and trans. Quintin Hoare and Geoffrey Nowell Smith (New York: International Publishers, 1971); Perry Anderson, "The Antinomies of Antonio Gramsci," *New Left Review* 100 (Nov. 1976–Jan. 1977); Raymond Williams, *Marxism and Literature* (Oxford: Oxford University Press, 1977); Stuart Hall, "Culture, the Media and the 'Ideological Effect,' " in James Curran, Michael Gurevitch, and Janet Woollacott, eds., *Mass Communication and Society* (Beverly Hills: Sage, 1979); and Todd Gitlin, op. cit.
26. R. Hart Phillips, "Havana Drums Up Fear of Invasion," *NYT*, Oct. 28, 1960, p. 10.
27. David Halberstam, *The Making of a Quagmire* (New York: Random House, 1965), p. 275.

"A Legitimate Part of That Global Commitment"

1. David Halberstam, *The Making of a Quagmire* (New York: Random House, 1965), p. 319.
2. Tom Wicker, *On Press* (New York: Viking, 1978), p. 92.
3. *Pentagon Papers*, Senator Gravel, ed. (Boston: Beacon Press, 1971), Vol. II, p. 36.
4. Ibid., pp. 21–22.
5. Jacques Nevard, "U.S. 'Copter Units Arrive in Saigon," *NYT*, Dec. 12, 1961.
6. Malcolm Browne, interview, Oct. 20, 1983; Stanley Karnow, "The Newsmen's War in Vietnam," *Nieman Reports* 17:4 (Dec. 1963), p. 6.
7. *Pentagon Papers*, II, pp. 102–3.
8. Guenter Lewy, *America in Vietnam* (New York: Oxford University Press, 1978), p. 24.
9. "The docking of the Core in Saigon during the late afternoon promenade hour with thousands watching, was regarded by the [International Control Commission] as a 'deliberate insult' and a 'slap in the face.' " Jacques Nevard, "U.S. Aid to Saigon Irks Truce Group," *NYT*, Dec. 13, 1961.
10. See Daniel Ellsberg, "The Quagmire Myth and the Stalemate Machine," in *Papers on the War* (New York: Simon and Schuster, 1972); James C. Thompson, Jr., Peter W. Stanley, and Curtis Perry, *Sentimental Imperialists: The American Experience in East Asia* (New York: Harper & Row, 1982), ch. 18; and Leslie H. Gelb with Richard K. Betts, *The Irony of Vietnam: The System Worked* (Washington, D.C.: Brookings, 1979).
11. John E. Mueller, *War, Presidents and Public Opinion* (New York: Wiley, 1973), ch. 3.

12. *Pentagon Papers*, II, p. 92; and see Gen. Maxwell D. Taylor, *Swords and Plowshares* (New York: W. W. Norton, 1972), pp. 238–44.
13. *Pentagon Papers*, II, p. 108.
14. Quoted in ibid., p. 82. The story was apparently from an edition of the *Times* not available to me, for I was unable to find it. But it is typical of the period. Cf. "Kennedy Seen Reluctant on Asia Troops," *Washington Post*, Oct. 15, 1961, p. A4; and "Taylor Cautious on GIs for Asia/Departs for South Vietnam—Hints U.S. Reluctance to Commit Troops," *NYT*, Oct. 16, 1961, p. 1. It is interesting to note that reporters often missed or ignored pointedly evasive answers by Taylor that seemed to hint strongly that there was disagreement in the administration. In the *Times* story of Oct. 16—"Taylor Hints U.S. Reluctance . . ."—Taylor was *asked* by reporters to comment on reports that the *president* was reluctant. He replied simply, "Any American would be reluctant to use troops unless absolutely necessary." Taylor's "populous country" remark in the Nov. 4 story quoted below seems equally evasive. Perhaps reporters could not imagine that the administration would mislead them about General Taylor's views; perhaps they thought it was not their place to challenge the president's authority by drawing attention to the discrepancy.
15. E. W. Kenworthy, "President Cool on Asia Aid; Sees Gen. Taylor," *NYT*, Nov. 4, 1961, p. 1.
16. E W. Kenworthy, "U.S. to Help Saigon with More Experts and Planes," *NYT*, Nov. 17, 1961, p. 1.
17. *Pentagon Papers*, II, p. 117.
18. Ibid., II, pp. 78, 112.
19. The story did not appear in the *Times* until several days later, in the fourth paragraph of an AP dispatch: "G.I.'s in Vietnam Observe Yule Despite Peril of Red Guerrillas," Dec. 27, 1961, p. 7.
20. "On one occasion," wrote Malcolm Browne, who covered Vietnam during this period for the Associated Press, "U.S. military authorities reported to newsmen that an Army enlisted man had 'slightly injured his arm,' on 'a training exercise with Vietnamese troops, when he accidentally tripped over a wire.' But about one week later I learned that the man involved was a sergeant friend of mine, and I looked him up at a hospital. It turned out that he'd been on patrol with Vietnamese troops, all right, and he had tripped over a wire. He had tripped because the wire was connected to an electrically detonated land mine, which had blown away half his elbow." "Vietnam Reporting: Three Years of Crisis," *Columbia Journalism Review*, Fall 1964, p. 6.
21. "U.S. Copter Crashes in Combat in Vietnam," *NYT*, Feb. 7, 1962, p. 3.
22. John Mecklin, *Mission in Torment* (Garden City, N.Y.: Doubleday, 1965), p. 115.
23. This was how Kennedy put it in his news conference of Feb. 14, 1962. *Public Papers of the Presidents of the United States: 1962* (Washington, D.C.: U.S. Government Printing Office, 1963), p. 136.
24. Jack Raymond, "G.O.P. Asks Candor on Vietnam War," *NYT*, Feb. 14, 1962, p. 1.
25. *Public Papers of the Presidents*, p. 136.
26. "The Truth About Vietnam," Feb. 14, 1962. James Reston, writing the same day, was more critical.
27. Felix Belair, Jr., "Senators Warn of Growing Risks in Vietnam War," *NYT*, Feb. 25, 1963, p. 1.
28. Halberstam, op. cit., p. 268.
29. Quoted in Mecklin, op. cit., p. 120.
30. Ibid.
31. "The Media's War," Feb. 10, 1982.
32. *NYT*, May 21, 1964.

33. David Halberstam, *The Powers That Be* (New York: Knopf, 1979), p. 449.

34. The argument that the administration's troubles with the press were rooted in the public relations dilemmas of limited war is advanced in a perceptive essay by Philip Geylin, "Limited War in an Open Society," in Anthony Lake, ed., *The Vietnam Legacy: The War, American Society and the Future of American Foreign Policy* (New York: New York University Press, 1976).

35. For a review of the literature on limited war and an interpretation of Vietnam in terms of this literature, see Wallace J. Thies, *When Governments Collide: Coercion and Diplomacy in the Vietnam Conflict, 1964–1968* (Berkeley: University of California Press, 1980). The military was always opposed to this sort of strategy, and actual policy was never entirely clear or consistent. The way the notion of "persuasion" through the limited use of military force was put into effect varied over the course of the war, alternating between a strategy of convincing the opponent he could not win by "slugging it out on the battlefield" and one of convincing him primarily by threats or demonstrative applications of force intended to signal military consequences that could ensue in the future (cf. Thies, pp. 7–8), with plenty of confusion within each period. During the Kennedy period, officials believed American intervention would turn the tide against the guerrillas in South Vietnam on the battlefield, convincing North Vietnam and its backers in Peking and Moscow to give up the struggle there. By 1964 it had become clear that the tide was not turning on the battlefield in the South, and the emphasis turned first to threats and then to the use of "graduated military pressures" directed against North Vietnam. From the middle of 1965 through 1968, the emphasis was once again on the battlefield in the South; and then from 1969 to 1973, as U.S. ground forces began to be withdrawn from the South, it shifted once again to threats and "expressive" applications of force.

36. "McNamara to Join Parley on Vietnam," *NYT*, Jan. 13, 1962, p. 1.

37. E. W. Kenworthy, "Pentagon Sets Up Vietnam Command Under a General," *NYT*, Feb. 9, 1962, p. 1.

38. E. W. Kenworthy, "Prolonged Fight Seen in Vietnam," *NYT*, Feb. 17, 1962, p. 1.

39. Austin C. Wehrwein, "McNamara Warns Soviet to Beware of Limited Wars," *NYT*, Feb. 18, 1962, p. 1.

40. "Robert Kennedy Assures Vietnam," *NYT*, Feb. 19, 1962, p. 1.

41. *NYT*, Jan. 12, 1963.

42. Phillip Knightley, *The First Casualty* (New York: Harcourt Brace Jovanovitch), ch. 14; James Aronson, *The Press and the Cold War* (Boston: Beacon Press, 1970), ch. 7.

43. This point is based on a review of *New York Times* coverage of Korea by my research assistant, Christy Drale. A useful account, which differs in important ways from those of Knightley and Aronson, cited above, can be found in *Battle Lines: Report of the Twentieth Century Fund Task Force on the Military and the Media* (New York: Priority Press Publications, 1985), ch. 3. It is worth noting that despite the censorship (which didn't extend to stories written in the United States) there were security breaches and also a fair amount of "negative" reporting during the divisive Korean War. Control of information was stronger than in Vietnam but clearly not air-tight.

44. Mecklin, op. cit., pp. 129–41; David Halberstam, "Curbs in Vietnam Irk U.S. Officers," *NYT*, Nov. 22, 1962, p. 6.

45. Mecklin, op. cit., p. 110; Halberstam, *The Powers That Be*, pp. 450–51.

46. Mecklin, op. cit., p. 111.

47. Halberstam names a number of his sources in "The Press in Vietnam and El Salvador," *Wall Street Journal*, Feb. 23, 1982. "They were all loyal officers," he writes, "discreet and suspicious at first with reporters, but as their reporting was

disregarded by their superiors, a pattern developed, and they would finally turn
to the reporters and talk with great candor." See also *The Making of a Quagmire*,
passim. Mecklin describes the journalists' sources, whose greater accuracy compared to the information released officially he recognizes, as "plentiful, and many
of them . . . malcontents: resentful aircraft crews who were taking most of the
American casualties, incompetent officials seeking recognition that had been denied in public service, neurotics whose vanity was massaged by the attention . . .
or sincerely indignant officers who believed the Kennedy Administration was leading the U.S. to disaster in Vietnam and were willing to risk a jail term (by com-
promising secrets) to appeal their case to the U.S. public" (op. cit., p. 118).

48. For example, *Pentagon Papers*, III, pp. 20–32; Mecklin, op. cit., pp. 99–105; Dean
Rusk, quoted in Montague Kern, Patricia W. Levering, and Ralph B. Levering,
The Kennedy Crises: The Press, the Presidency and Foreign Policy (Chapel Hill,
N.C.: University of North Carolina Press, 1983), p. 152.

49. This is the impression that emerges from soldiers' comments to reporters following
the exclusion of the press from the invasion of Grenada; for example, David
Smollar, "Pendleton Marines Give News Media Low Marks," *Los Angeles Times*
(San Diego County Edition), Nov. 27, 1983, Part II, p. 1; Robert Dietrich, "Ad-
miral Says Officer Corps Resents Press," San Diego *Tribune*, Dec. 14, 1983, p. 1.

50. Homer Bigart, "Denial of Purple Heart to G.I. Angers 'Copter Men in Vietnam,"
NYT, April 24, 1962, p. 10.

51. Many soldiers in Vietnam resented the fact that their involvement in the fighting
was being kept quiet by the adminstration. One particularly embarrassing episode
for the Johnson administration, which at first tried to maintain the fiction that U.S.
troops were not in combat, occurred in 1964 when *U.S. News and World Report*
(May 4, 1964) published letters a pilot killed in Vietnam had written to his wife:
"What gets me most is that they won't tell you people what we do over here.
. . . We—me and my buddies—do everything. The Vietnamese 'students' we have
on board are airmen basics [raw recruits]. The only reason they are on board is
in case we crash there is one American 'advisor' and one Vietnamese 'student.' "
Quoted in Mecklin, op. cit., p. 116.

52. David Halberstam, "Red Border Bases Plague Vietnam," *NYT*, March 16, 1963,
p. 1.

53. The Green Berets in the Central Highlands seemed to be a favorite subject of
Halberstam's. Similar stories on their activities appeared in the *Times*, for instance,
on Dec. 21, 1962, and Feb. 13, 1963.

54. March 11, 1963. This is actually a Monday. *Times* production workers in New
York were on strike from December 11, 1962, until the end of March 1963. All
citations during this period are from the Western Edition. The Western Edition
was only published Monday through Friday, so the Week in Review was published
on Monday.

55. A good summary of the events of this period can be found in Stanley Karnow,
Vietnam: A History (New York: Viking, 1983), ch. 8.

56. *Time*, Sept. 20, 1963, p. 62.

57. Journalists themselves become self-conscious about their roles, worried about becoming "part of the story," during such periods. See, for instance, Malcolm W.
Browne, op. cit.

58. Kern, et al., op. cit., p. 158.

59. Mecklin, op. cit., pp. 163–64.

60. David Halberstam, *The Powers That Be*, p. 449.

61. A piece by Robert Trumbull in the *New York Times Magazine* concluded, "Official
Americans here, though often impatient with some of Ngo's repressive policies
and his apparent reluctance to effect reforms, appear to have concluded that his
leadership in the present emergency is an irreplaceable asset. Some Westerners

who have made a specialty of studying the Vietnamese mind have suggested that a mandarin is really what most of the people want." " 'Mandarin' Who Rules South Vietnam," Jan. 7, 1962, p. 87. And see Aronson, op. cit., ch. 13.

62. Homer Bigart, "Vietnam Victory Remote Despite U.S. Aid to Diem," *NYT*, July 25, 1962, p. 1.

63. For example, Max Frankel, "U.S. May Call Home Envoy if Saigon Refuses Reforms," *NYT*, Dec. 1, 1961, p. 1; Max Frankel, "Vietnam Reform Is Sought by U.S.," *NYT*, April 5, 1963, p. 3.

64. These data exclude brief filler stories. The three reports counted as political include one on government officials involved in civic action and two on an amnesty program the government had instituted. All could be called favorable to the Diem administration. There were, from time to time, brief hints of stories that might have been covered if South Vietnamese politics had been a priority. On May 17, 1962, for instance, the *Times* ran on page 15 a two-paragraph Reuters dispatch on a series of arrests of opposition politicians charged with involvement in a 1960 coup against Diem. The *Times* own story that day, a report by Homer Bigart on the same page, summarized a South Vietnamese government communiqué reviewing battle activities. The next day, when Diem issued a decree banning unauthorized public meetings, the story again appeared only in a brief AP dispatch (p. 2).

65. "Though most of the reporters had been trained in political rather than military reporting," Halberstam wrote later, "it was an irony of Vietnam that their military reporting was generally a good deal better than their political reporting. They had the best possible military sources in the country, but their political reporting was limited by the absence of serious skilled Asia experts in the American Embassy. The McCarthy era had taken care of that" (*The Powers That Be*, p. 452). It is possible that other reporters had more extensive Vietnamese sources. Malcolm Browne, for example, who worked for the AP at the time, told me when asked about Halberstam's listing of major sources that he, at least, relied much more on Vietnamese ones (interview, Oct. 20, 1983). Browne was one of the few U.S. reporters who spoke Vietnamese.

66. Mecklin, op. cit., p. 172.

67. A comment in Taylor's memoirs, which provide a good account of the period from the point of view of the pro-Diem faction, gives a good idea of the bitterness of this conflict. Of one cable that originated in the State Department he writes, "As if some of the conspiracy-laden atmosphere of Saigon had found its way back to Washington, a small group of anti-Diem activists picked this time to perpetrate an egregious 'end-run' in dispatching a cable of the utmost importance to Saigon without obtaining normal departmental concurrences, an action which created extremely hard feeling among President Kennedy's advisors at a time when he badly needed their harmonious cooperation." Maxwell D. Taylor, op, cit., p. 292.

68. Mecklin, op. cit., p. 169.

69. *Pentagon Papers*, II, pp. 228–32; Stanley Karnow, op. cit., pp. 280–81.

70. "U.S. Affirms Aid for Diem Regime," *NYT*, July 10, 1963, p. 1.

71. "Crisis in South Vietnam Deepens as Diem's Forces Raid Pagodas; U.S. Sees Its Troops Endangered," *NYT*, Aug. 21, 1963, p. 1.

72. Tad Szulc, "U.S. Denounces Vietnam for Drive on Buddhists; Charges Breach of Vow," *NYT*, Aug. 22, 1963, p. 1.

73. The story of Vietnam reporting in this period is sometimes told as though the split between Washington reporting and reporting from the field were crucial. "The Kennedy White House . . . began a publicity campaign to sell Saigon through Washington-based reporters," Halberstam writes. "Day after day the White House could win this kind of confrontation, it had all the great names on its side, it could put on any member of that dazzling administration at prime time to explain how well the war was going" (*The Powers That Be*, p. 450). Whether the big names in

Washington dominated television coverage we cannot now know. It was true that the administration engaged in a campaign to discredit the Saigon press corps through their contacts with Washington reporters (Wicker, op. cit., p. 130; Max Frankel, interview, Sept. 17, 1984). It was also true that much Washington reporting blandly accepted official statements that were directly contradicted by information from the field. On January 9, 1963, for instance, *Times* pentagon correspondent Jack Raymond reported, "Secretary [of the Air Force Eugene M.] Zuckert emphasized that the United States Air Force officers and men do not themselves fly combat missions but train the South Vietnamese in doctrine and tactics." Three months earlier—to take one of many examples of contradictory information from the field—an AP dispatch on an air force plane shot down by Vietcong ground fire (*NYT*, Oct. 17, 1962, p. 1) had reported, "South Vietnam is short of pilots and it is estimated that in 30 percent of all the combat missions flown by Vietnamese Air Force planes, Americans are at the controls." Nevertheless, the image of an "absurd mismatch" between the big names in Washington and the "young and unheard-of" reporters in Saigon seems overdrawn, at least as far as *New York Times* coverage is concerned. Before the Buddhist crisis, the administration simply was not talking loudly enough about Vietnam to dominate the headlines "day after day." The periodic pronouncements that all was going well—like most Vietnam news—tended to appear on inside pages. During the Buddhist crisis, when the Kennedy administration did begin, as it certainly could do when it wished, to put its views on the front page more regularly, those views increasingly converged with what the anonymous sources in the field had been saying.

74. Tad Szulc, "U.S. Spurns Denial by Diem on Crisis," *NYT*, Aug. 29, 1963, p. 1. 76; Taylor, op. cit., p. 295.
75. Cf. Kern, et al., op. cit., pp. 167–73.
76. Ibid., ch. 14.
77. Charles Mohr, interview, Aug. 18, 1981; Halberstam, *The Powers That Be*, pp. 453–67.
78. Taylor, op. cit., p. 289. Whether Alsop's and Higgins's visits, specifically, were "sponsored" or solicited by the administration I do not know. See also Knightley, op. cit., pp. 379–80. Alsop, incidentally, concluded like many others that Diem had to go, and told Kennedy so on his return to the United States. Kern, et al., op. cit., pp. 174–75.
79. Karl Marx, *The Eighteenth Brumaire of Louis Bonaparte*, in *Surveys from Exile*, David Fernbach, ed. (New York: Vintage, 1974), p. 146. It is in the same passage that Marx ascribes to Hegel the observation that all history occurs twice, the first time as tragedy, the second as farce.
80. My own favorite account of the development of the Cold War world view is Daniel Yergin, *Shattered Peace: The Origins of the Cold War and the National Security State* (Boston: Houghton Mifflin, 1977). What I give here is obviously a very truncated account. Many political forces were pushing the Cold War for many different reasons.
81. "What Does Russia Want?" *Time*, April 1, 1946, p. 27. For the story behind this article, see Yergin, op. cit., p. 171.
82. The Soviet Union, of course, had its own verison of this ideology, and the two reinforced each other. Khrushchev's Jan. 6, 1961, speech on wars of national liberation fit neatly into the American view that they were to be seen as a challenge by the East to the West.
83. Daniel Bell, *The End of Ideology: On the Exhaustion of Political Ideas in the Fifties* (Glencoe. Ill.: Free Press, 1960); Seymour Martin Lipset, *Political Man: The Social Bases of Politics* (Garden City, N.Y.: Doubleday, 1963). See also Godfrey Hodgson, *America in Our Time* (Garden City, N.Y.: Doubleday, 1976), ch. 4.

84. See also ch. 4 below and Daniel C. Hallin, "When World Views View the World," *NACLA Report on the Americas*, July/August 1983.

85. Hanson W. Baldwin, "SOVIET POLICY: Khrushchev Presses for Victory in Many Areas by All Means Short of War," *NYT*, Sept. 16, 1962, p. E3.

86. *NYT*, Nov. 18, 1962, p. E3.

87. This information was available to policymakers, but it was among the many bits of information ignored because they did not fit the existing assumptions. See, for instance, Thies, op. cit., pp. 38–39.

88. "Tenacious Vietnamese: Ngo Dinh Diem," *NYT*, May 13, 1961, p. 2.

89. Robert Trumbull, "Taylor Surveys Peril in Vietnam," *NYT*, Oct. 20, 1961, p. 6.

90. Homer Bigart, "U.S. Role in Vietnam," *NYT*, April 1, 1962, p. E5.

91. Homer Bigart, "Villagers Cheer Diem During Tour," April 15, 1962, p. 9.

92. For example, David Halberstam, "In Vietnam: 'Not Bad,' " *NYT*, March 11, 1963, p. 13.

93. Homer Bigart, "Peasants Resist Shift by South Vietnam," *NYT*, April 20, 1962, p. 2.

94. Robert Trumbull, "Red Guerrillas War on South Vietnam," *NYT*, March 16, 1961, p. 1.

95. "Friction Affects Vietnam Fighting" (AP), *NYT*, Aug. 19, 1962, p. 3.

96. David Halberstam, "G.I.'s Set Up a Training Camp in Midst of Vietcong Sanctuary," *NYT*, Feb. 13, 1963, p. 3.

97. Robert Trumbull, "Vietnam Conflict Feeds on Unrest," *NYT*, May 28, 1961, p. 6.

98. Samuel L. Popkin, *The Rational Peasant: The Political Economy of Rural Society in Vietnam* (Berkeley: University of California Press, 1979); Jeffrey Race, *War Comes to Long An: Revolutionary Conflict in a Vietnamese Province* (Berkeley: University of California Press, 1972). Popkin and Race emphasize, as I have here, the appeal of the Communists to the "material" interests of the peasants. There is another school of thought that emphasizes their appeal to the political traditions of the village; this school is represented by John T. McAlister and Paul Mus, *The Vietnamese and Their Revolution* (New York: Harper & Row, 1970), and Francis FitzGerald, *Fire in the Lake: The Vietnamese and the Americans in Vietnam* (Boston: Little, Brown, 1972). See also Douglas Pike, *Viet Cong: The Organization and Technique of the National Liberation Front of South Vietnam* (Cambridge: MIT Press, 1966).

99. "The lessons of Long An," writes Jeffrey Race, "are that violence can destroy, but cannot build: violence may explain the cooperation of a few individuals, but it cannot explain the cooperation of a whole social class, for this would involve us in the contradiction of 'Who is to coerce the coercers?' " (op. cit., p. 196).

100. Terror tended to be directed, according to Race, at both the best and the worst, the most and the least corrupt government officals (ibid., pp. 83–84; Pike, op. cit., pp. 246–52).

101. Homer Bigart, "Safety Improving in Rural Vietnam," *NYT*, Feb. 19, 1962, p. 10. On Thao, see Karnow, Vietnam, p. 38. The other reference was in an AP story on the guerrillas, which explained that most fought either because they had been offered land in the future or because the Vietcong had threatened them or their families. "Vietcong Rebel: Small and Wary," *NYT*, June 16, 1962, p. 4. The *New York Times Magazine* also ran an article by stringer Jerry A. Rose, "The Peasant is the Key to Vietnam," April 8, 1962.

102. Milton E. Osborne, *Strategic Hamlets in South Vietnam* (Ithaca, N.Y.: The Cornell University Southeast Asia Program, 1965), pp. 63–66. The discussion of Strategic Hamlets here is based primarily on Osborne; Race, op. cit.; and Douglas Blaufarb, *The Counterinsurgency Era: U.S. Doctrine and Performance, 1950 to the Present* (New York: Free Press, 1977).

103. To quote Race again, "The lesson of Long An is that what was attacked was a particular form of social organization, and only consequentially the government itself. But because the government relied on a certain constellation of social forces, it died when its host died." Op. cit., p. 208.

"It Does Not Imply Any Change of Policy Whatever"

1. *Pentagon Papers,* Senator Gravel, ed. (Boston: Beacon Press, 1971), Vol. III, p. 703.
2. James Reston, *The Artillery of the Press: Its Influence on American Foreign Policy* (New York: Harper & Row, 1967), p. 63.
3. *Pentagon Papers* II, p. 182.
4. Ibid., III, p. 485.
5. *Public Papers of the Presidents of the United States: 1965* (Washington, D.C.: U.S. Government Printing Office, 1966), Vol. 2, pp. 794–95.
6. Ibid., p. 801.
7. James Reston, "Washington: The Undeclared and Unexplained War," *NYT*, Feb. 14, 1965.
8. John D. Morris, "House, 408–7, Votes Funds for Vietnam," *NYT*, May 6, 1965, p. 1.
9. John E. Mueller, *War, Presidents and Public Opinion* (New York: Wiley, 1973), p. 81.
10. "Washington: The Undeclared and Unexplained War," loc. cit.
11. Tom Wicker, interview, Sept. 11, 1984.
12. Kate Webb, *On the Other Side: 23 Days with the Viet Cong* (New York: Quadrangle, 1972), pp. 103–4.
13. Alexis de Tocqueville, *Democracy in America* (Garden City, N.Y.: Doubleday, 1969), p. 182.
14. Chalmers Roberts, *The Washington Post: The First Hundred Years* (New York: Houghton Mifflin, 1977), p. 5.
15. Ibid.
16. Ibid.
17. Michael Schudson, *Discovering the News: A Social History of American Newspapers* (New York: Basic Books, 1978). See also Anthony Smith, *Goodbye Gutenberg: The Newspaper Revolution of the 1980's* (New York: Oxford University Press, 1980), ch. 5.
18. Lincoln Steffens, *Autobiography* (New York: Harcourt, Brace and World, 1931), p. 317.
19. Quoted in Schudson, op. cit., p. 154.
20. *Columbia Journalism Review,* July/August 1982, p. 26.
21. Schudson, op. cit., pp. 156–57.
22. Cf. Gaye Tuchman, "Objectivity as a Strategic Ritual: An Examination of Newsmen's Notions of Objectivity," *American Journal of Sociology* 78:3 (Nov. 1972).
23. Peter Arnett, for example, who covered Vietnam for the Associated Press for many years, gave an impassioned defense of what he called "establishment journalism" in an interview with the author, August 1979.
24. Bernard Cohen, *The Press and Foreign Policy* (Princeton: Princeton University Press, 1963). See also Robert Batscha, *Foreign Affairs News and the Broadcast Journalist* (New York: Praeger, 1975).
25. Discussion of the professional ideology of American journalism can be found in Leon V. Sigal, *Reporters and Officials: The Organization and Politics of Newsmaking* (Lexington, Mass.: D. C. Heath, 1973); Stephen Hess, *The Washington Reporters* (Washington, D.C.: Brookings, 1981); Herbert J. Gans, *Deciding What's*

News (New York: Pantheon, 1979), ch. 6; and John W. C. Johnstone, Edward J. Slawski, and William W. Bowman, *The News People: A Sociological Portrait of American Journalists and Their Work* (Urbana, Ill.: University of Illinois Press, 1976); as well as in many of the works cited above.

26. Wicker interview.
27. Sigal, op. cit., ch. 6.
28. Robert Weissberg, *Public Opinion and Popular Government* (Englewood Cliffs, N.J.: Prentice-Hall, 1976), 234–37.
29. See Schudson, op. cit., pp. 144–59.
30. About 25% of the public reads the average editorial, according to a study commissioned by the American Newspaper Publishers' Association, and about 20% the average political column. The general average for all types of content in this study was 25%. Assuming that readership of the front page is much higher than average, readership of the front page is obviously much greater than readership of editorials and columns. The data are from Galen Rarick, ed., *News Research for Better Newspapers* (Washington, D.C.: ANPA Foundation, 1975), Vol. 7, pp. 35–39. Studies of the impact of news on public opinion have generally found front page content a powerful predictor, though none have compared it directly with the editorial page. See Richard A. Brody and Benjamin I. Page, "The Impact of Events on Presidential Popularity: The Johnson and Nixon Administrations," in Aaron Wildavsky, ed.; *Perspectives on the Presidency* (Boston: Little, Brown, 1975); Arthur H. Miller, Lutz Erbring, and Edie N. Goldenberg, "Type-set Politics: Impact of Newspapers on Public Conference," *American Political Science Review* 73:1 (1979). Given what we know about the effects of mass communication on political beliefs in general, it make sense that the front page should have greater impact than columns or editorials: people are less affected by media messages they perceive as attempts to persuade than by messages they perceive as informational. See Carl I. Hovland, Irving L. Janis, and Harold H. Kelly, *Communication and Persuasion* (New Haven: Yale University Press, 1953).
31. Joseph and Stuart Alsop, *The Reporter's Trade* (New York, Renal and Co., 1958), p. 5.
32. James Reston, "North Vietnam's Motives," *NYT*, Aug. 6, 1964, p. 8.
33. Johan Galtung and Marie Ruge, "The Structure of Foreign News: The Presentation of the Congo, Cuba and Cypress Crises in Four Foreign Newspapers," *Journal of International Peace Research* 1 (1965).
34. Peter Grose, "Sabotage Raids on North Confirmed by Saigon Aide," *NYT*, July 23, 1954, p. 1.
35. On the administration's "signals" to Hanoi during this period, see Wallace J. Thies, *When Governments Collide: Coercion and Diplomacy in the Vietnam Conflict, 1964–1968* (Berkeley: University of California Press, 1980), pp. 30–41.
36. Rusk's, Laird's, and Johnson's statements are all reported in Hedrick Smith, "President Reasserts Aim to Defend Southeast Asia," *NYT*, June 3, 1964, p. 1.
37. Max Frankel, "U.S. Stressing It Would Fight to Defend Southeast Asia," *NYT*, June 20, 1964, p. 1.
38. Jack Raymond, "U.S. Reinforcing Arms Stockpiles at Thailand Base," *NYT*, June 21, 1964, p. 1.
39. Hedrick Smith, "Rusk Eases Tone of U.S. Warning on Asia War Risk," *NYT*, July 2, 1964, p. 1.
40. *Public Papers of the Presidents*, 1963–64, Vol. II, p. 1164.
41. *Pentagon Papers*, III, p. 251.
42. Robert L. Galluci, *Neither Peace Nor Honor: The Politics of American Military Policy in Vietnam* (Baltimore: Johns Hopkins University Press, 1975), p. 35.
43. *Pentagon Papers*, III, p. 192. Cf. Leslie Gelb, *The Irony of Vietnam: The System Worked* (Washington, D.C.: Brookings, 1979, p. 108.

44. Galluci, op. cit., p. 44; Gelb, op. cit., p. 109.
45. *Pentagon Papers,* III, p. 229.
46. Charles Mohr, "Johnson Directs Taylor to Press Vietnam on War," *NYT*, Dec. 2, 1964, p. 1.
47. Larry Berman, *Planning a Tragedy* (New York: W. W. Norton, 1982), p. 35.
48. Max Frankel, "Campaign Effect on Vietnam Policy is Denied by Rusk," *NYT*, Oct. 9, 1964, p. 1.
49. James Reston, "What Are Our War Aims in South Vietnam?" *NYT*, Oct. 2, 1964, p. 36; Hanson W. Baldwin, "U.S. Weighs Vietnam Course," Nov. 29, 1964, Sec. V, p. 5.
50. Reston, "What Are Our War Aims?"
51. "President Calls U.S. Open-Minded on Nuclear Fleet; Also Joins in Putting Damper on Idea of Wider Vietnam War," *NYT*, Nov. 29, 1964, p. 1.
52. *Pentagon Papers*, III, p. 193.
53. Ibid., p. 202.
54. Berman, op. cit., p. 36.
55. Gelb, op. cit., p. 117; cf. *Pentagon Papers*, III, p. 296.
56. Berman, op. cit., p. 37.
57. Tom Wicker, "U.S. Jets Attack North Vietnam in Reprisal for Vietcong Raids," *NYT*, Feb. 8, 1965, p. 1.
58. Charles Mohr, "Questions on Air Strikes," *NYT*, Feb. 8, p. 14. Mohr's information on the carriers was just slightly out of date: two had been removed after the DESOTO patrol had been canceled, according to Galluci, op. cit., p. 45.
59. "Reprisal in Vietnam," *NYT*, Feb. 8, 1965, p. 24.
60. Tad Szulc, "U.S. Widens Basis for Retaliation," *NYT*, Feb. 10, 1965, p. 9.
61. *Pentagon Papers*, III, p. 323.
62. Max Frankel, "U.S. Stops Raids to Assess Effect," *NYT*, Feb. 9, 1965, p. 1.
63. *Pentagon Papers*, III, p. 309. When Bundy had left for Saigon, Max Frankel had reported that a growing sense of "pessimism and frustration" over Vietnam "was said . . . to account" for his trip. "Rising Pessimism on Vietnam Spurs Mission by Bundy," *NYT*, Feb. 3, 1965, p. 1. This earlier reporting was not referred to when Bundy returned.
64. James Reston, "Tension and Restraint," *NYT*, Feb. 9, 1965, p. 13.
65. Szulc, "U.S. Widens Basis for Retaliation."
66. Hanson W. Baldwin, "Value of U.S. Raids," *NYT*, Feb. 10, 1965, p. 8.
67. Tom Wicker, "Peril for Washington," *NYT*, Feb. 11, 1965, p. 12.
68. Max Frankel, "Capital Debates Policy on Raids," *NYT*, Feb. 13, 1965, p. 1.
69. Max Frankel, "China and U.S.—A Continuing Struggle for Asia," *NYT*, Feb. 14, 1965, p. E3.
70. *Pentagon Papers*, III, p. 324.
71. Max Frankel, interview, Sept. 17, 1984.
72. Max Frankel, "U.S. White Paper Brands Hanoi as 'Aggressor' and Hints at Air Attacks," *NYT*, Feb. 27, 1965, p. 1.
73. John W. Finney, "Hanoi Aggression Detailed by U.S. in White Paper," *NYT*, Feb. 28, 1965, p. 1.
74. "Storm Signals Over Asia," *NYT*, Feb. 28, 1965.
75. James C. Thompson, Jr., Peter W. Stanley, and Curtis Perry, *Sentimental Imperialists: The American Experience in East Asia* (New York: Harper & Row, 1981), pp. 262–63; James C. Thompson, interview, Oct. 24, 1983.
76. E. W. Kenworthy, "Johnson's Policy in Vietnam—Four Positions in Congress," *NYT*, July 25, 1965, p. E3.
77. Max Frankel, "Future of the Teach-In," *NYT*, May 17, 1965, p. 3.
78. Max Frankel, "Bundy Says U.S. Must Block Reds," *NYT*, June 21, 1965, p. 1;

Max Frankel, "Vietnam Debate Heard on 100 Campuses," May 16, 1965, p. 1; "Debate Sponsors Challenge Bundy to New Teach-In," May 17, 1965, p. 1.

79. Berman, op. cit., and Galluci, op. cit., are among the strongest statements of this view.

80. For example, Peter Grose, "Hanoi's Objectives," *NYT*, March 10, 1965, p. 4.

81. "Kennan Bids U.S. Reduce Asia Role," *NYT*, Feb. 26, 1965, p. 3; see also Felix Belair, Jr., "Kennan Cautious on Vietnam Raids," *NYT*, Feb. 27, 1965, p. 3.

82. *Pentagon Papers*, III, pp. 311, 690.

83. Galluci, op. cit., pp. 52–53.

84. See, for example, Gen. Earle Wheeler's assessment, quoted in Berman, op. cit., pp. 51–52.

85. John W. Finney, "U.S. Is Considering a Troop Increase in South Vietnam," *NYT*, Feb. 14, 1965, p. 1.

86. "The One-Way Street," *NYT*, March 7, 1965.

87. *Pentagon Papers*, III, p. 703.

88. Quoted in Berman, op. cit., pp. 57–58.

89. Jack Langguth, "U.S. Army Division Is Expected to Go to South Vietnam," *NYT*, March 13, 1965, p. 1.

90. Tad Szulc, "President Asserts Strategy on Vietnam Is Unchanged," *NYT*, April 1, 1965, p. 1.

91. Charles Mohr, "Johnson Refuses to Halt Bombing; Again Asks Talks," *NYT*, April 18, 1965, p. 1.

92. Max Frankel, "Johnson Renews Bid on Vietnam, Defends Bombing," *NYT*, April 28, 1965, p. 1.

93. Max Frankel, "Hanoi Proposes a Plan for Talks; Washington Cool," *NYT*, April 14, 1965, p. 1.

94. *NYT*, May 19, 1965.

95. Max Frankel, "U.S. Urges Hanoi to Answer Pleas by Neutral Lands," *NYT*, April 15, 1965, p. 1. Cf. George C. Herring, ed., *The Secret Diplomacy of the Vietnam War: The Negotiating Volumes of the Pentagon Papers* (Austin: University of Texas Press, 1983), pp. 107–9. See Also David Kraslow and Stuart H. Loory, *The Secret Search for Peace in Vietnam* (New York: Random House, 1968).

96. Berman, op. cit., p. 61.

97. At the time of the bombing pause, Johnson cabled to Taylor, "You should understand that my purpose in this plan is to begin to clear a path either toward a restoration of peace or toward increased military action. . . ." Quoted in Herring, op. cit., p. 111.

98. Ibid., pp. 120–21. Kohler, who was to deliver the message to the North Vietnamese ambassador in Moscow, believed the message "invited rebuff," and had recommended it be softened.

99. Tom Wicker, "U.S. Raids North Vietnam After 6-Day Lull Brings No Overture from Hanoi," *NYT*, May 19, 1965, p. 1.

100. "President Johnson and his closest advisors," Max Frankel wrote in his April 15 story, quoted above, "have been trying hard to hold down the pace of military escalation so as not to reach the point at which all negotiation becomes impossible."

101. A Reston column of April 25 is a good illustration. "How, then, is this aggression by subversion to be stopped?" Reston writes. "This is the main point." The answer Reston suggests is to "give private diplomacy a chance."

102. Berman, op. cit., pp. 62–63.

103. Tom Wicker, "U.S. Likely to Spur Ground Warfare in South Vietnam," *NYT*, April 22, 1965, p. 1.

104. See also Jack Langguth, "U.S. Forces in Vietnam May Rise to 60,000 in June," *NYT*, May 24, 1965, p. 1.

105. Jack Raymond, "U.S. Command in Saigon Backs Increase in Troops," *NYT*, July 18, 1965, p. 1.
106. Jack Raymond, "McNamara 'Launches' Carrier Strike," *NYT*, July 19, 1965, p. 1.
107. For example, Leslie Gelb, "The Essential Domino: American Politics and Vietnam," *Foreign Affairs* 50:3 (April 1972): "Gradualism . . . was the product of the old consensus game. Everyone was to be given the illusion that the war would soon be over. The Right was to be given escalation. The Left was to be given occasional peace overtures. The middle would not be asked to pay for the war."
108. John W. Finney, "Active U.S. Combat Role in Vietnam Acknowledged," *NYT*, June 6, 1965, p. 1.
109. John W. Finney, "U.S. Denies Shift on Troop Policy in Vietnam War," *NYT*, June 10, 1965, p. 1.
110. This, at least, is the impression one gets from the summaries of editorial opinion published in the Sunday edition of the *Times*.
111. E. W. Kenworthy, "Fulbright Urges a Holding Action in Vietnam War," *NYT*, June 16, 1965, p. 1.
112. James Reston, "Washington: The Politics of Vietnam," *NYT*, June 16, 1965.
113. "Vietnam and the Republicans," *NYT*, July 9, 1965, p. 28.
114. "Build-up in Vietnam," *NYT*, July 21, 1965.
115. "Johnson Weighing Reserve Call-Up to Assist Saigon," *NYT*, July 14, 1965, p. 1.
116. Week in Review, *NYT*, July 25, 1965.
117. Berman, op. cit., pp. 99ff.
118. Hanson W. Baldwin, "Military Disappointed," *NYT*, July 29, 1965, p. 11.
119. E. W. Kenworthy, "Most in Congress Relieved by the President's Course," *NYT*, July 29, 1965, p. 1.

The War on Television

1. Quoted in Michael Mandelbaum, "Vietnam: The Television War," *Daedalus* 111:4 (Fall 1982), p. 157.
2. Michael Arlen, *Living-Room War* (New York: Penguin, 1982), p. 8.
3. The controversy over these broadcasts is recounted in Montague Kern, Patricia W. Levering, and Ralph B. Levering, *The Kennedy Crises: The Press, the Presidency, and Foreign Policy* (Chapel Hill, N.C.: University of North Carolina Press, 1983), pp. 165–66.
4. Mandelbaum, op. cit.
5. Robert Harris, *Gotcha! The Media, the Government, and the Falklands Crisis* (London: Faber and Faber, 1983), pp. 61–65.
6. See, for instance, Guenter Lewy, *America in Vietnam* (New York: Oxford University Press, 1978), pp. 433–34; Peter Braestrup, *Big Story: How the American Press and Television Reported and Interpreted the Crisis of Tet 1968 in Vietnam and Washington* (Boulder, Col.: Westview Press, 1977); and Peter B. Clark, "The Opinion Machine: Intellectuals, the Mass Media and American Government," in Harry Clor, ed., *Mass Media and American Democracy* (Chicago: Rand-McNally, 1974).
7. Mandelbaum, op. cit., provides a good list of places where this view of television and Vietnam can be seen. To it I would add: Samuel Huntington, *American Politics: The Promise of Disharmony* (Cambridge, Mass.: Harvard University Press, 1981); Austin Ranney, *Channels of Power: The Impact of Television on American Politics* (New York: Basic Books, 1983); Martin Esslin, *The Age of Television* (San Francisco: W. H. Freeman, 1982); Bob Greene, "How Do You Fight a War with TV

Looking On?" *Los Angeles Times*, April 13, 1982; Kathleen J. Turner, *Lyndon Johnson's Dual War: Vietnam and the Press* (Chicago: University of Chicago Press, 1985), p. 4.

8. Cited in Ranney, op. cit., pp. 13–14.
9. United States Senate, Committee on Governmental Operations, *Confidence and Concern: Citizens View American Government* (Washington, D.C.: Government Printing Office, 1973), p. 79.
10. Richard F. Carter and Bradley Greenberg, "Newspapers or Television: Which Do You Believe?" *Journalism Quarterly* 42:1 (Winter 1965).
11. Peter Clarke and Lee Ruggels, "Preferences Among News Media for Coverage of Public Affairs," *Journalism Quarterly* 47:3 (Autumn 1970).
12. *Confidence and Concern*, p. 33. Here are the proportions of people responding that they had a "great deal of confidence" in the people running the institutions relevant to this discussion:

	1966	1972	1973
Military	62%	35%	40%
Executive branch	41	27	19
Press	29	18	30
Television news	25	17	41

13. Lawrence W. Lichty, "Video versus Print," *The Wilson Quarterly* 6:5 (1982), p. 55.
14. Lawrence W. Lichty, "The War We Watched on Television: A Study in Progress," *American Film Institute Report* 4:4 (Winter 1973).
15. W. Russell Neuman, "Patterns of Recall Among Television News Viewers," *Public Opinion Quarterly* 40:1 (Spring 1976).
16. For example, Herbert E. Krugman, "The Impact of Television Advertising: Learning Without Involvement," *Public Opinion Quarterly* 29:3 (Fall 1965); Shanto Iyengar, Mark D. Peters, and Donald R. Kinder, "Experimental Demonstrations of the 'Not-so-Minimal' Consequences of Television News Programs," *American Political Science Review* 76:4 (December 1982).
17. Arthur H. Miller, Edie N. Goldenberg, and Lutz Erbring, "Type-Set Politics: Impact of Newspapers on Public Confidence, *American Political Science Review* 73:1 (March 1979); M. J. MacKuen and S. L. Coombs, *More than News: Media Power in Public Affairs* (Beverly Hills: Sage, 1981); Iyengar, et al., op. cit.
18. Ranney, op. cit., p. 5.
19. For example, Michael J. Robinson, "American Political Legitimacy in an Age of Electronic Journalism," in Douglass Cater and Richard P. Adler, eds., *Television as a Social Force* (New York: Praeger, 1975).
20. The sample was stratified by time periods: eight, ten, or twelve dates were selected randomly from each month, and for each date one network was then selected randomly. The Defense Department Kinescopes were sampled more heavily (ten dates a month) because, in part due to limitations of that archive, certain types of stories occur relatively rarely (see below). The 1968 election campaign was also sampled heavily, to permit separate analysis. Statistics combining these sampling periods are weighted to correct for the sampling difference.
21. See George A. Bailey, *The Vietnam War According to Chet, David, Walter, Harry, Peter, Bob, Howard, and Frank: A Content Analysis of Journalistic Performance by the Network Television Evening News Anchormen, 1965–1970*, Ph.D. dissertation, University of Wisconsin, Madison, 1973.
22. One partial solution to this problem frequently employed in content analysis is to use multiple coders, which makes it possible at least to report intercoder reliability

scores, showing the degree of consensus in the coding of a variable. This, however, was a low-budget study, and the expense of that procedure made it impossible. All coding was done by the author.

The "Uncensored War"

1. See Part II, Table I, p. 112.
2. *Pentagon Papers*, Senator Gravel, ed. (Boston: Beacon Press, 1971), Vol. IV, p. 33.
3. See Daniel C. Hallin, "The Media, the War in Vietnam and Political Support: A Critique of the Thesis of an Oppositional Media, *Journal of Politics* 46:1 (February 1984).
4. Quoted in Edward Jay Epstein, *News From Nowhere* (New York: Vintage, 1974), p. 64.
5. Talcott Parsons, *The Social System* (New York: Free Press, 1951).
6. These stories were almost always inside the paper, but at least one had a significant political impact. A widely reported statement by Staughton Lynd, a radical historian who with two other dissenters had made his own peace mission to Hanoi (the *Times* still put *peace* in quotation marks in this context; here we were on the *outer* edge of the Sphere of Legitimate Controversy), that the United States had not contacted Hanoi directly led the administration to disclose the secret contact in Rangoon. John D. Pomfret, "Hanoi Accepted Secret U.S. Note, Washington Says," *NYT*, Jan. 11, 1966, p. 1.
7. Paul Weaver, "Newspaper News and Television News," in Douglass Cater and Richard P. Adler, eds., *Television as a Social Force* (New York: Praeger, 1975); Michael J. Robinson and Margaret A. Sheehan, *Over The Wire and on TV: UPI and CBS in Campaign '80* (New York: Russell Sage Foundation, 1983); Daniel C. Hallin and Paolo Mancini, "Speaking of the President: Political Structure and Representational Form in U.S. and Italian TV News," *Theory and Society* 13:6 (November 1984).
8. For example, Michael J. Robinson, "American Political Legitimacy in an Age of Electronic Journalism," in Cater and Adler, eds., op. cit.
9. Michael P. Getler, "U.S. Navy Fighters Shoot Down Two Libyan Jets;" Don Oberdorfer, "U.S. Has Sought to Pressure Quaddafi," both *Washington Post*, Aug. 20, 1981, p. 1.
10. CBS, Aug. 19, 1981. All references are to the evening news unless otherwise indicated.
11. NBC, Jan. 3, 1966.
12. "U.S. Officers Killed in Blast During Truce," *NYT*, Jan. 22, 1966, p. 1.
13. Av Westin recounts a struggle for time at CBS between New York newswriters, who preferred for Cronkite to tell the news, and the film and tape people, in *Newswatch: How TV Decides the News* (New York: Simon and Schuster, 1982), pp. 72–73.
14. Max Frankel, "Elusive Peace Keys," *NYT*, Jan. 1, 1966, p. 2; Drew Middleton, "Thant Suggests a Vietcong Role in Future Regime," *NYT*, Jan. 21, 1966, p. 1.
15. George C. Herring, ed., *The Secret Diplomacy of the Vietnam War: The Negotiating Volumes of the Pentagon Papers* (Austin: University of Texas Press, 1983), pp. 121–22.
16. *NYT*, Jan. 2, 1966.
17. For example, Jack Langguth, "Brutality Is Rising on Both Sides in South Vietnam," *NYT*, July 7, 1965, p. 7.
18. John P. Robinson, "Public Reaction to Political Protest: Chicago, 1968," *Public Opinion Quarterly* 34:1 (Spring 1970).

19. For example, Michael J. Robinson, "Public Affairs Television and the Growth of Political Malaise: The Case of 'The Selling of the Pentagon,' " *American Political Science Review* 70:2 (June 1967); and "American Political Legitimacy," op. cit.

20. Peter Braestrup, *Big Story: How the American Press and Television Reported and Interpreted the Crisis of Tet 1968 in Vietnam and Washington* (Boulder, Col.: Westview Press, 1977), Vol. 1, pp. 11–12.

21. Phillip Knightley, *The First Casualty* (New York: Harcourt Brace Jovanovich, 1975), p. 23.

22. John Hohenberg, *Foreign Correspondence: The Great Reporters and Their Times* (New York: Columbia University Press, 1964), p. 361.

23. Ibid., p. 139.

24. Ibid., pp. 216–17.

25. The Twentieth Century Fund's recent policy study on the military and the media, *Battle Lines* (New York: Priority Press Publications, 1985), says in its summary report, "Imperfect though it is, our independent press serves as the vital link between the battlefield and the home front, reporting on the military's successes, failures and sacrifices. By doing so, the media have helped to foster citizen involvement and support, which presidents, admirals and generals have recognized as essential to military success" (p. 4).

26. Studs Terkel, *"The Good War": An Oral History of World War II* (New York: Pantheon, 1984), p. 364.

27. Knightley, op. cit., p. 346. See also James Aronson, *The Press and the Cold War* (Boston: Beacon Press, 1970), chs. 7, 8; and, on the political use of censorship in World War II, Fletcher Pratt, "How the Censors Rigged the News," *Harpers*, February 1946.

28. Francis Faulkner, *Bao Chi: The American News Media in Vietnam, 1960–1975*, Ph.D. dissertation, University of Massachusetts, 1981, p. 117.

29. Ibid., pp. 223–28. See also *Battle Lines*, op. cit., p. 66.

30. William C. Westmoreland, *A Soldier Reports* (Garden City, N.Y.: Doubleday, 1976), p. 275.

31. Gene Roberts, "U.S. 'Ground Rules' Keep Rein on War Reporting," *NYT*, July 2, 1968, p. 6. Barry Zorthian, who was Sidle's predecessor, serving as head of the Public Affairs Office from 1964 to 1968, also recalled only four or five security violations during those years. See *Battle Lines*, op. cit., p. 65.

32. Department of Defense news release, Aug. 23, 1984.

33. Faulkner, op. cit., pp. 282–84. Faulkner gives many examples of disputes between the press and the U.S. mission over information and access.

34. No journalist I interviewed ever told me that military restrictions on access had a major impact on coverage.

35. Braestrup, op. cit., dedicaton.

36. Faulkner, op. cit., p. 236. In December, 1967 CBS presented a long report with film of Vietcong bodies being carried off for disposal. CBS received many complaints from viewers. NBC declined to show similar footage. "A Viet Nam Register," *Columbia Journalism Review*, Winter 1967–1968, p. 13.

37. Michael Herr, *Dispatches* (New York: Knopf, 1978).

38. Here is an excerpt from a dispatch from Don Whitehead of the Associated Press, who landed at Normandy on D-Day, recently quoted in the *New Yorker* (Nov. 5, 1984, pp. 37–38): "Snipers and machine gunners were picking off our troops as they came ashore. . . . Wounded men, drenched by cold water, lay in the gravel, some with water washing over their legs. . . . 'Oh, God, lemme aboard that boat,' whimpered a youth in semi-delirium. Near him a shivering boy dug with bare fingers into the gravel." In discussing news coverage in World War II and Korea, I lean heavily on the work of my research assistant, Christy Drale, and on many papers written for me by students.

39. Susan Sontag makes a similar argument about photography in general in *On Photography* (New York: Delta, 1977).
40. Quoted from a transcript of the *CBS Evening News*, Aug. 3, 1965.
41. David Halberstam, *The Powers That Be* (New York: Knopf, 1979), pp. 488–91.
42. Ibid., p. 490.
43. CBS, Aug. 5, 1965, as transcribed by CBS. Robert Elegant ("How to Lose a War," *Encounter* Aug. 1981, p. 78) implies—*insinuates* is probably the more correct word—that Safer staged the incident in a training village, but this contradicts the military's own version, which can be found in Guenter Lewy, *America in Vietnam* (New York: Oxford University Press, 1978, pp. 52–53). Lewy claims that Safer's report did not mention that the marines had taken fire from the village, but Safer did report they had been fired on. Safer's own reports leave it somewhat ambiguous whether the marines burned the village because they took fire or went in initially with orders to burn it. According to Halberstam, it turned out that it was burned at the request of the province chief, because the villagers had not paid their taxes. For a soldier's account, see Walter Terry, *Bloods* (New York: Random House, 1984), pp. 3–5. Vietnamese houses—hootches Americans called them—do not, incidentally, take a lifetime to build; this is a good example of the way a foreign correspondent, reporting on a strange society he or she has known only a matter of months, will often assimilate that reality to a cultural shorthand that will make it familiar to the home audience.
44. Rather was doing a follow-up on Cam Ne, which became the most heavily covered village in Vietnam. "Make no mistake," Rather reported, "they're holding this village by force, not through the pacification program. . . . The pacification program hasn't taken hold in Cam Ne. And until it does take hold here and a lot of other places in South Vietnam, nobody can feel very good about this dirty little war." CBS, Dec. 1965 (exact date not ascertained).
45. ABC, April 13, 1967.
46. Besides the controversy over whether the bombing was good policy to begin with, there was also a controversy over how it should be conducted: many in the military and in Congress complained about restrictions imposed by the civilian leadership. Many pilots presumably shared these complaints, but they did not mention them in on-the-record television interviews. Coverage of "hawkish" criticism of administration policy will be covered in Chapter 5.
47. Murray Fromson, CBS, April 11, 1967.
48. David Burrington, NBC, July 12, 1966.
49. ABC, July 5, 1966.
50. Peter Jennings, ABC, Mar. 8, 1966.
51. Bob Schieffer of CBS, for instance, told me he particularly liked the pilots, because they were "professional" and "daring . . . like cowboys" (Interview, Washington, D.C., August 1978). I should add that Schieffer, as CBS Pentagon correspondent, produced the most substantial piece of reporting on the air war to appear on the evening news for any network, a five-part series CBS did in December 1968, which did cover some of the generally neglected political issues.
52. "From time to time we show reports like that not to show what good guys Americans are, but to show what men are," said Chet Huntley, following a story on troops flying to the rescue of a Catholic village surrounded by the Vietcong, heavy on shots of GIs picking up the village children and giving them candy. One never saw such reports about men who did not happen to be Americans, however. NBC, Jan. 24, 1966.
53. For example, Nov. 1, 1965; Nov. 14, 1966.
54. NBC, Jan. 7, 1966.
55. NBC, Jan. 11, 1966.
56. World War II "was well reported in the sense that never before had so much

attention been given to the individual soldier or sailor with his individual home address and next of kin, but in that sense alone. Of the larger issues of the war, of the way it was fought, of what actually happened both on the home and the military fronts, most Americans, in the service or out, remained profoundly ignorant." Fletcher Pratt, op. cit., p. 99.

57. NBC, Sept. 9, 1965.
58. Peter Davis's documentary *Hearts and Minds* is a good representation of the connection between the ideology of war and popular culture. There is very little scholarly work on the subject.
59. CBS, May 2, 1967.
60. NBC, July 5, 1966.
61. CBS, Apr. 28. 1967.
62. NBC, Sept. 10, 1965.
63. NBC, Jan. 11, 1966.
64. CBS, Feb. 1, 1966.
65. NBC, Feb. 2, 1966.
66. CBS, Jan. 12, 1967.
67. CBS, Apr. 11, 1967.
68. Edward Jay Epstein quotes an ABC News directive to its correspondents in Saigon advising them that "the main source of hard news is the daily press briefing given by the Joint United States Public Affairs Office." Op. cit., p. 250.
69. One decision about the scoring of this measure should be mentioned. Stories are coded for the way they are written, which will usually, but not always, coincide with what actually happened: it is the side that is the primary actor in the story that is coded as having the military initiative. So, for instance, "Marines killed 30 Communists . . ." is scored as U.S. initiative, even if it is not reported who actually started the battle.
70. Lewy, op. cit., pp. 82–83.
71. Since assessments of the overall military situation are often reported in Washington stories, many are probably left out of the sample due to omissions from the Defense Department Kinescopes. It is hard to say whether this would substantially bias the figures, since coverage of both administration and opposition statements is undersampled.
72. Richard Nixon, *The Memoirs* (New York: Grosset and Dunlap, 1978), p. 499.
73. Late in the war, when the issue of participation of the NLF in peace talks put them on the edge of the Sphere of Legitimate Controversy and this forced journalists to use their official name, the anchor would usually explain that the NLF was the "political arm of the Vietcong" (e.g., CBS, Nov. 21, 1970). This would be a bit like Hanoi radio explaining that the South Vietnamese government was the "political arm of the puppet forces."
74, "Aide Says Liberation Front Is Independent of the North," *New York Times*, Jan. 5, 1967, p. 1.
75. "A Viet Nam Register," op. cit., p. 4; Aronson, op. cit., pp. 253–61.
76. I have chosen not to report on significance levels each time a statistical comparison is made in the text or in tables. But almost all such comparisons reported in this chapter and the next are significant at the .05 level or better (usually tested against a null hypothesis of even "balance." In this chapter the exceptions are the figures in Table 2 for comments about the GVN, for journalists' comments about the domestic opposition, and for comments on film about the DRV and NLF. For the latter, if the null hypothesis is even balance between favorable and unfavorable comments, $p < .09$ (two-tailed test).
77. These figures differ from those presented in Hallin, op. cit., Table 7, due to a different, more complicated method of estimating the time devoted to various actors. This estimate is made on the basis of the subjects of stories and is quite

rough, so the exact numbers should not be taken too seriously. A number of different methods of estimating, however, each produced something close to a linear transformation of the figures shown here, preserving the pattern of differences among the figures for different actors. Basically, the estimates used here are produced by adding the amount of time devoted to subjects primarily concerned with the activities of each actor, and then dividing the time in stories that cannot obviously be assigned to a specific actor—for example, those on ground combat or peace talks—according to the proportions given by comparison coverage of the U.S., DRV, and GVN policies (Variable 12, Codes 59, 51, and 41 in Appendix B).

78. NBC, July 8, 1966.
79. The pattern is complicated, however, and by one measure (Variable 30 in the Code Book) there is actually a decline in the proportion of positive assessments of the performance and capacity of DRV and NLF forces, perhaps reflecting the weakening of the latter after Tet.
80. ABC, Oct. 6, 1970.
81. The words actually coded in the sample are listed in the notes to Variable 47 in the Code Book.
82. Guenter Lewy (op. cit,. pp. 450ff.) estimates the proportion of civilian deaths in the Vietnam War at between 28% of the total number of deaths, assuming that all those reported by the United States and South Vietnam as enemy forces KIA were in fact military, and 45% assuming that one-third of them were civilians. These figures he compares with estimates of 40% civilian casualties in World War II and 70% (!) in Korea. By either of Lewy's estimates, television substantially *underrepresented* the proportion of civilian casualties: less than 25% of all references to casualties and about 16% of the wounded and dead shown on film were civilian.
83. William Shawcross, *Sideshow: Nixon, Kissinger and the Destruction of Cambodia* (New York: Simon and Schuster, 1979), figure following p. 216. On the effects of American firepower, see Bernard Fall, "The Impersonal War," in *Viet-Nam Witness* (New York: Praeger, 1966); Rafael Littauer and Norman Uphoff, eds., *The Air War in Indochina* (Boston: Beacon Press, 1972); Daniel Ellsberg, *Papers on the War* (New York: Simon and Schuster, 1972).
84. See for example, Daniel Lang, *Casualties of War* (New York: McGraw-Hill, 1969).
85. See Lewy on the Phoenix program, op. cit., pp. 280–81.
86. Ibid., p. 65.
87. Jonathan Schell, *The Military Half* (New York: Vintage, 1968), pp. 14–15.
88. Quoted from a column by Murrey Marder in Aronson, op. cit., p. 255.
89. Lewy (op. cit., p. 447) presents figures on civilians treated in South Vietnamese hospitals which, based on the nature of the wounds, suggest that while in 1967 a majority of these casualties were caused by U.S. and South Vietnamese action, by 1970 a majority were caused by the North Vietnamese and NLF. I'm skeptical of these figures as a representation of the causes of civilian casualties in South Vietnam as a whole, since it seems to me it is likely to overrepresent those living in government-controlled areas (perhaps the time trend is accounted for in part by the increase in the latter). But no doubt they do capture a significant trend.
90. CBS, Dec. 11, 1968.
91. CBS, Feb. 14, 1966.
92. ABC, Oct. 1965 (exact date not ascertained).
93. For example, NBC, Jan. 11, 1966.
94. For example, CBS, June 19, 1968; NBC, Sept. 21, 1965.
95. For example, CBS, Apr. 10, 1967.

"We Are on Our Way Out"

1. Jean Lacouture, *Hô Chi Minh* (Paris: Editions du Seuil, 1967), p. 143.
2. Herbert Y. Schandler, *The Unmaking of a President: Lyndon Johnson and Vietnam* (Princeton: Princeton University Press, 1977), p. 41.
3. *Pentagon Papers*, Senator Gravel, ed. (Boston: Beacon Press, 1971), Vol. 4, pp. 348–94.
4. Todd Gitlin, *The Whole World Is Watching: Mass Media in the Making and Unmaking of the New Left* (Berkeley: University of California Press), p. 205.
5. The leaks are discussed in *Pentagon Papers*, IV, pp. 511–12.
6. *Weekly Compilation of Presidential Documents* (Washington: Government Printing Office, 1967), pp. 1014–15.
7. Quoted on NBC news, Sept. 25, 1967.
8. Reprinted in Peter Braestrup, *Big Story: How the American Press and Television Reported and Interpreted the Crisis of Tet 1968 in Vietnam and Washington* (Boulder, Colo.: Westview Press, 1977), Vol. II, pp. 3–10.
9. Associated Press, *What You Should Know About Vietnam*, 1967.
10. Don Oberdorfer, *Tet!* (Garden City, N.Y.: Doubleday, 1971); George C. Herring, *America's Longest War: The United States and Vietnam, 1960–1975* (New York: Wiley, 1979), pp. 183–90; Stanley Karnow, *Vietnam: A History* (New York: Viking, 1983), pp. 534–93; Braestrup, op. cit.
11. Samuel L. Popkin, "Pacification: Politics and the Village," *Asian Survey* 10:8 (Aug. 1970); Samuel L. Popkin, "Internal Conflicts—South Vietnam," in Kenneth Waltz and Steven Spiegel, eds., *Conflict in World Politics* (Cambridge, Mass.: Winthrop, 1971).
12. David Halberstam, *The Powers That Be* (New York: Knopf, 1979), p. 514.
13. Quoted in Karnow, op. cit., p. 639.
14. John E. Mueller, *War, Presidents and Public Opinion* (New York: Wiley, 1973), ch. 3.
15. Burns W. Roper, "What Public Opinion Polls Said," in Braestrup, op. cit., pp. 674–704.
16. Mueller, op. cit., 58–59; Richard A. Brody, "That Special Moment: The Public Response to International Crises," paper presented at the 1983 Annual Meeting of the Western Political Science Association, Seattle, Wa., March 24, 1983; Richard A. Brody, "International Crises: A Rallying Point for Presidents?" *Public Opinion*, Dec./Jan. 1984.
17. Quoted in Schandler, op. cit., p. 202. Schandler gives a good account of the origins of the story and the reaction to it.
18. Roper, op. cit., Table 24.
19. Robert Weissberg, *Public Opinion and Popular Government* (Englewood Cliffs, N.J.: Prentice-Hall, 1976), pp. 234–37.
20. "Who, What, When, Where, Why: Report from Vietnam by Walter Cronkite," Feb. 27, 1968, reprinted in Braestrup, op. cit., Vol. II, pp. 188–89.
21. Quoted in Austin Ranney, *Channels of Power: The Impact of Television on American Politics* (New York: Basic Books, 1983), p. 5. And see Kathleen J. Turner, *Lyndon Johnson's Dual War: Vietnam and the Press* (Chicago, University of Chicago Press, 1985), p. 232.
22. Harry McPherson, quoted in Turner, op. cit., p. 220.
23. Quoted in Schandler, op. cit., p. 162.
24. Ibid., pp. 256–65.
25. Ibid., p. 111; Herring, op. cit., pp. 190–92.
26. CBS, Feb. 14, 1968.

27. Quoted in Braestrup, op. cit., p. 254.
28. The transcript appears in George A. Bailey and Lawrence W. Lichty, "Rough Justice on a Saigon Street: A Gatekeeper Study of NBC's Tet Execution Film," *Journalism Quarterly* 49:2 (Summer 1972).
29. Quoted in Braestrup, op. cit., p. 308.
30. The U.S. mission in Saigon, a former official told me, was divided roughly along generational lines, with younger people generally feeling the official claim of victory was, as he put it, "a brave cover story." On the journalists' understanding of Tet, see Peter Arnett, "Tet Coverage: A Debate Renewed," *Columbia Journalism Review*, Jan./Feb. 1978, and Charles Mohr, "Once Again—Did the Press Lose Vietnam?" *Columbia Journalism Review*, Nov./Dec. 1983.
31. Roper, op. cit., p. 689; When the Nixon administration came into office, a survey of policymakers showed an "optimist" group, which estimated it would take the Saigon government about eight years to get the war under control, and a "pessimist" group, which guessed thirteen years. Karnow, op. cit., p. 589.
32. See Braestrup, op. cit., ch. 5.
33. Cited in ibid., p. 403.
34. Ibid., pp. 338–39.
35. Karnow, op. cit., p. 541.
36. Lou Davis, NBC, Aug. 4, 1970.
37. NBC, Mar. 24, 1972.
38. Richard Threlkeld, CBS, Sept. 30, 1969.
39. Richard Threlkeld, CBS, Oct. 1, 1968.
40. This terminology is set down in a fascinating memo from MACV directing the Armed Forces Vietnam Network on "correct" and "incorrect" terms to be used in reporting the war. The term *Hamburger Hill*, not surprisingly, was among those banned. The memo was reprinted in the *Columbia Journalism Review*, Winter 1970–71, p. 37. The media picked up the term *search and clear* to some degree; NBC's Jack Russell, for instance, used it in a story on June 11, 1969.
41. Schandler, op. cit., pp. 273ff.
42. Cited in Edward Jay Epstein, *News from Nowhere* (New York: Vintage, 1973), pp. 17–18. Epstein reports that the memo led to a significant decline in combat coverage, and that seems plausible. Overall, despite Tet, the total amount of combat footage shown in 1968 was considerably lower than in 1967.
43. Excluded from these data are statements coded "other" and those appealing to the authority or sincerity of policymakers, loyalty to the country, and the balance of opinion polls.
44. Guenter Lewy, *America in Vietnam* (New York: Oxford University Press, 1978), pp. 136ff.
45. See, for instance, George Esper and the Associated Press, *The Eyewitness History of the Vietnam War* (New York: Ballantine, 1983), pp. 120–23.
46. CBS, March 21, 1969.
47. Lewy, op. cit., pp. 146–47.
48. Ibid., p. 156. And see Robert D. Heinl, "The Collapse of the Armed Forces," *Armed Forces Journal*, June 7, 1971.
49. ABC, May 28, 1970.
50. Edward M. Opton, Jr., "It Never Happened, and Besides, They Deserved It," in Nevitt Sanford, Craig Comstock, and associates, *Sanctions for Evil* (San Francisco: Jossey-Bass, 1971).
51. Jim Bennet, ABC, April 13, 1972.
52. On Nixon's Vietnam policy I have relied on Karnow, op. cit.; Lewy, op. cit.; Herring, op. cit.; Seymour N. Hersch, *The Price of Power: Kissinger in the Nixon White House* (New York: Summit, 1983); Jonathan Schell, *The Time of Illusion* (New York: Knopf, 1976); Robert Shaplen, *The Road From War: Vietnam 1965–*

71 (New York: Harper & Row, 1971); Tad Szulc, *The Illusion of Peace: Foreign Policy in the Nixon Years* (New York: Viking, 1978); Richard Nixon, *The Memoirs* (New York: Grosset & Dunlap, 1978); Henry Kissinger, *The White House Years* (Boston: Little, Brown, 1979); and H. R. Haldeman, *The Ends of Power* (New York: Dell, 1978).

53. Karnow, op. cit., p. 577.
54. This is illustrated by the reaction of Congress and the press to Nixon's October 1970 peace proposal, discussed below.
55. Haldeman, op. cit., p. 122.
56. Gallup Opinion Index, July 1972.
57. *Statistical Abstract of the United States: 1979* (Washington, D.C.: U.S. Government Printing Office, 1979), p. 375.
58. Howard Schuman, "Two Sources of Anti-War Sentiment in America," *American Journal of Sociology* 78:3 (Nov. 1972).
59. On Oct. 27, 1969, ABC reported results of a poll which showed 80% of the public favoring continued withdrawal, and at the same time 52% favoring reescalation to win. I have not seen the wording of the questions.
60. Daniel Boorstin, *The Image* (New York: Atheneum, 1962).
61. CBS, May 15, 1969.
62. Quoted in William E. Porter, *Assualt on the Media: The Nixon Years* (Ann Arbor: University of Michigan Press, 1976), p. 59.
63. Haldeman, op. cit., p. 122.
64. Herring, op. cit., pp. 223–24.
65. Robert B. Semple, Jr., "Nixon Bids B-52's Resume Bombing After Brief Halt," *NYT*, Sept. 13, 1969, p. 1; Max Frankel, "Nixon and Vietnam," *NYT*, Sept. 13, 1969, p. 3.
66. On CBS, the network I watched for that day.
67. On NBC.
68. Hersch, op. cit., pp. 130–32. Other accounts note that the administration also was not optimistic that massive escalation would succeed in forcing North Vietnamese concessions, for example, Herring, op. cit., p. 224.
69. Gallup Opinion Index, July 1972.
70. W. Russell Neuman, "Patterns of Recall among Television News Viewers," *Public Opinion Quarterly* 40:1 (Spring 1976).
71. Weissberg, op. cit., p. 235.
72. Karnow, op. cit., pp. 627–28.
73. Kissinger, op. cit., p. 980.
74. NBC, June 12, 1969.
75. CBS, July 10, 1971.
76. See especially Porter, op. cit.
77. Herbert Gans, *Deciding What's News* (New York: Pantheon, 1979), p. 187.
78. In the sample for CBS in the pre-Tet period there were eleven stories on Republican opposition, nine on liberal Democratic opposition.
79. Schandler, op. cit., p. 59. "Although [Johnson] never approved the strategy the Joint Chiefs continued to recommend," Schandler writes, "he never completely ruled it out either. He allowed the military chiefs a gradual increase in their combat forces and held out the possibility of a greater combat authority in the future."
80. CBS, Aug. 17, 1967.
81. Nelson Polsby, "Interest Groups and the Presidency: Trends in Political Intermediation in America," in Walter Dean Burnham and Martha Wagner Weinberg, eds., *American Politics and Public Policy* (Cambridge, Mass.: MIT Press, 1978); Samuel P. Huntington, *American Politics: The Promise of Disharmony* (Cambridge, Mass.: Harvard University Press, 1981), pp. 184ff.
82. NBC, Oct., 1965 (exact date not ascertained).

83. CBS, Dec. 8, 1967.

84. Gitlin, op. cit., p. 119.

85. The civil rights movement also found it necessary to "provoke" violence in order to get news coverage. See David Garrow, *Protest at Selma* (New Haven: Yale University Press, 1978). The flag was carried by a member of the U.S. Committee to Aid the National Liberation Front. On the ability of this group to "hype" the media, see Gitlin, op. cit., pp. 118–19.

86. Schuman, op. cit.

87. See, for instance, Schell, op. cit., pp. 127–31. On Nixon's success with the "Silent Majority," a good general analysis is Godfrey Hodgson, *America in Our Time* (Garden City, N.Y.: Doubleday, 1976), pp. 412–28.

88. "How to Be Immoral and Ill, Pathetic and Dangerous All at the Same Time: Mass Media and the Homosexual," in Stanley Cohen and Jock Young, eds., *The Manufacture of News* (Beverly Hills: Sage, 1973).

89. CBS, Apr. 19, 1982.

90. I elaborate on this argument in "Hegemony: The American News Media from Vietnam to El Salvador, a Study of Ideological Change and Its Limits," in David Paletz, ed., *Political Communication* (Norwood, N.J.: Ablex, forthcoming).

91. CBS, June 16, 1967.

92. Philip E. Converse, et al., "Continuity and Change in American Politics: Parties and Issues in the 1968 Election," *American Political Science Review* 63 (December 1969).

93. *Time*, Mar. 22, 1968, p. 13.

94. This occurred in a story on underground newspapers published by GIs, CBS, May 9, 1969.

96. Quoted in Gitlin, op. cit., p. 91.

97. CBS, Oct. 15, 1969. Gans discusses the media's emphasis on the disruption and reestablishment of order in *Deciding What's News*, pp. 53–55. For an analysis of British media coverage showing a similar emphasis, see James D. Halloran, Philip Elliot, and Graham Murdock, *Demonstrations and Communication* (Hammondsworth: Penguin, 1970).

98. CBS, May 1, 1970.

99. Antiwar movement stories are those coded 63 or 66–72 on Variable 12 (see Appendix B). All those with at least one statement coded 21-72 or 81-98 on Variable 40 are counted as containing substantial discussion of the war.

100. ABC, Oct. 7, 1968.

101. I found this consistently in my interviews. And see Gans, op. cit., p. 187.

102. Don Baker, ABC, May 22, 1969.

103. Walter Cronkite, CBS, Mar. 31, 1966.

104. Karnow, op. cit., p. 446.

105. Cf. Edward S. Herman and Frank Broadhead, *Demonstration Elections: U.S.-Staged Elections in the Dominican Republic, Vietnam and El Salvador* (Boston: South End Press, 1984), pp. 81–91.

106. This is not to say television *never* covered the political views of the opposition in South Vietnam. The CBS rundown for Oct. 5, 1967, for instance, shows a story on Buddhist leader Thich Tri Quang. But this is not the typical story on South Vietnamese politics.

107. Tom Streithorst, NBC, Aug. 20, 1972.

108. ABC, July 16, 1969.

109. CBS, Dec. 11 and 16, 1968.

110. Ed Fouhy, interview, Oct. 11, 1983.

111. I elaborate on this argument in "The American News Media: A Critical Theory Perspective," in John Forester, ed., *Critical Theory and Public Life* (Cambridge, Mass.: MIT Press, 1985).

112. See my "The Media Go to War—From Vietnam to Central America." *NACLA Report on the Americas*, July/August 1983.

113. Cronkite, for instance, concluded his Tet broadcast, "The only rational way out . . . will be to negotiate, not as victors, but as an honorable people who lived up to their pledge to defend democracy." Another important occasion was April 1975, when the war finally ended. See Noam Chomsky, "The Remaking of History," *Ramparts*, August 1975; Larry Lichty, "The Night at the End of the Tunnel," *Film Comment*, July/August 1975.

114. The number of references here is a simple total, counting every reference equally rather than minor references as one-half. One of the other references in the total is a particularly good example of what happens to political issues in a campaign story. On June 30, 1972, ABC reported a stement by candidate George McGovern that President Nixon was "perpetrating a hoax on the American people" by promising that bombing would help get back the POWs. Like most campaign stories, however, the ABC report focused not on the substance of what the candidate said, but its impact on his chances to win. The story began, "There had been fears that George McGovern's angry outburst over yesterday's Credentials Committee ruling and hurt the candidate's image. So today it was a calm, confident, and self-assured McGovern speaking out on a favorite campaign theme."

115. Steve Knoll, "When TV Was Offered the Pentagon Papers." *Columbia Journalism Review*, March/April 1972.

116. One study of Watergate found that those who followed the crisis on television were more likely than those who did not to lay the blame on individuals rather than "the system." Jack McLeod et al., "Decline and Fall at the White House: A Longitudinal Analysis of Communication Effects," *Communication Research* 4 (1977). And see David Paletz and Robert Entman, *Media Power Politics* (New York: Free Press, 1981), ch. 9.

117. Jack Perkins, NBC, Sept. 7, 1965.

118. This was true, for example, of the 1971 CBS special *The Changing War in Indochina*, which also was primarily concerned with the progress or lack of progress being made in various areas by U.S. and South Vietnamese programs.

119. Don Baker took parachute training with South Vietnamese airborne troops in an ABC story shown Jan. 2, 1969.

Conclusion

1. Memorandum to Johnson, March 21, 1968, quoted in Kathleen J. Turner, *Lyndon Johnson's Dual War: Vietnam and the Press* (Chicago: University of Chicago Press, 1985), p. 243.

2. James Clay Thompson, *Rolling Thunder: Understanding Policy and Program Failure* (Chapel Hill, N.C.: University of North Carolina Press, 1980), pp. 76–77.

3. Richard Nixon, *The Memoirs* (New York: Grosset & Dunlap, 1978), p. 382; Henry Kissinger, *The White House Years* (Boston: Little Brown, 1979), pp. 249–52.

4. "The reason for secrecy," Kissinger writes (op. cit., p. 252), "was to prevent the issue from becoming an international crisis, which would almost certainly have complicated our diplomacy or war effort." He is vague about what form this crisis would take and how it would have complicated either diplomacy or the war. What he implies is that protests from the North Vietnamese and Sihanouk would cause political opposition at home and around the world, and that the North Vietnamese might become more intransigent in the peace talks. The talks, however, were going nowhere at this point. Kissinger also talks about "press leaks of military operations . . . needlessly endangering American lives." Again he is vague on how American

lives were endangered, but the argument seems to be this: "our bombing saved American . . . lives"; press leaks endangered it politically; therefore press leaks endangered American lives.

5. John E. Mueller, *War, Presidents and Public Opinion* (New York: Wiley, 1973), ch. 3.

6. Background briefing of Feb. 9, 1968, quoted in Francis Donald Faulkner, *Bao Chi: The American News Media in Vietnam, 1960–1975*, Ph.D. dissertation, University of Massachusetts, 1981.

7. Gabriel A. Almond and Sidney Verba, *The Civic Culture: Political Attitudes and Democracy in Five Nations* (Princeton: Princeton University Press, 1963), p. 478.

Bibliography

I. Interviews

Journalists are identified by the news organizations they worked for during the Vietnam period. A number of other people preferred not to be identified and are not listed here. My notes do not indicate the exact date of some early interviews.

Peter Arnett (AP), New York, July, 1978.
Steve Bell (ABC), Washington, August, 1978.
Malcolm Browne (AP, ABC, *New York Times*), New York, October 20, 1983.
Ed Fouhy (CBS), Washington, October 11, 1983.
Max Frankel (*New York Times*), New York, September 17, 1984.
Charles Mohr, (*Time, New York Times*), Washington, August 18, 1981.
Ron Nessen (NBC), Bethesda, Md., August 7, 1978.
Don Oberdorfer (Knight Newspapers, *Washington Post*), Washington, August 19, 1981.
Robert Pierpoint (CBS), Washington, August 17, 1981.
Bill Plante (CBS), Washington, December 21, 1978.
James Reston (*New York Times*), telephone, September 13, 1984.
Dick Rosenbaum (ABC), Washington, August, 1978.
Morley Safer (CBS), New York, October 18, 1983.
Tony Sargent (CBS), Washington, August, 1978.
Bob Schieffer (Fort Worth *Star-Telegram*, CBS), Washington, August, 1978.
Bernard Weinraub (*New York Times*), Washington, December 18, 1978.
Tom Wicker (*New York Times*), New York, September 11, 1984.

II. Personal Correspondence

Malcolm Browne, February 2, 1979.
J. William Fulbright, August 23, 1984.

III. Books and Articles

Adams, William, and Schreibman, Fay, eds. *Television Network News: Issues in Content Research*. Washington, D.C.: School of Public and International Affairs, George Washington University, 1978.

243

Alexander, Jeffrey C. "The Mass Media in Systemic, Historical and Comparative Perspective," in Elihu Katz and Tamas Szeskö, eds. *Mass Media and Social Change*. Beverly Hills: Sage, 1981.

Alsop, Joseph and Stuart. *The Reporter's Trade*. New York: Renal and Co., 1958.

Anderson, Charles R. *The Grunts*. New York: Berkley Books, 1984.

Arlen, Michael. *Living-Room War*. New York: Penguin, 1982.

———. *The View From Highway 1*. New York: Farrar, Straus & Giroux, 1976.

Arnett, Peter. "Reflections on Vietnam, the Press and America." *Neiman Reports* 26:1. March 1972.

———. "Tet Coverage: A Debate Renewed." *Columbia Journalism Review*. January/February 1978.

Aronson, James. *The Press and the Cold War*. Boston: Beacon Press, 1970.

Associated Press. *What You Should Know About Vietnam*, 1967.

Bailey, George A. *The Vietnam War According to Chet, David, Walter, Harry, Peter, Bob, Howard and Frank: A Content Analysis of Journalistic Performance by the Network Television Evening News Anchormen 1965–70*, Ph.D. dissertation. University of Wisconsin, Madison, 1973.

Bailey, George A., and Lichty, Lawrence W. "Rough Justice on a Saigon Street: A Gatekeeper Study of NBC's Tet Execution Film." *Journalism Quarterly* 49:2. Summer 1972.

Baker, Mark. *Nam: The Vietnam War in the Words of the Men and Women Who Fought There*. New York: Berkley Books, 1983.

Ball, George W. *The Past Has Another Pattern*. New York: Norton, 1982.

Barnet, Richard J. *The Roots of War*. New York: Penguin, 1973.

Batscha, Robert. *Foreign Affairs News and the Broadcast Journalist*. New York: Praeger, 1975.

Berman, Larry. *Planning a Tragedy*. New York: W. W. Norton, 1982.

Bernstein, Victor, and Gordon, Jesse. "The Press and the Bay of Pigs." *Columbia University Forum*. Fall 1967.

Blaufarab, Douglas. *The Counterinsurgency Era: U.S. Doctrine and Performance, 1950 to the Present*. New York: Free Press, 1977.

Boorstin, Daniel. *The Image*. New York: Atheneum, 1962.

Braestrup, Peter. *Big Story: How the American Press and Television Reported and Interpreted the Crisis of Tet 1968 in Vietnam and Washington*. Boulder, Colo.: Westview Press, 1977.

Brody, Richard A. "International Crises: A Rallying Point for Presidents?" *Public Opinion*. December/January 1984.

Brody, Richard A., and Page, Benjamin I. The Impact of Events on Presidential Popularity: The Johnson and Nixon Administrations," in Aaron Wildavsky, ed. *Perspectives on the Presidency*. Boston: Little, Brown, 1975.

Browne, Malcolm W. *The New Face of War*. Indianapolis, Ind.: Bobbs-Merrill, 1968.

———. "Vietnam Reporting: Three Years of Crisis." *Columbia Journalism Review*. Fall 1964.

Carter, Richard F., and Greenberg, Bradley. "Newspapers or Television: Which Do You Believe?" *Journalism Quarterly* 47:3. Autumn 1970.

Cater, Douglass. *The Fourth Branch of Government*. New York: Vintage, 1958.

Chomsky, Noam. "The Remaking of History." *Ramparts*. August 1975.

Clark, Peter B. "The Opinion Machine: Intellectuals, the Mass Media and American Government," in Harry Clor, ed. *Mass Media and American Democracy*. Chicago: Rand-McNally, 1974.

Clark, Peter, and Ruggels, Lee. "Preferences Among News Media for Coverage of Public Affairs." *Journalism Quarterly* 47:3. Autumn 1970.

Cohen, Bernard. *The Press and Foreign Policy*. Princeton: Princeton University Press, 1963.

Cohen, Stanley, and Young, Jock, eds. *The Manufacture of News*. Beverly Hills: Sage, 1973.

Colby, William, and Forbath, Peter. *Honorable Men: My Life in the CIA*. New York: Simon and Schuster, 1978.

Crozier, Michel J., Huntington, Samuel P., and Watanuki, Joji. *The Crisis of Democracy*. New York: New York University Press, 1975.

Davidson, W. Phillips. "Making Sense of Vietnam News." *Columbia Journalism Review*. Winter 1966/1967.

Desmond, Robert W. *Tides of War: World News Reporting 1931–1945*. Iowa City: University of Iowa Press, 1984.

———. *Windows on the World: The Information Process in a Changing Society 1900–1920*. Iowa City: University of Iowa Press, 1980.

Duncan, David Douglas. *I Protest!* New York: Signet, 1968.

Elegant, Robert. "How to Lose a War." *Encounter*. August 1981.

Ellsberg, Daniel. *Papers on the War*. New York: Simon and Schuster, 1972.

Emerson, Gloria. *Winners and Losers: Battles, Retreats, Gains, Losses and Ruins from the Vietnam War*. New York: Harcourt Brace Jovanovich, 1976.

Epstein, Edward J. *Between Fact and Fiction: The Problem of Journalism*. New York: Vintage, 1975.

———. *News from Nowhere*. New York: Vintage, 1973.

Esper, George, and the Associated Press. *The Eyewitness History of the Vietnam War*. New York: Ballantine, 1983.

Esslin, Martin. *The Age of Television*. San Francisco: W. H. Freeman, 1982.

Fall, Bernard B. *Last Reflections on a War*. Garden City, N.Y.: Doubleday, 1967.

———. *The Two Vietnams*. New York: Praeger, 1967.

———. *Viet-Nam Witness, 1953—66*. New York: Praeger, 1966.

Faulkner, Francis Donald. *Bao Chi: The American News Media in Vietnam, 1960–1975*. Ph.D. dissertation, University of Massachusetts, 1981.

FitzGerald, Francis. *Fire in the Lake: The Vietnamese and the Americans in Vietnam*. Boston: Little, Brown, 1972.

"Four Saigon Correspondents Ask: Are We Getting Through." *Columbia Journalism Review*. Fall 1966.

Friendly, Fred W. *Due to Circumstances Beyond Our Control . . . .* New York: Vintage, 1968.

Galluci, Robert. *Neither Peace Nor Honor: The Politics of American Military Policy in Vietnam*. Baltimore: Johns Hopkins University Press, 1975.

Galtung, Johan, and Ruge, Marie. "The Structure of Foreign News: The Presentation of the Congo, Cuba and Cypress Crises in Four Foreign Newspapers." *Journal of International Peace Research* 2:7. 1965.

Gans, Herbert J. *Deciding What's News*. New York: Pantheon, 1979.

Gelb, Leslie H., and Betts, Richard K. *The Irony of Vietnam: The System Worked*. Washington, D.C.: Brookings, 1979.

Geylin, Philip. "Limited War in an Open Society," in Anthony Lake, ed. *The Vietnam Legacy: The War, American Society and the Future of American Foreign Policy*. New York: New York University Press, 1976.

Gitlin, Todd. *The Whole World Is Watching: Mass Media in the Making and Unmaking of the New Left*. Berkeley: University of California Press, 1980.

Goulden, Joseph C. *Truth Is the First Casualty: The Gulf of Tonkin Affair— Illusion and Reality*. New York: Rand McNally, 1969.

Goulding, Phil. *Confirm or Deny: Informing the People on National Security*. New York: Harper & Row, 1970.

Greene, Bob. "How Do You Fight a War with TV Looking On?" *Los Angeles Times*. April 13, 1982.

Halberstam, David. *The Best and the Brightest*. New York: Random House, 1972.

———. *The Making of a Quagmire*. New York: Random House, 1965.

———. *The Powers That Be*. New York: Knopf, 1979.

Haldeman, H. R. *The Ends of Power*. New York: Dell, 1978.

Hallin, Daniel C. "The American News Media: A Critical Theory Perspective," in John Forester, ed. *Critical Theory and Public Life*. Cambridge, Mass.: MIT Press, 1985.

———. "The Media Go to War—From Vietnam to Central America." *NACLA Report on the Americas*. July/August 1983.

———. "The Media, the War in Vietnam, and Political Support: A Critique of the Thesis of an Oppositional Media." *Journal of Politics*. February 1984.

Hallin, Daniel C., and Mancini, Paolo. "Speaking of the President: Political Structure and Representational Form in U.S. and Italian TV News." *Theory and Society* 13:6. November 1984.

Halloran, James D., Elliot, Philip, and Murdock, Graham. *Demonstrations and Communication*. Hammondsworth: Penguin, 1970.

Harris, Robert. *Gotcha! The Media, the Government and the Falklands Crisis*. London: Faber and Faber, 1983.

Hasford, Gustav. *The Short-Timers*. New York: Bantam, 1980.

Heinl, Robert D. "The Collapse of the Armed Forces." *Armed Forces Journal*. June 7, 1971.

Herman, Edward S., and Broadhead, Frank. *Demonstration Elections: U.S.-Staged Elections in the Dominican Republic, Vietnam and El Salvador*. Boston: South End Pres, 1984.

Herr, Michael. *Dispatches*. New York: Knopf, 1978.

Herring, George C., ed. *The Secret Diplomacy of the Vietnam War: The Negotiating Volumes of the Pentagon Papers*. Austin: University of Texas Press, 1983.

———. *America's Longest War: The United States and Vietnam, 1950–1975*. New York: Wiley, 1979.

Hersch, Seymour N. *The Price of Power: Kissinger in the Nixon White House*. New York: Summit, 1983.

Herz, Martin F., with Rider, Leslie. *The Prestige Press and the Christmas*

Bombing, 1972: Images and Reality. Washington, D.C.: Ethics and Public Policy Center, 1980.

Hess, Stephen. *The Washington Reporters.* Washington, D.C.: Brookings, 1981.

Hilsman, Roger. *To Move a Nation: The Politics of Foreign Policy in the Administration of JFK.* Garden City, N.Y.: Doubleday, 1967.

Hodgson, Godfrey. *America in Our Time.* Garden City, N.Y.: Doubleday, 1976.

Hohenberg, John. *Foreign Correspondence: The Great Reporters and Their Times.* New York: Columbia University Press, 1964.

Hoopes, Townsend. *The Limits of Intervention.* New York: David McKay, 1973.

Houghton, Neal D. "The Cuban Invasion of 1961 and the U.S. Press in Retrospect." *Journalism Quarterly.* Summer 1965.

Huntington, Samuel P. *American Politics: The Promise of Disharmony.* Cambridge: Harvard University Press, 1981.

Iyenger, Shanto, Peters, Mark D., and Kinder, Donald R. "Experimental Demonstrations of the Not-so-Minimal Consequences of Television News Programs." *American Political Science Review* 76:4. December 1982.

Johnson, Lyndon B. *The Vantage Point: Perspectives of the Presidency, 1963— 1969.* New York: Holt, Rinehart and Winston, 1971.

Johnstone, John W. C., Slawski, Edward J., and Bowman, William. *The News People: A Sociological Portrait of American Journalists and Their Work.* Urbana, Ill.: University of Illinois Press, 1976.

Kahin, George McTurnan, and Lewis, John W. *The United States in Vietnam.* New York: Dial Press, 1969.

Karnow, Stanley. "The Newsmen's War in Vietnam." *Nieman Reports* 17:4. December 1963.

———. *Vietnam: A History.* New York: Viking, 1983.

Kernell, Samuel. *Going Public.* Washington: Congressional Quarterly Press, 1985.

Kissinger, Henry. *The White House Years.* Boston: Little, Brown, 1979.

Knightley, Phillip. *The First Casualty.* New York: Harcourt Brace Jovanovitch, 1975.

Knoll, Steve. "When TV Was Offered the Pentagon Papers." *Columbia Journalism Review.* March/April 1972.

Kovic, Ron. *Born on the Fourth of July.* New York: Pocket Books, 1976.

Kraslow, David, and Loory, Stuart H. *The Secret Search for Peace in Vietnam.* New York: Random House, 1968.

Lacouture, Jean. *Hô Chi Minh.* Paris: Editions du Seuil, 1967.

Lang, Daniel. *Casualties of War.* New York: McGraw-Hill, 1969.

Lefever, Ernest W. *TV and National Defense.* Chicago: Institute for American Strategy, 1974.

Lewy, Guenter. *American in Vietnam.* New York: Oxford University Press, 1978.

Lichty, Lawrence W. "The Night at the End of the Tunnel." *Film Comment.* July/August 1975.

———. "Video versus Print." *The Wilson Quarterly* 6:5. Special Issue, 1982.

———. "The War We Watched on Television: A Study in Progress." *American Film Institute Report* 4:4. Winter 1973.

Littauer, Rafael, and Uphoff, Norman, eds. *The Air War in Indochina*. Boston: Beacon Press, 1972.

Mandelbaum, Michael. "Vietnam: The Television War." *Daedalus* 111:4. Fall 1982.

McAlister, John T., Jr. *Vietnam: The Origins of Revolution*. New York: Knopf, 1969.

McAlister, John T., Jr., and Mus, Paul. *The Vietnamese and Their Revolution*. New York: Harper & Row, 1970.

McCartney, James. "Must the Media Be 'Used'?" *Columbia Journalism Review*. Winter 1969–70.

McLaughlin, John. "War News Out of Perspective." *Columbia Journalism Review*. Winter 1968/1969.

Mecklin, John. *Mission in Torment*. Garden City, N.Y.: Doubleday, 1965.

Milstein, Jeffrey S. *Dynamics of the Vietnam War: A Quantitative Analysis and Predictive Computer Simulation*. Columbus: Ohio State University Press, 1974.

Minor, Dale. *The Information War*. New York: Hawthorn Books, 1970.

Mohr, Charles. "Once Again— Did the Press Lose Vietnam?" *Columbia Journalism Review*. November/December 1983.

Mueller, John E. *War, Presidents and Public Opinion*. New York: Wiley, 1973.

Neuman, W. Russell. "Patterns of Recall Among Television News Viewers." *Public Opinion Quarterly* 40:1. Spring 1976.

Neustadt, Richard E. *Presidential Power: The Politics of Leadership with Reflections on Johnson and Nixon*. New York: Wiley, 1976.

Nixon, Richard M. *The Memoirs*. New York: Grosset & Dunlap, 1978.

Oberdorfer, Don. *Tet!* Garden City, N.Y.: Doubleday, 1971.

———. "Tet: The Turning Point," *Washington Post Magazine*. January 29, 1978.

Opton, Edward M., Jr. "It Never Happened, and Besides, They Deserved It," in Nevitt Sanford, Craig Comstock, and Associates, eds. *Sanctions for Evil*. San Francisco: Jossey-Bass, 1971.

Osborne, Milton E. *Strategic Hamlets in South Vietnam*. Ithaca, N.Y: The Cornell University Southeast Asia Program, 1965.

Paletz, David, and Entman, Robert. *Media Power Politics*. New York: Free Press, 1981.

The Pentagon Papers. Senator Gravel, ed. Boston: Beacon Press, 1971.

Pike, Douglas. *Viet Cong: The Organization and Technique of the National Liberation Front of South Vietnam*. Cambridge: MIT Press, 1966.

Popkin, Samuel L. "Internal Conflicts—South Vietnam," in Kenneth Waltz and Steven Spiegel, eds. *Conflict in World Politics*. Cambridge, Mass.: Winthrop, 1971.

———. "Pacification: Politics and the Village." *Asian Survey* 10:8. August 1970.

———. *The Rational Peasant: The Political Economy of Rural Society in Vietnam*. Berkeley: University of California Press, 1979.

Porter, William E. *Assault on the Media: The Nixon Years*. Ann Arbor: University of Michigan Press, 1976.

Powers, Thomas. *The War at Home: Vietnam and the American People*. New York: Grossman, 1973.

Pratt, Fletcher. "How the Censors Rigged the News." *Harper's*. February 1946.

Race, Jeffrey. *War Comes to Long An: Revolutionary Conflict in a Vietnamese Province*. Berkeley: University of California Press, 1972.

Ranney, Austin. *Channels of Power: The Impact of Television on American Politics*. New York: Basic Books, 1983.

Rather, Dan, with Herskowitz, Mickey. *The Camera Never Blinks: Adventures of a TV Journalist*. New York: William Morrow, 1977.

Reston, James. *The Artillery of the Press: Its Influence on American Foreign Policy*. New York: Harper & Row, 1967.

Roberts, Chalmers. *The Washington Post: The First Hundred Years*. New York: Houghton Mifflin, 1977.

Roberts, Gene. "U.S. 'Ground Rules' Keep Rein on War Reporting." *New York Times*, July 2, 1968.

Robinson, John P. "Public Reaction to Political Protest: Chicago, 1968." *Public Opinion Quarterly* 34:1. Spring 1970.

Robinson, Michael J. "American Political Legitimacy in an Age of Electronic Journalism," in Douglass Cater and Richard P. Alder, eds. *Television as a Social Force*. New York: Praeger, 1975.

———. "Public Affairs Television and the Growth of Political Malaise: The Case of 'The Selling of the Pentagon.' " *American Political Science Review* 70:2. June 1976.

Robinson, Michael J., and Sheehan, Margaret A. *Over the Wire and On TV: UPI and CBS in Campaign '80*. New York: Russell Sage Foundation, 1983.

Rosenberg, Milton J., Verba, Sidney, and Converse, Phillip E. *Vietnam and the Silent Majority*. New York: Harper & Row, 1970.

Salisbury, Harrison, *Without Fear or Favor: An Uncompromising Look at The New York Times and Its Times*. New York: Ballantine, 1980.

Scheer, Robert. "Tonkin—Dubious Premise for a War." *Los Angeles Times*. April 28, 1985.

Schell, Jonathan,. *The Military Half*. New York: Vintage, 1968.

———. *The Time of Illusion*. New York: Knopf, 1976.

Schudson, Michael. *Discovering the News: A Social History of American Newspapers*. New York: Basic Books, 1978.

Schuman, Howard. "Two Sources of Anti-War Sentiment in America." *American Journal of Sociology* 78:3. November 1972.

Schurmann, Franz, Scott, Peter Dale, and Zelnick, Reginald. *The Politics of Escalation in Vietnam*. New York: Fawcett, 1966.

Szulc, Tad. *The Illusion of Peace: Foreign Policy in the Nixon Years*. New York: Viking, 1978.

Shaplen, Robert. *The Road From War: Vietnam 1965–71*. New York: Harper & Row, 1971.

———. *The Lost Revolution*. New York: Harper & Row, 1966.

Shawcross, William. *Sideshow: Nixon, Kissinger and the Destruction of Cambodia*. New York: Simon and Schuster, 1979.

Sigal, Leon V. *Reporters and Officials: The Organization and Politics of Newsmaking*. Lexington, Mass.: D.C. Heath, 1973.

Small, William. *To Kill a Messenger: Television News and the Real World*. New York: Hastings House, 1970.

Smith, Steven Phillip. *American Boys*. New York: Avon, 1984.

Stavins, Ralph, Barnet, Richard J., and Raskin, Marcus G. *Washington Plans an Aggressive War*. New York: Random House, 1971.

Steffens, Lincoln. *Autobiography*. New York: Harcourt, Brace and World, 1931.

Stone, I. F. *In a Time of Torment*. New York: Random House, 1967.

———. *Polemics and Prophecies 1967–1970*. New York: Random House, 1970.

Summers, Col. Harry G. *On Strategy: A Critical Analysis of the Vietnam War*. Novato, Calif.: Presidio, 1982.

"Survey: A Salisbury Chronicle." *Columbia Journalism Review*. Winter 1966/1967.

Sweezy, Paul M., Huberman, Leo, and Magdoff, Harry. *Vietnam: The Endless War*. New York: Monthly Review, 1970.

Talese, Gay. *The Kingdom and the Power*. New York: World Publishing, 1969.

Taylor, Maxwell D. *Swords and Plowshares*. New York: W. W. Norton, 1972.

Taylor, Telford. *Nuremburg and Vietnam: An American Tragedy*. Chicago: Quadrangle, 1970.

Terkel, Studs. *'The Good War': An Oral History of World War II*. New York: Pantheon, 1984.

Terry, Wallace. *Bloods: An Oral History of the Vietnam War by Black Veterans*. New York: Random House, 1984.

Thies, Wallace J. *When Governments Collide: Coercion and Diplomacy in the Vietnam Conflict, 1964–1968*. Berkeley: University of California Press, 1980.

Thompson, James C. *Rolling Thunder: Understanding Policy and Program Failure*. Chapel Hill, N.C.: University of North Carolina Press, 1980.

Thompson, James C., Jr., Stanley, Peter W., and Perry, Curtis. *Sentimental Imperialists: The American Experience in East Asia*. New York: Harper & Row, 1982.

Tuchman, Gaye. "Objectivity as a Strategic Ritual: An Examination of Newsmen's Notions of Objectivity." *American Journal of Sociology* 78:3. November 1972.

Turner, Kathleen J. *Lyndon Johnson's Dual War: Vietnam and the Press*. Chicago: University of Chicago Press, 1985.

Twentieth Century Fund. *Battle Lines: Report of the Twentieth Century Fund Task Force on the Military and the Media*. New York: Priority Press, 1985.

United States Senate, Committee on Governmental Operations. *Confidence and Concern: Citizens View American Government*. Washington, D.C.: U.S. Government Printing Office, 1973.

"Vietnam: What Lessons?" *Columbia Journalism Review*. Winter 1970–71.

Vo Nguên Giap. *People's War, People's Army*. New York: Praeger, 1962.

Weaver, Paul. "Newspaper News and Television News," in Douglass Cater and Richard P. Adler, eds. *Television as a Social Force*. New York: Praeger, 1975.

Webb, James. *Fields of Fire*. Englewood Cliffs, N.J.: Prentice-Hall, 1978.

Webb, Kate. *On the Other Side: 23 Days with the Viet Cong*. New York: Quadrangle, 1972.

Weissberg, Robert. *Public Opinion and Popular Government*. Englewood Cliffs, N.J.: Prentice-Hall, 1976.

Welch, Susan. "The American Press in Indochina, 1950–56," in Richard L.

Merritt, ed. *Communication in International Politics*. Urbana, Ill.: University of Illinois Press, 1972.

Westmoreland, William C. *A Soldier Reports*. Garden City, N.Y.: Doubleday, 1976.

White, Ralph K. *Nobody Wanted War: Misperception in Vietnam and Other Wars*. New York: Anchor, 1970.

Wicker, Tom. *On Press*. New York: Viking, 1978.

Windchy, Eugene V. *Tonkin Gulf*. Garden City, N.Y.: Doubleday, 1971.

Appendix A

Abbreviations

AFRVN	Armed Forces of the Republic of [South] Vietnam
APC	Armored Personnel Carrier
ARVN	Army of the Republic of [South] Vietnam
DMZ	Demilitarized Zone
DRV	Democratic Republic of [North] Vietnam
FUNK	National United Front of Kampuchea, Khmer Rouge
GVN	Government of [South] Vietnam
HES	Hamlet Evaluation System
JCS	Joint Chiefs of Staff
KR	Khmer Rouge (see FUNK)
KIA	Killed in Action
MACV	Military Advisory Command, Vietnam; later Military Assistance Command, Vietnam
MIA	Missing in Action
NLF	National Liberation Front [of South Vietnam], Vietcong
NSAM	National Security Action Memorandum
PAVN	Peoples' Army of [North] Vietnam
PL	Pathet Lao
POW	Prisoner of War
RVN	Republic of [South] Vietnam
USG	United States Government
VC	Vietcong, NLF

Appendix B

Code Book with Marginals for Some Variables

Note: Marginal frequencies are unweighted raw data and cannot be directly interpreted.

Variable   1:   Character Case ID
Variable   2:   Numeric Case ID
Variable   3:   Year of Broadcast
Variable   4:   Month and Day of Broadcast
Variable   5:   Day of Week
Variable   6:   Network
  668   1.   ABC
  938   2.   CBS
  880   3.   NBC
Variable   7:   Date of Coding
Variable   8:   Elapsed Time of Story
          In tens of seconds.

> *Note:* Dividing a television broadcast into separate stories for content analysis is a matter of judgment. A television broadcast often flows from one topic to another, more or less related, without a clear break. Sometimes, in attempting to identify individual "stories," each with distinct topics, this analysis will, for example, divide thirty seconds of reporting by the anchorman into two or three stories; sometimes it will combine several lengthy film reports which follow one another without interruption, and the anchorman's introduction to them, into a single story. This means that "elapsed time of story" is to some extent a subjective measure—as subjective as the definition of a "story." Measures of the aggregate amount of time devoted to any subject are not, of course, affected by these decisions about dividing the content into units.

Variable   9:   Lead Story?
 1870   0.   Not lead story
  214   1.   Lead story
  402   9.   Not ascertained (Defense Dept. sample only)
Variable 10:   Type of story
 1528   1.   Anchorman in studio
   26   2.   Interview only
  109   3.   Voice-over narration by anchor

716	4.	Film report by correspondent
0	5.	Conversation with correspondent(s) in studio
46	6.	Commentary from studio
3	7.	Commentary from scene
Variable	11:	Country
2070	1.	Vietnam
142	2.	Cambodia
80	3.	Laos
55	4.	General Indochina
29	8.	Not ascertained
·110	9.	Inappropriate—strictly a domestic story

Note: Coded for country referred to in story or where events actually took place. Coded for domestic stories as well as stories from Indochina, if those stories refer to events or policies in Indochina.

Variable	12:	Primary Subject of Story
58	00.	No Vietnam story
465	01.	Ground combat (and river combat, close air support, coastal patrol)
197	02.	Strategic bombing and shelling of DRV and infiltration routes in Laos, Cambodia
43	03.	Bombing and shelling within RVN (or Laos or Cambodia, interdiction of infiltration routes excluded) not directly in support of ground action (applies to U.S., allied action)
66	04.	Artillery attacks, sabotage, etc., against military, gov't, and logistical targets; booby traps (applies to DRV, NLF action)
38	05.	Attacks on civilian targets; terrorism (applies to DRV, NLF action)
23	07.	Assessment of particular tactical situation
45	08.	Assessment of strategic situation
6	09.	Evaluation of strategy and tactics, ground and general
0	10.	Evaluation of strategy and tactics, strategic bombing, shelling
10	11.	Truces
8	12.	Other military action
6	13.	Infiltration
8	14.	Effects of combat, general
132	15.	Body count
43	16.	Military casualties (not classifiable under type of combat, above)
41	17.	Civilian casualties (except DRV)
5	18.	Civilian casualties in DRV
1	19.	Environmental destruction
15	20.	Deployment of new troops (excluding normal rotation of troops, which is scored 23)
29	21.	Troop withdrawals (excluding normal rotation and R&R)
26	22.	GVN and Laotian, Cambodian gov't troops: recruitment, training, tactics, technology, etc.
32	23.	U.S. troops, general
10	24.	Military tactics and technology, ground and naval (excluding strategic bombardment)

21	26.	Military tactics and technology: air
9	28.	Morale, discipline, etc., of U.S. troops
12	29.	Drug use by U.S. troops
4	30.	Opinions of U.S. troops
5	31.	Relations between U.S. troops and Vietnamese
3	32.	Race relations among U.S. troops
4	34.	DRV, NLF, PL, KR troops, military technology, tactics, etc.
0	35.	DRV, NLF, PL, KR: political organizing
0	36.	DRV, NLF, PL, KR: history, political goals
17	37.	DRV, NLF, PL, KR troops as POWs
5	38.	DRV, NLF, PL, KR: other
12	40.	RVN (or Laos or Cambodia, depending on country coded in Var. 11, above), general
65	41.	GVN (or Laotian or Cambodian) policy
65	42.	RVN (Laotian, Cambodian) politics (elections, demonstrations, coups, etc.)
7	43.	RVN (Laotian, Cambodian) economy
1	45.	U.S. impact in Indochina (prostitution, etc.)
2	46.	Impact of U.S. withdrawal
15	47.	Pacification, psychological warfare, *Chieu Hoi*, support for GVN in countryside, etc.
31	51.	DRV, NLF, PL, KR policy
159	59.	U.S. policy-making, statements of policy, etc.
80	60.	Political debate in U.S.
58	61.	Campaign stories with reference to war
9	62.	Campaign stories involving confrontations between candidate and demonstrators
19	63.	Antiwar movement as an issue (statements about movement, hearings, etc.)
3	64.	Antiwar activity and statements: electoral
28	65.	: Legislative
35	66.	: Peaceful mass action and organizing (including lobbying by "grass roots" groups)
5	67.	: Civil disobedience
9	68.	: Mass action involving violence
0	69.	: Terrorism
6	70.	: Individual resistance
26	71.	: In military
4	72.	: Other
0	73.	Statements and actions by hawk critics of administration: electoral and legislative
1	74.	: Other
3	75.	Statements and actions by supporters of administration: candidates and public officials
3	76.	: Group spokespeople and letter-writers
3	77.	: Mass action and organizing
6	78.	Actions of authorities vis-à-vis antiwar movement, police tactics, etc.

4	79.	Miscellaneous domestic stories
13	81.	GIs at home (jobs, hospitals, benefits, Medal of Honor ceremonies, etc.)
3	82.	Families of GIs
3	83.	Effect of war on economy
8	84.	The draft
18	85.	POWs, general
22	86.	POWs in North Vietnam
19	87.	POWs, releases and homecomings
11	88.	Families of POWs
31	89.	War crimes trials, hearings, etc.
172	90.	Negotiations, diplomatic activity
7	91.	International public opinion, general
16	92.	International opposition to U.S. policy
2	93.	International support
7	94.	U.S. allies in Vietnam, sending troops, etc.
1	95.	U.S. allies refusing troops, asking money, etc.
5	96.	Effect of war on détente
48	98.	Other

Variable 13: Secondary Subject of Story

Same coding categories as above except code 00 not used; code 99 = No secondary subject.

Variable 14: Focus of Story

75	0.	Vietnam and domestic debate not a major focus
2353	1.	Vietnam and domestic debate a major focus of story
58	9.	Not applicable—no Vietnam story

Notes: Some stories which are not primarily about the Vietnam War or the domestic debate but which contain important references to the war are included in the sample and coded 0 in this variable. The most common of these are campaign stories and stories on presidential press conferences and summit meetings.

All stories in the sampled broadcasts in which the war and the domestic debate are a major focus are coded. Some stories on related issues which grew out of the war are excluded, however. Specifically:

1. Trials and hearings on war crimes are included when they are first announced. After that, stories on these topics are not coded unless they contain significant information or statements about the incidents in question or the war in general: stories that deal exclusively with legal issues, etc., are not included.

2. Trials and hearings on the antiwar movement (e.g., the Chicago conspiracy trial) are treated similarly.

3. Stories about the draft are not coded if they refer exclusively to problems of administration, fairness of application of the law, etc., and do not refer directly to the war.

4. Stories about the military budget, military technology, and preparedness are treated similarly.

Variable 15: Nature of Story

3	0.	"Light" story

2044	1.	Report of event, current situation or policy announcement
41	2.	Report on reaction to event or statement
142	3.	Report of statement
59	4.	Report on ongoing process, situation, or policy
34	5.	Background report
49	6.	Analysis or commentary
22	7.	"Human-interest" story
34	8.	Other (including interview)
58	9.	Not applicable—no Vietnam story
Variable	16:	Film of Demonstrations and Organizing
31	02.	Interview
8	11.	Organizing (people working in offices, speaking to small groups, handing out leaflets, etc.
4	12.	Meetings, conventions
6	13.	News conferences
16	20.	Crowds in marches or rallies
7	21.	Tight shots of demonstrators, general
12	22.	Tight shots of "neat" demonstrators
14	23.	Tight shots of "scruffy" demonstrators
4	24.	Demonstrators with NLF flags, signs, slogans
2	25.	People "frolicking" at demonstrations
0	26.	Nudity, "obscene gestures," etc.
3	27.	Tight shots of people speaking at rallies, no sound
9	28.	Tight shots of people speaking at rallies, with natural sound
4	31.	Crowds engaging in civil disobedience
2	32.	Tight shots of people engaging in civil disobedience
0	33.	Draft cards being burned
4	41.	Demonstrators heckling
1	42.	Tight shots of "neat" demonstrators heckling
2	43.	Tight shots of "scruffy" demonstrators heckling
1	50.	Demonstrators practicing violence
1	51.	Crowds engaging in violence
0	52.	Tight shots of demonstrators engaging in violence
2	53.	Police lines standing, no violence
1	54.	Police lines advancing, maneuvering
3	55.	Police engaging in violence
1	56.	Police engaging in violence, tight shots
7	57.	Combat between police and demonstrators
1	58.	Demonstrators being arrested violently
2	59.	Arrests, no violence
4	61.	Injured demonstrators
2	62.	Injured demonstrators, tight shots, faces visible
2	63.	Injured police
0	64.	Injured police, tight shots, faces visible
1	70.	Counterdemonstrators organizing
1	71.	Crowd shots of counterdemonstrators
0	72.	Tight shots of counterdemonstrators
0	73.	Counterdemonstrators heckling
1	74.	Counterdemonstrators heckling, tight shots

0	75.	Counterdemonstrators engaging in violence
0	76.	Counterdemonstrators engaging in violence, tight shots
2	77.	Combat between demonstrators and counterdemonstrators
1	78.	Confrontations between police and counterdemonstrators
0	79.	Injured counterdemonstrators
0	80.	Injured counterdemonstrators, tight shots
18	81.	Tight shots of signs, readable
2	82.	Tight shots of counterdemonstrators' signs
4	98.	Other
—	99.	Inappropriate—no film of demonstrations and organizing

Note: A maximum of six codes could be scored for a single story.

Variable 17: Film in Variable 16 Refers To:

71	1.	Antiwar demonstrations, organizing
4	2.	Prowar demonstrations, organizing
2411	3.	Inappropriate

Variable 18: Film of Americans Helping Vietnamese

751	0.	Film does not show Americans helping Vietnamese civilians
17	1.	Film shows Americans helping Vietnamese civilians (giving medical aid, giving candy to children, etc.)
1717	9.	Inappropriate—no film report

Variable 19: Combat Film

662	0.	Film does not show combat
106	1.	Film does show combat
1717	9.	Inappropriate—no film report

Note: Scored 1 for all film of incoming and outgoing fire, except: scored 0 when outgoing fire or distant air strikes are shown only briefly.

Variable 20: Casualties on Film

60	01.	Bodies, faces not visible (including body bags, coffins, graves)
8	02.	Bodies, faces shown
1	03.	Body, isolation on single individual, face shown
41	11.	Wounded, faces not shown
45	12.	Wounded, faces shown
52	13.	Wounded, isolation on single individual, face shown
0	21.	Person wounded or killed on camera, face not shown
0	22.	Wounded or killed on camera, face shown
1	23.	Wounded or killed on camera, isolation on single individual, face shown
9	31.	Refugees, in crowds
22	32.	Refugees, tight shots
1	41.	Violent prisoner interrogations
34	51.	Destruction of homes, etc.
2	98.	Other
—	99.	No casualties shown on film

Notes: 1. Scored for casualties shown in United States as well as in Vietnam, for example, wounded vets at home, coffins shipped back to the United States, etc.

2. The basic unit of analysis for scoring was the film "shot." At times, however, when a sequence of similar shots was edited to-

gether, usually corresponding to one line of narration, they would be scored together. This was most common in stories on refugees.

3. A maximum of six codes scored for any story. This limitation applies for Variables 20 and 22 through 24, which were scored together. On those rare occasions when more than six film sequences or verbal references to casualties appeared, casualties on film would be scored before verbal references, and more dramatic sequences or references were scored first (e.g., tight shots rather than long shots).

		Variable 21: Film of Survivors Grieving
2	1.	U.S. civilians
9	2.	RVN, Laotian, Cambodian civilians
0	3.	North Vietnamese civilians
0	4.	U.S. GIs
0	5.	ARVN, Laotian, Cambodian gov't soldiers
1	6.	Others
—	9.	No film of survivors grieving

		Variable 22: Whose Casualties Referred To
20	0.	Not ascertained
286	1.	U.S. only
88	2.	GVN, Cambodian, Laotian gov't troops only
174	3.	DRV, NLF, PL, KR troops only
214	4.	Both sides
16	5.	U.S. and GVN, etc., troops only
221	6.	Indochinese civilians, except DRV
14	7.	North Vietnamese civilians
29	8.	Others
—	9.	Inappropriate, no reference to casualties.

Notes: 1. Both verbal and visual references to casualties scored, including references made in domestic stories.

2. References to "light" casualties not coded; references to "moderate" and "heavy" casualties coded.

3. Extremely vague references (e.g., statement that "people are getting killed") not scored.

4. References to casualties in stories on war crimes trials scored only when testimony about specific incidents is described.

5. Announcements of troops missing or captured are scored. Otherwise, references to POWs and MIAs not scored.

6. Announcements of aircraft lost not scored if fate of crew not reported.

7. References to casualties in "Hanoi radio claimed . . ." stories not coded.

		Variable 23: Responsibility for Casualties
88	0.	Not attributed, no clear responsibility
149	1.	Attributed or clearly linked to U.S. ground action
44	2.	Attributed or clearly linked to U.S. air action, naval bombardment, etc.
47	3.	Attributed or clearly linked to ARVN, etc.
397	4.	Attributed or clearly linked to DRV, NLF, PL, KR

22	5.	Accidental
15	6.	Attributed or clearly linked to "friendly fire"
2	7.	Attributed or clearly linked to "war," etc.
123	8.	Attributed or clearly linked to both sides
—	9.	No reference to casualties; casualties not attributable

Notes: 1. Scored 9 when numerical body count only is given.

2. Codes 1 and 2 take precedence over code 3 when both attributions are made, or when casualties attributed only to "allies."

Variable 24: Type of Reference to Casualties

156	01.	Military, quantitative only
406	02.	Military, minimal elaboration or context
171	03.	Military, with context (description of situation, identity of victim, etc.)
9	06.	Wounded vets at home
0	07.	Effects on families in U.S.
4	08.	Military, interview with victim
4	11.	Civilian, quantitative only
62	12.	Civilian, minimal elaboration or context
44	13.	Civilian, with context
0	15.	Abuse of civilians (stealing, etc.)
25	16.	Kidnapping, assassination, murder of civilians
19	17.	Massacre
15	18.	Murder, torture or abuse of prisoner
36	19.	Refugees
1	20.	Orphans
0	21.	Life for survivors
2	22.	Interview with civilian victim
39	23.	Destruction of homes, etc.
7	31.	VIP casualty
61	98.	Other
—	99.	No reference to casualties

Notes: 1. Soldier referring to death of buddy without details scored 02.

2. All casualties shown on film scored "with context."

3. Code 17 scored only if event is specifically described as a massacre.

Variable 25: Military Initiative

10	0.	U.S., ARVN, etc., advance, no combat
8	1.	DRV, NLF, PL, KR advance, no combat
211	2.	U.S., etc., attack
254	3.	DRV, etc., attack
79	4.	Mutual advance or attack
5	5.	Expect U.S., etc., offensive or operation
44	6.	Expect DRV, etc., offensive or operation
179	7.	U.S. air, artillery, or naval attack (not close support)
37	8.	Downing of U.S. aircraft
1659	9.	No report indicating military initiative

Notes: 1. This variable is scored for the way the story is written, which will usually, but not always, coincide with the actual events.

It is the side which is the primary *actor* in the news story as it is written that is scored as having the initiative. So, "marines killed 30 Communists," is scored 2 even if the story does not say who initiated the battle, and so is "allied forces beat back a North Vietnamese assault." "U.S. and North Vietnamese forces battled for three hours" is coded 9, even if the story mentions in passing which side initiated the battle.

2. Mixed references scored 9, unless there is a clear preponderance of initiative on one side or the other.

3. References to expected offensives or major operations take precedence over other references.

4. Military initiative not scored if it is merely mentioned in passing that troops were involved in an operation.

5. Attacks on government and civilian targets are scored.

6. References in "Hanoi radio claimed . . ." stories are not coded.

Variable 26:   Troops Involved in Military Operation
476	1.	U.S. only
134	2.	ARVN, Laotian, Cambodian gov't troops only
2	3.	Other U.S. allies only
113	4.	1 and 2
5	5.	1 and 3
2	6.	2 and 3
19	7.	"Allied," unspecified
30	8.	Not ascertained
1705	9.	Inappropriate, no report of military operation involving U.S. or allied troops

Notes: 1. Not scored when troops are merely passive victims of artillery attacks, etc.

2. Not scored when story reports only casually that troops were involved in military operation.

Variable 27:   Description of Military Results
690	0.	No description in terms of success or failure
95	1.	Operation results in success for U.S., allies
52	2.	Operation results in success for DRV, etc.
36	3.	Results inconclusive, mixed, or stalemate
6	4.	No contact, "frustration" for U.S., allies
1	5.	No contact, success for U.S., allies
4	6.	Enemy "cleared out" but "will return"
5	7.	U.S. troops "sweep through" area, otherwise no description in terms of success or failure
1597	9.	Inappropriate, no report of military operation

Note: Coded only if story clearly states or implies a judgment about the outcome of the operation described.

Variable 28:   Assessment of Military Situation
36	1.	Progress, success for U.S., RVN
12	2.	Loss of ground, failure for U.S., RVN
4	3.	Stalemate
0	4.	U.S., RVN "cannot win"
2	5.	DRV, NLF "cannot win"

4	6.	Hope for future (for U.S., RVN)
7	7.	Concern about future
4	8.	Mixed
2414	9.	No assessment of military situation

Note: Scored for assessment of *overall* military situation only. This includes assessment of the success or failure of major operations and offensives.

Variable 29: References to Performance and Capacity of AFRVN

12	1.	Negative reference, major theme of story
8	2.	Negative reference, not major theme
4	3.	Major neutral or mixed reference
4	4.	Minor neutral or mixed reference
34	5.	Major positive reference
27	6.	Minor positive reference

Note: Coded both for verbal references, by journalists and other speakers, and for subject of story. For example, story of major ARVN defeat scored as negative reference even if no general conclusions are drawn about ARVN capacity.

Variable 30: References to Performance and Capacity of DRV, NLF Forces
Same coding categories as above.

Variable 31: References to Morale of U.S. Troops
Same coding categories as above.

Variable 32: References to Success of Pacification
Same coding categories as above.

Variable 33: References to Performance and Capacity of GVN
Same coding categories as above.

Variable 34: References to Democracy in South Vietnam
Same coding categories as above.

Variable 35: References to U.S./South Vietnam Relations
Same coding categories as above.

Note: Scored both for relations between governments and relations between individuals, for example, relations between U.S. troops and civilians.

Variable 36: References to Peace Hopes
Same coding categories as above.

Variable 37: References to Escalation or Deescalation
Same coding categories as above.

Notes: 1. Coded primarily for escalation or deescalation of *U.S. role* in war. Thus a report on an increase in the strength of the ARVN, which suggested that this would enable U.S. troops to go home sooner, would be scored positive, that is, as deescalation.
2. "Holding the line" coded positive.

Variable 38: Identity of People Speaking or Cited on Television

40	01.	President or president-elect
13	02.	Vice president
137	03.	Other civilian administration officials
53	04.	Military officials
24	05.	Supporters of administration, general

28	06.	Legislators supporting administration
1	07.	Candidates supporting administration
43	11.	Antiwar demonstrators, demonstration organizers
13	12.	Other nongovernmental antiwar critics
27	13.	Individual war resisters
103	14.	Antiwar legislators
29	15.	Antiwar candidates
7	16.	Campaign workers for antiwar candidates
0	21.	Hawk critics of administration, general
3	22.	Hawk legislators
11	23.	Hawk candidates
6	31.	Other legislators
43	32.	Other candidates
4	41.	Police, National Guard spokesmen, and military spokesmen in trials of war resisters
6	42.	Local government officials, university administrators, and other authorities (not expressing a view on the war)
37	51.	GVN officials
2	52.	Laotian, Cambodian gov't officials
5	53.	ARVN, etc., soldiers
11	54.	South Vietnamese oppositionists
6	55.	Other Indochinese civilians
2	56.	GVN legislators
39	61.	DRV, NLF, PL, KR officials
0	62.	DRV civilians
7	63.	PAVN, etc., soldiers
277	71.	U.S. soldiers, lower-ranking officers, POWs, vets, and lower-level civilian officials in the field (pacification advisors, etc.)
38	72.	Families of above
28	73.	Other U.S. civilians, not otherwise classifiable
2	81.	Foreign supporters of U.S. policy
11	82.	Foreign critics
8	83.	Other foreign
9	91.	Experts, etc., not identified with positions on the war
1	97.	Reporter at a news conference
28	98.	Other
—	99.	Inappropriate, no one speaking or cited

Notes: 1. Everyone who appears on film making a statement is coded. People whose statements are quoted or cited are also coded, unless they are merely announcing a policy or event or make a statement entirely tangential to the debate over the war. Also, brief citations of statements about peace talks, etc., which are essentially only statements of acceptance or rejection of a negotiating position, are not coded—for example, "North Vietnamese negotiator Xuan Thuy termed the American proposal 'a small carrot concealing big guns.' "

2. Code 04 usually refers to general officers, and all lower-ranking officers are coded 71. However, lower-ranking officers who have

major and visible command roles (e.g., commander of U.S. forces at Khe Sanh, a colonel) are coded 04. Military public information officers are also coded 04 regardless of rank.

3. Official spokespeople are coded according to the identity of those they represent.

4. Collective "persons" are coded when they make substantive statements about war policy or domestic debate, for example, Hanoi radio; resolutions by trade unions or city governments.

5. People whose position on the war is not generally known, and who are not identified with a position, either explicitly or by the structure of the story, are generally coded 31, 32, 55, 71, 72, 73, or 83, regardless of the views they actually hold.

6. Statements by a maximum of six people are coded. On those rare occasions when more than six people appear in a story, people who make the most substantive statements and who do not repeat statements made by others are coded.

Variable 39: "Balancing" of Statements Coded Above
542   0. Statement not balanced
42   1. Newscaster gives counterarguments
88   2. Newscaster refers to specific opposing views
3   3. Newscaster balances by referring to public opinion (e.g., "but not everyone thinks that way . . .")
88   4. Statement balanced by one opposing statement
18   5. Statement balanced by two or more opposing statements
83   6. Statement balanced within context of broadcast as a whole (e.g., several arguments on each side, spread through various stories)
13   7. Other balancing
251   8. Inappropriate, statement not controversial
—   9. Inappropriate, no statement made

Notes: 1. Codes 4 and 5 are used when a statement is counterposed to one or more statements on film; code 2, when a statement is counterposed to one cited or quoted by the newscaster.

2. Code 8 is used when people made statements that are not controversial, for example, a GI saying he is glad to be home or a lieutenant describing a particular battle. It is used liberally for speakers coded 53, 63, 71, 72, and 73 in Var. 37: statements by people in these categories can manifest a political direction through their focus, terminology,etc., and still be coded as noncontroversial if they don't clearly imply an opinion or argument. It is used very sparingly for statements of high officials and direct participants in political debate.

Variable 40: Content of Statements on Vietnam Policy
8   11. Expression of hope for peace only, no policy position expressed or implied
73   21. Support for specific administration policy expressed or implied
39   22. Criticism of specific policy from dove point of view
2   23. Criticism of specific policy, hawk
22   24. Criticism of specific policy, not classifiable hawk or dove

42	31.	Support for general U.S. policy in Vietnam
94	32.	Criticism of general U.S. policy, dove
4	33.	Criticism of general U.S. policy, hawk
5	34.	Criticism of general U.S. policy, not classifiable
17	41.	Support for GVN
24	42.	Criticism of GVN
8	51.	Support for DRV, NLF, PL, KR
50	52.	Criticism of DRV, NLF, PL, KR
5	61.	Support for U.S. policy-making process
16	62.	Criticism of U.S. policy-making process
108	71.	Statement about facts or situation, favorable to administration
45	72.	Statement about facts or situation, unfavorable
9	74.	Statement about public opinion, favorable
13	75.	Statement about public opinion, unfavorable
34	81.	Statement about aims of U.S. policy, favorable (e.g., peace proposal is sincere; U.S. does not seek permanent military presence in RVN)
15	82.	Statement about aims of policy, unfavorable
8	83.	Statement about aims of policy, neutral
30	91.	Advocacy of alternative policy
16	92.	Criticism of alternative policy
111	98.	Other
—	99.	Inappropriate, no statement on Vietnam policy

Notes: 1. Codes 71 and 72 are used only when statements are made concerning issues of fact which are generally recognized as controversial (e.g., does U.S. bomb civilian areas in DRV?)

2. On rare occasions statements by journalists will be coded. This is done only when journalists express or clearly imply a position or conclusion about controversial issues; never when they are merely reporting on events, situations, or statements, even if a political position can be inferred from their selection of facts, terminology, tone of voice, etc. Coding for journalists' statements here will usually coincide with a code for interpretation in Var. 47.

3. Statements about minor policies, for example, policy on military leaves, not coded.

4. Statements which merely announce a policy or event not coded.

Variable 41: Criteria for Evaluating Policy

65	00.	No arguments used or implied, statement of opinion only
17	01.	Sincerity of policymaker (e.g., "political motivation," desire for peace)
4	02.	Authority of policymaker
5	03.	Loyalty of opponent of war
8	04.	Support for policy (public opinion, effect on reelection chances, etc.)
3	12.	South Vietnamese "don't want us there"
32	21.	Effectiveness of policy—whether it will achieve its ends
3	30.	Likely effects or costs of policy, whether intended or not

In this category code separately:

12	31.	Death, destruction in Indochina

18	32.	Loss of U.S. Lives
9	33.	Economic cost to U.S. and effect on other priorities
4	34.	Conflict within U.S.
2	35.	Militarization of U.S., repression, destruction of democracy
4	36.	Damage to U.S. world position, overextension
2	37.	Damage to U.S. world image
12	38.	Danger of wider war
6	41.	U.S. law, constitutionality
1	42.	International law
0	43.	Right to intervene in affairs of another country
0	44.	Morality, wisdom of war in general
2	60.	Aims of U.S. policy, aims cited but not discussed

In this category code separately:

11	61.	General aims of U.S. policy (e.g., stopping communism, self-determination for RVN, "just peace," etc.)
0	62.	Commitment to South Vietnam
9	63.	Protect U.S. troops
0	64.	Get back POWs
105	65.	End war quickly, reduce level of fighting, achieve peace
5	66.	Worthiness of GVN
21	67.	Imperialist aims, aggression, "world policeman" role, etc.
4	68.	Absence of aims
3	70.	Aims of policy, with argument about what aims really are or whether they are justified

In this category code separately same goals as under 60, above

3	81.	No choice because other side acts as it does
1	82.	Justified by misdeeds of other side
51	98.	Other
—	99.	Inappropriate, no statement about U.S. policy

Note: Coded for all statements of opinion about U.S. policy (not for statements about other parties to the conflict) and for statements which do not express an opinion but which argue or imply that certain criteria for evaluating policy are important. Statements by journalists which fit this description are coded.

Variable 42: Reasons for Fighting

8	01.	"Stop Communism," "halt aggression," "preserve freedom," etc., no further elaboration
3	02.	Domino theory
5	03.	Munich analogy
2	11.	Credibility, prestige (including confidence of allies)
0	21.	Fulfill commitment to South Vietnam
5	22.	Help people of South Vietnam
1	23.	Prevent bloodbath
1	24.	"Win hearts and minds"
5	41.	Imperialist, aggressive aims
1	42.	Save face of president
0	43.	Domestic political reasons
0	51.	No choice now—we are already there
0	52.	Protect U.S. troops; get back POWs

0   61. Mistake: quagmire sucked us in

5   71. No reason

1   98. Other

—   99. No presentation of reasons for fighting

Note: Coded for all statements about why U.S. is fighting in Indochina. Journalists' statements included.

Variable 43:   U.S. War Aims

7   01. Victory: "win the war," "defeat Communism," etc.

0   02. Halt aggression

3   03. Non-Communist South Vietnam

0   04. "Free and independent" South Vietnam

10   05. Right of self-determination for SVN; prevent North from taking over South by force

5   06. "Just and honorable peace"

15   07. End war, get out, achieve peace (unqualified)

0   08. Avoid defeat, humiliation

13   09. *Not* military victory; negotiated settlement; political settlement

5   10. Imperialist aims

1   11. U.S. has no aims, is confused about aims

2   21. Military victory—if talks fail

1   98. Other

—   99. No presentation of U.S. war aims

Note: Coded for all statements about what the U.S. seeks to achieve in Indochina. Journalists' statements included.

Variable 44:   Direction of Statements on Antiwar Movement

24   1. Support for antiwar Movement

55   2. Criticism of antiwar Movement

0   3. Support for goals; criticism of tactics

9   4. Support for actions of authorities

9   5. Criticism of actions of authorities

6   6. Mixed: differentiation between "good" and "bad" antiwar movement

0   7. Other mixed

0   8. Other

—   9. Inappropriate, no statement about antiwar movement or neutral statement only

Notes: 1. Statements on protest are coded only when they clearly include the antiwar movement. Thus a statement on "anarchists and revolutionaries" is not included.

2. On coding of journalists' statements, see notes to Var. 40.

Variable 45:   Focus of Statements on Antiwar Movement

8   00. Statement of approval or disapproval only

9   01. Public support: how many people does movement represent?

7   02. Public support: how many participate?

1   11. Tactics: will movement succeed in convincing public?

20   12. Tactics: succeed in changing policy?

0   13. Tactics: affect morale of troops?

5   14. Tactics: affect determination of enemy?

36	15.	Tactics: violence, disruption, legality
9	16.	Apperarance, style, etc.
1	17.	Tactics: wisdom of splitting Democratic party
6	21.	Loyalty: does movement want Communists to win?
5	22.	Loyalty: participation of Communists
3	23.	Right to dissent, criticize authority during war
20	41.	Political views: reasons for opposing war, alternative policies, etc.
4	42.	Knowledge, competence of antiwar movement people
14	51.	Background: organizing techniques, etc.
7	52.	Background: who activists are
23	61.	Tactics of authorities
20	98.	Other
—	99.	Inappropriate, no statement about antiwar movement

Notes: 1. Coded for all statements about the antiwar movement which focus attention on the issues listed, whether they express an opinion or not.

2. Coded for journalists' statements as well as those of nonjournalists. Journalists, of course, are always focusing and defocusing attention with their use of language and their selection of material. This variable is designed to measure the most explicit focusing. Journalists' statements are coded when they give particular emphasis to a given "angle," usually in the lead-in or wrap-up to the story or in interpretive remarks.

Variable 46: Object of Interpretation (see following variable)

9	0.	U.S. soldiers
176	1.	U.S. administration
86	2.	GVN
95	3.	DRV, NLF, PL, KR
0	4.	South Vietnamese oppositionist
40	5.	Opponent of war
5	6.	Supporter of war
3	7.	Police, etc., in U.S.
58	8.	Other
—	9.	No actor or no interpretation

Variable 47: Interpretation

53	120.	Impute a motive or strategy without source
17	201.	Imply doubt about a source
34	202.	Explicitly express doubt about a source
37	301.	Evaluate an action or policy as successful, or a situation as favorable
22	302.	Evaluate as unsuccessful or unfavorable
2	303.	Evaluate as inconclusive or stalemated
1	304.	Evaluate as mixed
7	305.	State that evaluation is impossible based on current information
44	310.	Speculate about future events
320, 40, 60.		Speculate on effects of action, policy, or event (see note below)
321, 41, 61.		: On military situation

322, 42, 62.	:	Civilian casualties
323, 43, 63.	:	"Hearts and minds"
324, 44, 64.	:	GVN morale
325, 45, 65.	:	GVN stability, efficiency
326, 46, 66.	:	GVN democracy
327, 47, 67.	:	South Vietnamese economy
328, 48, 68.	:	Enemy morale and intentions
329, 49, 69.	:	Peace talks, peace chances
330, 50, 70.	:	U.S. casualty level
331, 51, 71.	:	U.S. domestic situation
332, 52, 72.	:	U.S. domestic situation (conflict, dissent, political trouble for president)
333, 53, 73.	:	U.S. economy
334, 54, 74.	:	Intentions of U.S. policymakers
335, 55, 75.	:	Level and scope of war
336, 56, 76.	:	Détente

420–426. Point out what effects are important to look for, without speculation about what effects will actually be. Same effects coded as in 320–336, above. Favorability not coded.

5 441. Assert that whatever the outcome of the fighting, there will be more casualties

2 442. Assert that whatever the outcome of the fighting, civilians will suffer

28 500. Identify key question, policy problem or causal factor (e.g., "security is the key to pacification").

18 510. Evaluate importance of event, policy or action

600, 601, 602. Offer background or context, for example, reference to similar policy in the past, to underlying causes, etc. Coded for favorability to actor, as described in note. For example, story which points out contradiction between action or event and publicly stated policy coded unfavorable.

15 700. General opinionated newswriting, positive

27 701. General opinionated newswriting, negative

3 710. Loaded word choice, positive

25 711. Loaded word choice, negative

7 800. Explicit argument, general

1 801. : To end war

0 802. : To continue war

0 803. : To escalate

0 804. : To deescalate, offer more concessions, etc.

5 805. : For policy of object

12 806. : Against policy of object

900, 901, 902. Other interpretation, coded favorable, unfavorable, or neutral as above

— 999. No interpretation

Notes: 1. All news stories contain an underlying interpretive framework, and most implicitly express underlying political positions as well. This variable, however, is designed only to measure the clearest cases of news analysis and editorializing. It is therefore scored quite conservatively: all cases that seem marginal are scored "no interpretation." All interpretations or opinions that are attributed to a source, of course, are scored "no interpretation." In some cases interpretations or opinions are not explicitly attributed, but seem nevertheless to come from a source (assessments of victory or defeat in particular battles or the progress of peace talks are the most common examples). These, too, are coded "no interpretation." Obviously the line between stories that are "clearly" interpretive and those that are not is a fuzzy one. In general, directional categories, those considered favorable or unfavorable to the object, are the easiest to code objectively. Coding of neutral interpretation is somewhat more subjective.

2. The object of interpretation is an action, policy, or statement of the actor coded in Var. 46. If no actor is coded, the object is an event, fact, or situation, and favorability or unfavorability is coded with reference to their implications for U.S. policy.

3. Categories in the 320 to 376 series are scored for favorability to the actor coded in Var. 46. First code listed is for favorable interpretation; second, for unfavorable; third, for neutral. An effect is considered favorable to the actor if it (a) achieves the actor's ends (e.g., an NLF action threatens the security of the GVN) or (b) conforms with generally recognized political and moral standards (e.g., actions which cause civilian casualties are coded as unfavorable to the actor).

4. "Loaded word choice" is word choice which, in the context in question, has a clearly evaluative connotation and which is not attributed. Only strongly and clearly evaluative language is coded here. Following is a list of the language actually coded, with the context when necessary: Loaded word choice, positive: purpose of GVN policy is "education and understanding"; troops are "brave, firm" (use of terms *hero* and *heroic* was not coded if it occurred in a story on Medal of Honor ceremonies—it was then assumed to be attributed; as it turned out, it did not occur in the sample outside of such stories); area "liberated" from Communists. Loaded word choice, negative: "vengeance"; Soviet Union's "Vietnamese Communist *clients*"; "murder," "irrational murder" ("murder" not scored if it occurred in judicial context); "wild and vicious riot," "appalling wave of arson and looting," "frustrated militants," "wild violence," "suicide, suicidal" (said of military tactics); "acid-tongued evangelist"; "butchery"; "viciousness," "stubborn defiance" (said of negotiator); "brutal"; activities of antiwar group "exposed"; "so-called humanitarian reasons"; "fanatical"; "atrocity."

5. Interpretations of minor policies and statements, policies, and events which do not have to do with the war or domestic debate (e.g., president's campaign tactics) not coded.

6. This variable is adapted from George Baily, *The Vietnam War According to Chet, David, Walter, Harry, Peter, Bob, Howard and Frank: A Content Analysis of Journalistic Performance by the Net-*

work Television Evening News Anchormen, 1965–1970, Ph.D. dissertation, University of Wisconsin, Madison, 1973.

Variable 48:   References to Official Secrecy and Lying

12	1.	Reference to secrecy, major subject of story
3	2.	Reference to secrecy, not major subject
7	3.	Major reference to inaccuracy of official statements (no suggestion that officials intended to mislead)
15	4.	Minor reference to inaccuracy
2	5.	Major reference to intentional dishonesty
5	6.	Minor reference to intentional dishonesty
3	7.	Major reference to "credibility gap"
2	8.	Minor reference to "credibility gap"
2437	9.	No reference to official secrecy, inaccuracy or dishonesty

Notes: 1. Coded for statements by journalists and others.

2. Coded for references to U.S. officials only.

3. Secrecy here means withholding of information or interference with public access to it. It is only scored when a positive attempt to block public knowledge is alleged or implied. "It was not disclosed . . ." not scored.

Variable 49:   Standardized Decimal Weight

To correct different sampling densities used for National Archives and Vanderbilt Television News Archive data bases, and an overlay sample for the 1968 election campaign period. Values are 1.12 for Vanderbilt sample, 0.89 for National Archives sample, and 0.74 for campaign period. Unweighted $N = 2,428$; weighted $N = 2,446$.

Index